D1263522

Kristi,
May the bless & prosper your
days –

Michael Cannon
Gal. 2:20

Michael Cannon has given us new insights into the conversation between Jesus and his Father as described in John 17. Leading us into this very personal encounter, we get a glimpse of the power of prayer as he describes for us the process of moving through various emotions to the affirmation of faith, and then applies these principles for the reader.

—HUGHES OLIPHANT OLD
Erskine Theological Seminary

If one wishes to dig deeply into the subject of prayer as modeled by Jesus, this treatment of John 17 by Michael Cannon will be an enormous help. Cannon explores Jesus' prayer both exegetically and theologically with assistance from some noted Reformed scholars of the past. The result is strong Scripture-based teaching on the purpose, motivation, and meaning of prayer. This volume is especially strong in the integration of theology and praxis. I highly recommend this fine work.

—DONALD L. HAMILTON
Columbia International University Seminary and School of Missions

This study of Jesus' prayer in John 17 is firmly grounded in scripture and solid theology. The book takes concepts from the High Priestly prayer and ties them together with pertinent scripture passages to show how this chapter presents Jesus as the great High Priest, the second person of the trinity, and the Savior. The use of great teachers and preachers of the past helps the book avoid the shallow trendiness and novelty which is the bane of so many sermon and academic books today. The book is a treasure trove of material for sermons and Bible study.

This study of Jesus' High Priestly prayer in John 17 is a study of the great themes of Christianity as reflected in this parayer and ties together much of scripture and great preachers and thinkers from many Christian traditions. It systematically explores Christ's role and purpose and helps our understanding of John's presentation of Jesus.

—RAY K SUTHERLAND
University of North Carolina at Pembroke

The Prayer of Jesus

The Prayer of Jesus

An Expository and Analytical Commentary on John 17

MICHAEL CANNON JR.

RESOURCE *Publications* · Eugene, Oregon

THE PRAYER OF JESUS
An Expository and Analytical Commentary on John 17

Copyright © 2011 Michael Cannon Jr. All rights reserved. Except for brief quotations in critical publications or reviews, no part of this book may be reproduced in any manner without prior written permission from the publisher. Write: Permissions, Wipf and Stock Publishers, 199 W. 8th Ave., Suite 3, Eugene, OR 97401.

Resource Publications
An Imprint of Wipf and Stock Publishers
199 W. 8th Ave., Suite 3
Eugene, OR 97401

www.wipfandstock.com

ISBN 13: 978-1-60899-876-0

Manufactured in the U.S.A.

For my son . . . my friend whom I long to see

Contents

Preface

I AM CONVINCED THAT John Chapter 17 is unique in all the chapters of the Bible. Chapter 16 ends with a declaration of victory and an encouragement to take heart in the face of immanent difficulty. And then Jesus lifts his eyes to heaven and speaks with his Father in prayer. We become like a fly on the wall listening to an intimate exchange between Father and Son, between the first and second person of the Trinity, and between our Savior and our God. The sum of the mission of Christ is found in these verses as well as the sum of our position in him.

A careful study of these verses can yield a theology that will embrace the cardinal doctrines of the Christian faith. It's all here: incarnation theology, our union with Christ, sovereign decrees and election, propitiation, the atonement, the great commission and the communion of the saints. These and more are nested in the words of our savior as he prays to the Father. Is there any more sacred ground than to be present when the incarnate Lord speaks to the God of heaven? So remove the sandals from your feet and read the 17ᵗʰ chapter of the Gospel according to John over and over again. In that chapter you will come to know the heart of the Savior.

The greatest benefit to the work you now hold in your hand is the re-emergence of some of the greatest expositors of this chapter to have been published. Newton, Manton, Augustine, Jones, and others have invested their lifetime of study into interpreting this chapter for us. I am humbled to have access to such great works and hope that uniting them in this work will help to further the understanding of the Church.

I

When God Prays

(John 17:1)

THE BOOK OF JOHN, Chapter 17 is commonly referred to as the *High Priestly Prayer* for good reason. It presents something that is unique in all of Scripture, the prayer of God the Son to God the Father, a communication within the Trinity.

The apostle John has given us the ministry of Jesus Christ, and that ministry is being summed in this prayer. To truly understand this prayer, we need a grasp of the balance of John's Gospel because so much of what Jesus has said and done before is brought to full light here in His expression of prayer. When taken as part of the entire book, the Gospel of John breaks down roughly into two parts; John, Chapters 1–12 present Jesus to the world as the Christ who is salvation being presented for all men in all places to see and to hear. In John 13–21, Jesus then turns His attention toward the development of his disciples and is manifested more particularly to them—to His own.

So in the first half of the book, Jesus is presented to the world and in the second half, 13–21, Jesus is manifested to His own. In exploring these themes, we find that this Gospel takes the form of a sermon. In John 13, He is presented as our advocate. And, in Chapter 14, He is described as the promised Messiah and the object of our hope. In Chapter 15, Jesus is the Living Vine and we are the branches. It is Christ who strengthens us by giving us life and feeding us from the life that is in Himself. As we are abiding in Christ, we do His will just as His Word abides in us. In Chapter 16, we find He is the giver of the Holy Spirit.

This brings us to Chapter 17 where Jesus Christ is working as our High Priest. Even the crucifixion itself is presented in terms of the burnt offering, which was for those who were already in living relationship with God.

The first verse of Chapter 17 is the introduction to the rest of the prayer and merits considerable attention. "When Jesus had spoken these words, He lifted up His eyes to heaven, and said, "Father, the hour has come; glorify Your Son that the Son may glorify You.""

Most Christians can identify with the question with which the disciples approached Jesus, "Lord, teach us to pray." There are scores, volumes, stacks, and shelves of books written on prayer. While there is much agreement about prayer, there is also much disagreement about prayer. There are many who won't even agree on the use of prayer or the obligation to pray. Despite all the books and all the teachings on prayer, probably there is no spiritual discipline that is neglected more than prayer.

Regardless of the multiple views on prayer, they would fall between two extremes. If we exclude prayers which do not even address a personal God, but are simply expressions of meditation to calm the spirit, and include only those that actually address the Christian's conception of God, we would find these two extremes.

The first extreme is that prayer is something that is easy and that answers are guaranteed. According to this teaching, if you pray by a specific formula, perhaps even in the name of Jesus, then there will be an answer to all prayer. This teaching forgets all of the Scriptural teaching, which applies conditions to prayer. For example, there is in 1 Peter, a teaching that says, "Husbands, if your relationship with your spouse is not right, your prayers are not heard." Did you know of that condition? There is a condition of the human heart that is necessary for a prayer to be heard by God. We pray through Christ who is our mediator. Any teaching that tells you to close your eyes, utter a few words, and expect an answer is contrary to the Scriptural teachings on prayer.

The other extreme is an avoidance of prayer altogether in the belief that God is sovereign and God predestines all things. Since God already knows what's going to happen and even knows the substance of any prayer that I would make, why bother with that at all? I'll simply, as a sign of faith and trust, neglect prayer as a testimony that God is going to handle it according to His will. Why voice my will when God knows better than I what is His will?

Those who would follow that sort of teaching forget also the teaching of Scripture. They forget that we are commanded to pray. It's not something for us to contemplate whether we ought to or ought not to do; we are commanded to pray. Also, they are forgetting the proper object of prayer. Prayer is not about accomplishing our will or putting our will in conflict or in contest against God. Prayer is about glorifying God. Not only is prayer taught and exemplified in Scripture, but we have recorded the Lord's own prayer here in John 17.

We know that Jesus prayed on many occasions. In some instances, we are given the content or the purpose of the prayer, but here we are given a script of His prayer, a glimpse at the heart of God. The chapter from beginning to end is the Lord's Prayer. Usually when you hear someone refer to the Lord's Prayer, you think of the prayer Jesus taught His disciples which many congregations employ in their own services. This prayer is recorded in Luke 11 and the Sermon on the Mount. Some, particularly the Roman Church, refer to that prayer as the *Our Father*. A better designation would be the "Disciple's Prayer" because it was a model of prayer provided for the disciples to use as they prayed. It was taught by the Lord, but it was prayed by the disciples.

In John 17, we're presented the actual prayer of our Lord—the Lord's own prayer. The Lord's Prayer in John 17 is not one He taught us, but one He made for us. In His sinlessness, Jesus never actually prayed *with* people, but *for* people. He, for example, did not say with the disciples, "Forgive us our debts as we forgive our debtors," for as the sinless Son of God, He had no debts to be forgiven. He prayed *for* His people. This prayer follows the sermon He just delivered in chapters 14–16.

In that sermon, Jesus described the coming of the Holy Spirit. He gave His disciples the promise of their own future place of glory. He promised to intercede for them as their mediator. He exhorted them to obey and abide in Him and His Word. He placed all of this in the context of their union with Him. We speak often of Jesus making continual intercession with the Father, but here we see something of what that prayer might look like. It's Jesus praying a high priestly prayer to God the Father. Now Jesus turns His face from speaking with the disciples. He looks heavenward, symbolically lifting His eyes from the earth to the heavens, and begins to pray and speak to the Father. This passage, this chapter follows the tone and pattern of that prayer.

John has recorded an unambiguous connection between the prayer of Chapter 17, and the sermon in Chapters 14–16. The prayer is a consummation of all the promises Jesus has made to the disciples. It's a consummation of all the admonitions He has given. It's a consummation of all the predictions He has made and the basis for them is found in heaven. There is not one conditional sentence in this prayer. There is not one place you will find a Scripture that reads, "If you do this then I will do that." This is a prayer from Jesus to the Father.

We can model our own prayers after this prayer by learning it is a prayer to our Heavenly Father. The object of all prayer is to bring about God's glory that we may pray not only for ourselves, but others also as Jesus is doing. There is also a sense in which we cannot model our prayers after this prayer because this is in the first person as Christ is praying to God. The prayer of God incarnate is addressed to God the Father. There isn't any hint of a confession of sin in this prayer, but instead the exact opposite. Christ has been and remains perfectly obedient to the Father and that is reflected in this prayer.

Nevertheless, the Spirit seems to have made this prayer especially available to us because Jesus did pray it other times. We know that He prayed in Gethsemane, "Father, if there is any way to remove this cup then take it from Me, but nevertheless, Thy will not Mine be done." We know on the Cross, Jesus prayed. We know there were other times Jesus prayed, but here we are given both the form and the substance of all of His prayer as far as we know.

Thomas Manton, the great Puritan preacher said, "This prayer is a standing monument to Christ's affection to the church" (109). Martyn Lloyd-Jones, another wonderful preacher quoting a 17th century preacher said, "It is the greatest prayer that was ever offered on earth, and it follows the greatest sermon that was ever preached on earth" (11). We should approach all of Scripture with a sense of reverence and awe, all of Scripture because it is the very Word of God. Paul taught that to Timothy in 2 Timothy 3:16. "All Scripture is breathed out by God and is profitable for teaching, for reproof, for correction and for training in righteousness," yet there is something that seems to settle on us as we reflect on this prayer of Jesus—a conversation within the Trinity, a conversation between God the Father and God the Son, as God the Son who is incarnate is now lifting His eyes and focusing exclusively on His words to God the Father.

The Trinity existed in all eternity and yet here we hear conversation. We might have expected to be told that such a prayer occurred, but to be allowed to remain and listen is further indication of the reality of our union with Christ. It would be one thing if the Scriptures recorded simply, "Jesus retired and communed and prayed to God the Father, and perhaps was ministered to by the angels and the Spirit of God," but we're not given just that. We're allowed to listen as Christ speaks to God.

Many have treated John 17 as too sacred to preach. There are others such as John Knox who, as he was approaching death, had it read to him each and every day, and as he was passing begged his wife to read him John 17, and his life expired even while she was reading that passage to him. So great, so comprehensive are the truths in John 17, that again, Martyn Lloyd-Jones says, "If we had nothing but John 17, we would surely have more than enough to sustain us because our Lord has given us an insight into our whole position and into everything that is of importance and of value to us while we are in this world of time" (13).

If ever you were looking for Cliff Notes to the gospel, John 17 is your Cliff Notes. It presents the person of Christ. It presents the gospel. It presents us and who we are in Christ, as Christ prays for Himself and His disciples and the Church. John 17 begins, "After He spoke these words. . . ." What words? We are reminded again of these chapters, which were intended to establish and comfort the disciples through instruction. These words should be marked carefully as not for man, but from the Son of God. The Son of God preached a sermon in the verses and in the chapters leading up to this prayer. The sermon was intended to comfort the disciples with the words, "Let not your hearts be troubled. . . ." He doesn't stop with the words of instruction and assurance but goes on to pray for them, to commit them to the Father, saying in verse 11 of Chapter 17, "Keep them in your name which you have given me."

Such is the love of Christ that He first begins by settling, assuring and grounding His disciples in truth through instruction and teaching, and then He prays to the Father that they would be preserved. The disciples came to know not only the doctrines and truth concerning Christ, but the genuineness of His love, the genuineness of His compassion as He begins interceding for them even while He is still in the flesh, even in the moments before His betrayal and His crucifixion.

Thomas Manton observes, "Hitherto, Christ has dealt with man in the name of God, opening His counsel to us, but now He deals with God in the name of men, opening our case to Him" (110). He speaks *to* us in the Word and He speaks *for* us in prayer. That simple line is worth remembering. Christ speaks *to* us in His Word. He speaks *for* us in prayer. Our Christ prays for us, continually interceding for His people. Our Christ hasn't simply completed His work on earth and ascended and is seated at the right hand of God, but our Christ continues His ministry of prayer. We have that first prayer before us now in chapter 17.

In this prayer, in Chapter 17, we have three major divisions—three major subjects. First of all, taken as a whole, the prayer is for the Church because Christ Himself is the head and believers are the body. Christ is the head and all who are in Christ are the body. We might break it down more particularly.

Verses 1–5: Jesus is praying for Himself.

Verses 5–19: He prays for His disciples, those who were present with Him, those believers who brought to us these Scriptures and who carried the gospel out following the resurrection.

Verse 19 to the end: Jesus is praying for us, for future believers, for those who would hear the gospel and believe. He's praying, again, for His Church. Frederic Godet notes, "The shout of victory at the end of the sermon is an anticipation of the faith, and now Jesus turns to the one who is omnipotent and who can grant faith" (323). He ends His sermon with a strain of victory. He has overcome all things—a victorious note at the end of the sermon. Then He turns in prayer to the One who can grant the faith that is required for those of us who would enter into Christ.

Let's note first how immediately Jesus goes into prayer. He finishes His sermon, and He immediately moves to a time of prayer. He turns His eyes toward heaven, and He gazes into the heavens. His praying, in effect, is sealing His teaching with the acknowledgment that it was all taught in the presence of God the Father. Nothing was done in isolation. God the Father was there while Jesus was teaching, and now when He finishes teaching the disciples, He turns immediately to prayer to God the Father. He speaks plainly and directly when He teaches the disciples. He speaks plainly and directly when He speaks to God the Father.

We should be embarrassed that we are so quickly tired out from prayer. How many of us simply tire out from prayer. Any moment allowed for prayer in a service of worship will feel like an eternity to many, while idle conversation among peers passes quickly and effortlessly. In the few moments at the beginning of our service we have a time for silence; how many look forward to that, realizing that as we have come into the church and as we have come into the household of faith, as we've enjoyed greeting one another in faith, how many look forward to that 30–second window of prayer? To how many does it seem like 10 minutes because we tire out so easily in prayer?

In prayer, we pour out our whole soul to the glory of God. Is that expression of our soul limited to a few simple sentences? Is there no depth to our expression of praise to God? Is there no sense of our own inadequacy even as we enter into His presence for worship? There is too much time between our acts of devotion and our time for Christ-like work and activity; consequently our flame begins to die, and our heat grows cold. We do not turn immediately to a time of prayer. We let time lapse. What do we do in the time that lapses? We dwell in the world. We turn our attention to worldly things. So we wonder why our love of Christ has gone cold when we have walked so far away and for so long from the heat of His love. We allow the energy to engage in the holy activities of faith to diminish. We have weak spiritual fortitude because we are so unrehearsed in our times of prayer.

Manton compares Christians to birds who are foolish and leave their nests and, after straggling along and delaying, return to find that the eggs have cooled before they have hatched. So the church today has transitioned from a house of prayer to a place of fellowship, or to a concert hall, or to many other things, but rarely a house of prayer. We have much to say, but we have little to pray. When our hearts are warned by the teaching of Scripture, we ought to spend our time afterward in conversation with God. Isn't prayer testimony to the reality of our faith that God is present?

Prayer for one who does not believe God is present is hollow, rhetorical exercise, but if God is present, if God were manifest in flesh again and stood here supernaturally as He appeared in the Upper Room to the disciples, which one of us would only give a few seconds to Him then wonder, *Why must I be engaged in prayer with the Lord for so long? Can't we do this quicker?* Why are we tired so easily from being directly engaged with God in prayer? It's almost as if we beg, "Engage me with anything but God. Talk to me about God, but for me to be personally engaged with God through prayer? I tire and I'm wearied. I can't pray that long."

When our hearts are warned by the teaching of Scripture, we ought to spend our time afterward in conversation with God. Communion in

Scripture ought to follow naturally with communion in prayer because prayer is the ascension of the heart to God. The psalmist David understood. Psalm 25:1, *"To You, O Lord, I lift up my soul."* Why is it so precious to sing from the Psalms? It's not a condemnation of hymns. Hymns are wonderful expressions of faith. Hymns are wonderful encapsulations or summaries of Christian doctrine. They are wonderful for teaching. Psalms are words of prayer from psalmists. They teach us the language of prayer and the heart of prayer. "To You, O Lord, I lift up my soul." It's good that we lift up our voices, but so much the better when with understanding, and high and holy thoughts of God, we experience a true love and reverence that finds expression in prayer. Where there is no prayer, I would question genuine love and reverence.

If we are to pray, we ought to do so with certainty as Jesus does. Six times in His prayer He uses the term *Father*. There is no doubt concerning the relationship between God the Son and God the Father. We must pray as one of His own. Not only does He say *Father*, but in verse 11, He calls Him *Holy Father*. We have to remember with reverence and awe, our Father is holy.

Frederic Godet, again points out, "When Jesus prays for Himself, it's not His own person He prays for the work and glory of God" (323). Ponder that a moment. When Jesus prays for Himself, He is not praying for His own person, but for the work and the glory of God as manifest in His person. When He prays for His apostles, it is to commend them to God as agents to continue His work. He prays for their safety. He prays for their welfare so that they may continue the work of Christ to the glory of the Father. When He prays for us, those who at that time had yet to even be born, much less believe, it is because we are the objects of the work of the gospel where the glory of God shines forth. We can see the main concern throughout the whole prayer is the glory of God. This is God's purpose in our salvation—His own glory.

I love Lloyd-Jones' discussion on this point. It's bad news for the modern mind. He says, "The entire gospel of salvation is displayed in these first five verses of John, chapter 17. The gospel is focused on God's own glory, but that point is missed by most in the church today" (44).

> When Jesus had spoken these words, He lifted up His eyes to heaven, and said, 'Father, the hour has come; glorify Your Son that the Son may glorify You, since You have given Him authority over all flesh, to give eternal life to all whom You have given Him.

> And this is eternal life, that they know You the only true God, and Jesus Christ whom You have sent. I glorified You on earth, having accomplished the work that You gave me to do. And now, Father, glorify Me in Your own presence with the glory that I had with You before the world existed." (John 17:1–5)

The gospel, the entire gospel is being displayed in these first five verses.

Jones tells us that it used to be our fathers' delight to consider all of the gospel and all of its complexity and all of its simplicity. In every dimension and in every facet, its history, its expression. They used to take joy in spending an entire day simply exploring the gospel of salvation—something that even the angels marvel at as they look at it. But for us, it has become something small, something easily mastered, something so simple that we simply touch on it and then move on.

Jones says, "The trouble with us is, as I am never tired of pointing out, that we are so utterly subjective. We are always looking at ourselves, at how things affect us, and at what we want for ourselves. We are slaves to our own habits, and states, and desires and to our own likes and dislikes. And the result is that we approach everything from the standpoint of what it means to us" (42). He's saying everything in our religious life, everything in our religious expression and all that our minds are consumed with concerning the church and the gospel is all about what it means to *us*. So subjective is the modern mind. So centered is the world on *us* that everything is to be ordered as to what it means to me, to us.

As Jones says, "And we look at the gospel for what it has to say to me, how it can help me and we fail to hear what the gospel has to say about us. The gospel becomes subjective and small" (43). Jesus' prayer is an objective look at the gospel. Every subject of Jesus' prayer has the glory of God as the object. Do you want to know what the center of gravity for the gospel is? The glory of God. The center of gravity for God's purpose in salvation is not me. It's His own glory—the glory of God. The ultimate purpose in salvation has always been the glory of God. That's even revealed to us in salvation when we see it correctly—the glory of God.

Jesus, knowing the agony of the Cross was just ahead, in His humanity dreading the pain and the suffering, also sees the glory of God that will be manifest in the salvation that follows. When you see the gospel, you will see the holiness and the righteousness of God as well as God's mercy and compassion and love. The Cross is a symbol of God's unwillingness to permit sin and unrighteousness in His creation. His character is holy, and sin, which is worse than cancer in the body, must be destroyed. Because of the mercy and love demonstrated in the gospel, we are spared that destruction.

In the beginning of this prayer, we see the hour has arrived. Earlier in the gospels, Jesus often said, "It is not yet My time." But now, the time has come for Jesus' betrayal, His arrest, His crucifixion. The objective of all this which was on Jesus' mind is the glory of God. How much of our prayer is spent asking God that He be glorified in our lives versus the time spent asking for blessings, relief, cures, opportunities, wants, needs, desires? Out of the small amount of time we spend in prayer, how much of that is spent saying, "God, may You be glorified," versus how much time is spent saying, "Lord, I have needs, and I come to You because there is nowhere else for me to go."

In that appearance of piety, we somehow then become disbelievers in answered prayer because we have approached prayer with our own end in mind, with our own glory in mind as if God's whole purpose was simply to listen and obey our requests, and we have missed the whole purpose of the gospel, which was God's glory. Jesus' prayer was a model not only for us to follow, but to show us more clearly the nature and purpose of the gospel itself, which is God's glory.

2

Glory and Power

John 17:1–5

JOHN, CHAPTER 17 IS a conversation we are blessed to have received, a prayer offered by God incarnate, in Christ, to God the Father, a conversation between the Father and the Son given to us in great detail that we might know something of the mind of Christ in those moments before His arrest and crucifixion. We find expressed here His great love for the Father and His great love for you and for me as He prays for Himself and for the disciples, who were there present with Him, and He prays for the church, for those who would come to believe in the future. We have in Chapter 17 a preciousness of collected words which are the prayer of Christ. All Scripture is inspired by God, but isn't there something of the sense of hallowed and sacred ground as the Son speaks to the Father in prayer? It causes us to pause as we come to these verses.

> When Jesus had spoken these words, He lifted up His eyes to heaven, and said, "Father, the hour has come; glorify Your Son that the Son may glorify You, since You have given Him authority over all flesh, to give eternal life to all whom You have given Him. And this is eternal life, that they know You the only true God, and Jesus Christ whom You have sent. I glorified You on earth, having accomplished the work that You gave Me to do. And now, Father, glorify Me in Your own presence with the glory that I had with You before the world existed."

We determined in the previous chapter that the nature and goal of prayer, and of the gospel itself, is God's glory. In fact, as we study the Scriptures, God's glory begins to emerge more and more as the beginning and the end of all things in the Scriptures. We're remiss if we forget that the first of the Shorter Catechisms, which our children learn, asks us this question, "What is the chief end of man?" What we learned there at the very beginning of a Christian's journey in learning—if that learning is based upon the outline provided by our catechism—is that the chief end of those who have obtained eternal life through Christ to is to glorify God and enjoy Him forever; to glorify God, to cause His testimony to shine forth, and to live in the light of the truth of God.

We gather in our services to give God the *glory*, but we use the word so frequently that something about the meaning it has become lost, as so many words we use. We use a lot of language without reference really to the particular definition. We use language more in an adjectival sense. That is, we like to use it as a descriptive word, but rarely do we contemplate the weight of what we are saying. We say, "We gather to give God the glory," almost as if it's an aside in the Christian life; just one of the many things we do as Christians. We give God glory. We do so many things in our service to God and we list *giving Him glory* as one of them. But isn't it the *primary* work of the Christian? To give God the glory—a work in which everything else is then ordered beneath.

Glory and *light* are often used to describe God in the Scriptures. It is God's glory that Moses asked to see in Exodus 33:18. "God, Father show me Your glory." God's glory is what we are to proclaim, as we are told in 1 Chronicles 16:24, "Declare His glory among the nations. . . ."

What is it we are to be declaring when we declare His glory? If it had said, "Preach the Word among the nations," we would understand that quite clearly, and in fact we are to preach the Word among the nations, but how is it we *declare His glory*? If I could say to you, "Pull out a piece of paper and write down what is it distinctively you are declaring when you declare His glory," what would you say? What would you write? How would you respond?

In Psalm 96, verses 2 and 3 connect declaring God's glory with telling of His salvation. Explaining the salvation of God is a way of declaring His glory. In Ezekiel, Chapter 43, the glory of the Lord is described as something that comes and fills the temple. His glory and His person are the same. If you read *glory* throughout the Scriptures, particularly in the Old Testament, you come to know that glory is so closely identified with His person as to be inseparable. Glory is not just a characteristic; glory is a description of God. But do we understand that when we use that term?

Do we understand glory is a way of saying, "I'm speaking of God"? To see His glory and to tell of His glory means to see God.

In Isaiah 6:3 we read, "Holy, holy, holy is the LORD of hosts; the whole earth is full of His glory!" What are they saying there? *"The whole earth is full of His glory!"* I'm afraid we use that in much more of a sentimental sense than we do in a realistic sense. When we say, "The whole earth is full of His glory," do we mean it as some sort of a passionate way of saying, "Everything bears testimony to God"? Do we mean that God is wonderful, almost in a pantheistic way?

If we say, "The whole earth is full of His glory," without knowing what we are saying when we use the word *glory*, we may be abusing that word by assigning it in ways it simply is not intended to be used. The Scriptures say, "The whole earth is full of His glory!" But because of our misunderstanding of the word "glory," we distort that word by applying it in many other ways. We need to recognize that when we say "glory" we are saying, "The whole earth testifies to God. It bears a testimony to the truth of God."

In Romans, Chapter 1:23 we find that, in man, the glory of God has been exchanged for idolatry. In other words, our gaze has moved from God's glory to the glory of those things made by the hands of men, to our own lives. In some cases, they're actual crafted idols. We idolize and give glory and ascribe glory to many things which have nothing to do with God, and yet to God alone belongs the glory.

Romans 1 indicts us for it, saying we have taken the glory of God and exchanged if for idolatry. In Romans 3:23 Paul continues, "As creatures created in God's image our sin has brought us short of manifesting God's glory." Our very lives, our very persons are to manifest God's glory. This is tied into our being united to Christ an into our being indwelled by the Holy Spirit, being temples of the Holy Spirit. We are to manifest God's glory in our person as we are being changed day after day into the likeness of His image. Our lives are to bear testimony. In other words, our lives are to bear the *glory* of God as it testifies of God.

We can conclude at this point, at the very least, with Jonathan Edwards who said, "The great end of God's work, which is variously expressed in Scripture, is indeed but one. And this one end is most properly and comprehensively called the glory of God." The great end of God's work is comprehensively called the glory of God. So, in other words, the gospel, creation, salvation, the kingdom, all of it, all of it is under the great heading of, "An expression of the glory of God."

I hope now you're beginning to get a sense in which we really have not used the word *glory* properly. We speak of all of those subcategories, which together express the glory of God. God's glory is the subject of Jesus' first petition in His prayer. The very first petition in Jesus' prayer is that the Father would glorify Him, as the Son, in order that the Son would glorify the Father. What exactly is the *glory* Jesus is speaking of here? The prayer is confusing because Jesus had glory from eternity. It seems that He must have lost it when he became incarnate, since He is asking the Father to restore it in order that He Himself can glorify the Father. Yet, He does have glory on earth because He has revealed it to others in finishing the work God had given Him to do.

We can sort out the confusion if we begin with an understanding of the definition of the word "glory." The word in its English roots as well as in ancient languages means *to seem,* or *to appear,* or *to have an opinion.* The Greek word *doxa* is retained and preserved in English words as in the words "orthodox" or when you hear the word "heterodoxy." Orthodox means to have a correct opinion of something. Heterodox means to have a different opinion of something. Paradox refers to conflicting opinions.

In describing religion, we use the word *orthodox* to mean they have a right opinion about the revelation of God as it's contained in the Scriptures. If someone is celebrating or practicing a heterodoxy that means they have an opinion that is different from what is presented in the Scriptures. Of course if they are living with paradox that means they find themselves conflicted in their ability to understand what is going on in the Scripture and what is happening in life.

As the word developed historically it came to mean simply this, *that which is worthy of a good opinion.* Thus, when in your mind you arrive at the truth about the revelation of God in the Scriptures, you esteem that truth highly. You have something before you worthy of a good opinion.

In the Psalms, the word is used in connection with God's attributes. God is called the King of Glory because He is perfect in the divine attributes of being King. His truth, justice, and mercy are perfect in expression and so He is worth the highest opinion of men. As God reveals Himself in Scripture, our opinion of Him advances; it grows until He has the highest position and our highest commitment and dedication in our opinions regarding Him.

Glory then points to worth. As you say, "I glorify God," you are assigning God worth so all that can be known of God becomes an expression of His glory. On a personal level, when we say, "I did it for the glory," the meaning is, "I accomplished something to be known for it and so that in knowing, men would hold me in high regard." In manifesting his glory, God is showing His person and His work and making it publicly known, and in making it publicly known His expectation is that men would highly esteem it, thereby giving him the glory.

In chapter 17, verse 4, Jesus said, "I glorified You on earth, having accomplished the work that You gave Me to do." By completing His work in ministry, Jesus was revealing the character of God. He was showing people God so we can say that when we see Jesus we have seen the Father. That's why Jesus was dismayed when the people said, "Just show us the Father and it's enough." And Jesus said, "Have I been with you all this time and still you ask me, 'Show me the Father?'"

What we do as a church is so important because it always points to something. Everything we do in worship is meant to point to God and God alone. Anything we do that points to anything else takes the glory intended for God alone and assigns it to something else. It can be religious in function, it can be secular in function, but it takes the glory God requires to be given to Him alone, and gives it to idols. Everything we do is critically important, because it's an expression and a testimony of our esteem of God.

Jesus, in asking to be glorified, shows what Paul is teaching in Philippians 2. Jesus had a glory in all eternity past. He set that aside, a radiance, as it were, of light, or a garment of light. If you want to, think of glory as light—so often it's referred to in Scripture as that light—and so He took that off and put in its place the flesh of man, inglorious in appearance. He's speaking of the resurrection when He says to the Father, "Glorify Me with that glory that I had before." He is speaking of that time when God would raise Him from the dead and grant to Him a glorified body.

While in the flesh, Jesus showed the Father's glory. In 2 Corinthians 3:17, "Now the Lord is the Spirit, and where the Spirit of the Lord is, there is freedom. And we all, with unveiled face, beholding the glory of the Lord, are being transformed into the same image from one degree of glory to another." Isn't that an amazing truth? The prayer which Jesus prayed, "Father, glorify Me that I may glorify You," we also can pray, because we all with unveiled faces are beholding His glory, because we are united with Christ. Because the Spirit has indwelled us, we are being transformed day after day into the same glory.

We also will receive, at the resurrection, glorified bodies. Now that's not to confuse us with Christ who is the one and only begotten Son, who is One with the Father, a member of the Trinity. But it is to say that that same glory of the Father, which will be indwelling in us, will manifest testimony, not of our own glory, but of His. We will become living testimonies as we show forth the glory of God.

Jesus ascribed Glory to God by His teaching and obedience, the Cross showed God's justice, and the resurrection shows His mercy. Jesus glorified God by teaching and living God's character before men. In short, Jesus glorified God by illumining God to people, showing them God's glory in His own person that they might think rightly about God. The Scripture is now saying that we, who with unveiled faces behold the glory of the Lord, must also live to do the same.

Our life's calling is to show God's glory in our living, that our lives, our bodies, our thoughts, our speech will all bear testimony to the truth of Scripture and show the glory of God. For what other purpose do we exist? The chief end of man, the highest end of man, is to glorify God and enjoy Him forever. That involves a journey of self-denial, obedience, and suffering until we too are glorified in the resurrection.

The ideas of self-denial, obedience, and suffering may give pause to some. How are we to glorify God? By testimony, faith, obedience, worship—yes, worship is our testimony to God's glory, but that's not our only testimony. In Romans 8:16–17, "The Spirit Himself bears witness with our spirit that we are children of God, and if children, then heirs—heirs of God and fellow heirs with Christ, provided we suffer with Him in order that we may also be glorified with Him."

First Peter 4:12 and 13, "Beloved, do not be surprised at the fiery trial when it comes upon you to test you, as though something strange were happening to you. But rejoice insofar as you share Christ's sufferings, that you may also rejoice and be glad when His glory is revealed."

Romans 8:18 says much of the same thing, "For I consider that the sufferings of this present time are not worth comparing with the glory that is to be revealed to us."

Quoting from Luke 24:26, the great puritan, Thomas Manton said, "Shame, sorrow, and death is the roadway to glory, joy, and life. The

Captain of our salvation was thus made perfect and all the followers of the Lamb are brought in by that same method" (122).

> Hebrews 2:10, "For it was fitting that He, for whom and by whom all things exist, in bringing many sons to glory, should make the Founder of their salvation perfect through suffering."

Let me refer you to two other passages, lest you think that we are practicing what is called isogesis—that is picking a passage that just talks about suffering and then making it a doctrine. We see in Matthew, Chapter 5, "Blessed are you when others revile you and persecute you and utter all kinds of evil against you falsely on my account."

Matthew chapter 10, verse 16, 24, and 25, tell us, "Behold, I am sending you out as sheep in the midst of wolves, so be wise as serpents and innocent as doves . . . A disciple is not above his teacher, nor a servant above his master. It is enough for the disciple to be like his teacher. . . ." So Jesus commands us, "Take up your cross." Manton concludes, "It is the folly of some to think to be in heaven before they have done anything for God's glory upon earth. It is a trustworthy saying, if we are dead with Him, we shall also live with Him. If we suffer we shall reign with Him. We are too delicate. We would have our path strewn with roses and do not like the discipline" (122).

So we can conclude at this juncture as Jesus Himself was facing the Cross—and was praying that God would glorify Him in order that through the Cross and the resurrection He would glorify the Father—that those who are saved by grace, not by works lest any should boast, those who are redeemed by the atoning work of Christ, secured in His righteousness alone, regenerated by the work of the Holy Spirit, must also suffer. First Peter 4:13, "But rejoice insofar as you share Christ's sufferings, that you may also rejoice and be glad when His glory is revealed."

But where, among God's people is the suffering that we see in the Scriptures that is so indicative of a life in Christ? We know there have been, and there will be and are even today, many who are called to martyrdom, and we also know that many will not be called to martyrdom. Martyrdom is not the only means of suffering for Christ. Yet the world, we know, is also under the reign of the Prince of Darkness, and it is filled with spirits and principalities of evil that are constantly striving against the kingdom of heaven and against the glory of God and God's people. No Christian is at home in the world, but we are called to live as aliens and foreigners, sojourners, passing through this world.

Many who claim Christ live very comfortably and easily in the world, suffering absolutely no resistance and fighting no battles. Why? Why are those who call themselves Christians so comfortable in the world which ought to be a foreign and hostile place? The writer of Hebrews also wonders, "You have not resisted sin to the point of shedding blood." We observed that most Christians haven't even broken a sweat, much less resisted to the point of shedding blood.

I am reminded of the days of my youth when we would go to the beach together as a family. My parents would go out first and would put everything in place on the sands. There would be the towel with the distinctive colors, the cooler. Everything was prepared. We'd go down into the water where we played absently for a time. Suddenly, if we were not careful, we could look up and realize that the person watching from the beach was not our mother, not our father, and that the blanket was the wrong color. In fact, the hotel behind them was not even the place where we were staying. Somehow we had been moved down the shore. If we didn't look up once in a while and pay attention, we could find ourselves a hundred yards down the beach, moved by a knee-deep undertow, without even struggling against it.

We have moved far, far away from where we began, and we have to confess some seem at ease in the world because they don't see their place in the kingdom of God. They have lost their point of reference. They've simply waded into the world thinking that only going in knee-deep somehow would preserve their Christian integrity. They would stay right with God because they haven't gone in over their head. They haven't given themselves fully to the world, and so unbeknownst to them—and it would be a shock and a surprise to many of them—the undertow has indeed carried them far from where they began with Christ. And if they would only turn and begin to walk as Christ has called them to walk, they would realize the world, which they have settled so easily into and which seems to be offering so little resistance, actually now, when they turn to walk the path of Christ, is their fierce enemy and will push against them to the point of exhaustion.

The flesh of man always wants ease and self-glory. Self-glory is the opposite of humility and it is sin. Self-glory is the lifting up of ourselves rather than the Gospel. Self-glory is an unwillingness to go the way of

Christ but an adaptation to the way of man. When Jesus prays, "Glorify Me," He isn't speaking of the same vainglories of the world that men seek in its wealth, respect, position, pass-times and honor; He wants to be glorified with the Father.

First Peter 1:21, ". . . God, who raised Him from the dead and gave Him glory, so that your faith and hope are in God." This must be the focus of our own prayer as well. If we are risen with Christ, we must seek those things that are above. We must seek first the kingdom of God and the righteousness thereof. We must, like Christ, take our eyes off of that which is on earth and raise our eyes unto the heavens—whether it's physically in prayer, or whether it is spiritually—as we are changing our focal point in life from that which belongs to man and brings joy to man to that which belongs to God and gives glory to God.

This is the remedy to the tribulation and difficult times we face in life, the suffering we think we endure. We lift our eyes from the temporal suffering of this life and gaze on the hope, the blessings, of eternity. 2 Corinthians 4:17, "For this light, momentary affliction is preparing for us an eternal weight of glory beyond all comparison. . . ."

We could paraphrase Jesus' opening lines of His prayer this way: "Father, I have glorified You on earth. That is, I have shown them Your might and Your compassion. I have taught them Your love and Your salvation. I am the Word of God, a Light in the darkness. I have lived that man may see You. Now Father, glorify Me by raising Me from the grave, by causing Me to sit at Your right hand to rule, by fulfilling Your purpose in Me for the redemption and salvation of man by the covenant of grace in order that I may glorify You. There is no glory in My body that will remain in the grave, but when You raise Me, the glory is Yours and when I return to the glory I once had, I will return to Our own and dwell in them, that their lives would be testimonies of Your gospel and You will be known and in being known, You will be glorified for every knee shall bow and every tongue will confess that I am the Lord."

So to glorify God is to see God in truth and to hold a right opinion of Him. We are called also to glorify the Father, just as Christ was. "Let your light so shine before men that they will see your works and glorify God in heaven." How do we glorify God? We can summarize by reviewing these points that are offered, again, by Thomas Manton in his great discourse on this passage:

1. *We glorify God by reverence, and thought, and in worship.* We behave as if we truly believe that He is a sovereign and transcendent God.

2. *By acknowledging Him in speech.* John 7:18, "The one who speaks on his own authority seeks his own glory; but the One who seeks the glory of Him who sent Him is true, and in Him there is no falsehood." We close our sentences with, "God willing." "Speak of His wonder and might before others," we read in Isaiah 48:1–11, a wonderful discourse of declaring God's might before the world.

3. *We make the progress of the kingdom the end of all our labors.* Such as in 1 Corinthians 10:31, "Whether you eat or drink, whatever you do, you do all for the glory of God." Philippians 1:20, ". . . with full courage now as always Christ will be honored in my body . . ." So we make the progress of the kingdom the end of every labor.

4. *Is that we make God's glory the aim of all our prayers.* When we close our eyes in prayer, praying for strength and for a vision to glorify God in everything that we are and in everything that we do.

5. *We are content to suffer shame if it brings God glory.* Was there any greater shame than the Cross? Was there any greater inglorious moment than when the life of Christ was ebbing there in the shame of the Cross? And yet it was there on the Cross that the promise of God was being fulfilled, and so it was there on the Cross when Jesus was glorified. C.S. Lewis says, "The glory of God and, as our only means to glorifying Him, the salvation of human souls is the real business of life" (521), and so a further way to glorify God is to express the glory of God as we express the gospel.

6. *To impress upon others their own obligations to glorify God.* Do not remain silent about this Christian obligation. The only way we are able to glorify God is transformation. First, the transformation that comes through salvation as the Spirit of God takes our hearts and brings life to that which is still and stone and dead. Secondly we are being transformed day after day into His glorious image, as that which is broken and flawed is being restored to that which is glorious and beautiful before God. If we do these things, then we will know the objective of our chief end, and that is to glorify God; when we ourselves receive glorified bodies, then we will enjoy him forever.

3

Father's Gift to The Son

(John 17:1–2)

WHILE ALL SCRIPTURE IS inspired by God and all Scripture is profitable for reading, reproof, for training in righteousness, for correction, yet we must feel that we are treading upon a holy ground when we read the words of Christ as He pours out His own soul before God the Father. We pause upon each word, for which word spoken within the unity of the Trinity would we gloss over? Which word is not as important as the word that came before when spoken by Christ as a petition and a prayer to the Father?

The prayer is broken down into largely three subtopics: Christ's prayer for Himself, Christ's prayer for the disciples, which He gathered around Him then at that very time, and also His prayer for us, those who would come to believe, the Church, which was just then beginning to form.

> Verses 1 and 2, chapter 17: "When Jesus had spoken these words, He lifted up His eyes to heaven, and said, "Father, the hour has come; glorify Your Son that the Son may glorify You, since You have given Him authority over all flesh, to give eternal life to all whom You have given Him."

At the conclusion of Chapter 16, Jesus says, "In the world you will have tribulation. But take heart; I have overcome the world." He is sounding the victory at the conclusion of His teaching to the apostles. The last word to the apostles is, "We have secured, I have secured the victory." It's not, "Woe is Me as I now go to the Cross. You are about to see suffering and shame such as you've never seen before. Remember what you will see now as I am pinned to a tree and as I bleed and die for you." Those are not the sentiments Jesus leaves them with. Jesus leaves them on the high note of victory. He says, ". . . but take heart, I have overcome the world." Thus, in Chapter 17, he turns His eyes from them up to heaven and prays, "Father . . . glorify your Son that the Son may glorify You, since You have given Him authority over all flesh. . . ."

God here is giving Christ two gifts, two gifts at Christ's own request. On special occasions we also give gifts. We buy and we give gifts as tokens or expressions of support or affirmation, perhaps because of something that has occurred or some significant date that is passing. On birthdays we tend to consider an individual's taste and their life, perhaps their hobbies, and we try to support that through the gift we give them. At Christmas, gifts usually have a broader application. Sometimes we give one gift for a whole family, sometimes for a couple. On anniversaries we do the same.

When we think of the crucifixion and the event of Christ there on the Cross, we usually see suffering, the ugliness of sin, the murder of an innocent Man. We ask, "What did God see when He looked at the Cross?" At the conclusion of Chapter 16, Jesus is speaking of victory. He's speaking of triumph. I would suggest to you, that's what God sees. As Jesus is ending on a high note, He is not presenting the Cross, at this place, as a time of mourning and sadness, but as a time of rejoicing in the glory of God, of victory.

Our opinion of the crucifixion has become so dark and so gloomy that we have to pause for just a minute and reflect, so that we won't be so puzzled, over why it is the joy of Christ. If we think of the Lord's Supper, do we see the Lord's Supper as a time of mourning as a time of oppression or anxiety? Consider the communion table; it is a celebration of Christ's atonement for us in His body and in His blood, a place where we celebrate. Is it a somber celebration? Yes, it is. Is it a serious celebration? Yes, it is.

Yet it is not a time of sadness. It is a time of joy, a time of victory and of celebration as we gather at the marriage feast of the Lamb, where Christ through the crucifixion and by the anointing of His people with the Holy Spirit and its indwelling in them has consummated the marriage, as it will, and provided us with this symbolic celebration. Just as the wedding ring is the symbol of marriage, the Supper is the symbol of our unity with Him.

If this is a time of joy, if it is a time of glory being given to God here at the Cross, then what gift would be fitting for the Son of God on the occasion of His victory and of His conquest over sin? God, we read, has given Him the authority to rule and He has given Him a people for a kingdom. Jesus says, referring to Himself, "Since you have given Him authority over all flesh to give eternal life to all whom You have given Him." Authority over all flesh and the power to give life to all He has given to Him, as well as the unity in the Godhead, those are gifts which glorify the Son at the completion of His mission and also glorify the Father and the salvation of men through the completion of the covenant of grace.

Verse 2 has a vital connection with the concept of glorifying God the Father in verse 1. In verse 1, Jesus says, ". . . the hour has come; glorify your Son that the Son may glorify you, since you have given Him authority over all flesh. . . ." The glorifying of God is connected with this authority that is given to Jesus. Jesus will be glorifying the Father through the exercising of authority over all flesh and through the granting of life to all whom the Father has given Him.

In effect we might paraphrase this idea in this way. "I will glorify you to the degree that you have given me authority over all flesh and to the end that I will give eternal life to all you have predestined to salvation, all you have given me."

In Matthew 9:6, Jesus asserted that He had authority over sin to forgive sin. In Luke, Chapter 8, as the waves raged about the boat which the disciples were in, and they feared for their very lives, Jesus demonstrated authority over the waves and hence over creation itself. Then in Luke, Chapter 7, verses 6 through 9, the centurion, a Gentile, has called for Jesus to heal his servant:

> And Jesus went with them. When He was not far from the house, the centurion sent friends, saying to Him, "Lord, do not trouble yourself, for I am not worthy to have you come under my roof. Therefore I did not presume to come to you. But say the word, and let my servant be healed. For I, too, am a man set under authority, with soldiers under me: and I say to one, 'Go,' and he goes; and to another, 'Come,' and he comes; and to my servant, 'Do this,' and he does it."

Even the centurion, a Gentile, recognizes that if Jesus simply says the word, He has authority to heal. The centurion says, "I have authority myself and I know what that means. It means if I tell someone to do something, they go do it." Such is the way of one who is under authority, who has authority and so he recognizes Jesus' own authority.

Jesus has been establishing His authority all throughout His ministry. In some of the sermons during the 1600's and 1700's, a great deal of importance was placed on the concept of Jesus' authority. The Law of God is heavily emphasized. Our early preachers concentrated on the words of Christ, insisting that Jesus did not come to remove or rewrite the law, but to fulfill the Law.

Christ's people who are now in unity with Christ, who Himself is subject to the Law, are also obligated to obey the Law. God's past faithfulness to Christ is an encouragement to Him in an hour of trial. Jesus prays for these gifts. "Lord God grant to me authority over all flesh that I also would give eternal life to the people you have given to me." Authority and a people.

Where is Jesus' confidence in praying for these two gifts from the Father? He knows the Father and He knows the faithfulness of the Father, and He knows the Father will be faithful to do all He has promised to do. That should be also an encouragement to us.

Jesus knew that we would be susceptible to discouragement. But he also knew the truth of the teaching of Judges 13:23: "If the Lord had desired to kill us, He would not have accepted a burnt offering and a grain offering from our hands. . . ." In other words, if God did not care and if God's design was to ultimately leave us and abandon us or to destroy us in the judgment, then He would not have called us to worship. He would not have offered us the Lord's Supper. He would not have given us His Word. He would not have accepted our worship. He would not have called us to life in Christ. So all of these bear testimony of God's faithfulness to the end that He will love and He will bless His people in the end.

The foundation of our assurance is not our steadfastness in the Christian life, but God's own faithfulness, that God himself is faithful to do that which we cannot. God will accomplish His will and God will be faithful to grant all He has promised. If God was determined to save the people, to draw them out of Egypt and give them a land and send them a Messiah, then we should be confident and have an even greater faith that God who does not change will help us as well.

Second Corinthians 1, 9 through 10, "Yes, we had the sentence of death in ourselves, that we should not trust in ourselves but in God who raises the dead, who delivered us from so great a death, and does deliver us; in whom we trust that He will still deliver us." Where's your confidence? What gives you a sense of assurance?

We live in a day when people act as if they have no conscience, and they do not reflect upon these things. We work hard to fool ourselves into thinking our soul is at ease when we know it is not. We are so afraid to come before God. Perhaps He will not accept us. Perhaps we won't be good enough. He will accept us in Christ, and no, we are not good enough, not one. All have sinned and fallen short of the glory of God. Yet, God calls and saves still. How? Because He has given to His Son eternal life to save all the Father has given Him. Which ones will be saved that come to Christ? All. Who comes? All the Father has given Him. Those will be saved.

The same trust in God that allowed Paul to finish his ministry despite sickness, prison, stoning, death, and threats of death, was an encouragement to Christ who now faced betrayal, arrest, flogging, crucifixion, and it ought to be an encouragement to us as well in our daily lives as we live and serve God. As you have given, or since you have given, Jesus is also encouraged because His request is based on God's promise, God's faithfulness and God's promise to give Him a possession and administration of the kingdom.

Psalm 2, verse 7 and 8, ". . . You are my Son, today I have begotten you. Ask of me, and I will give you the nations for your inheritance, And the ends of the earth for your possession." Jesus was encouraged in His prayer to ask God for authority and a kingdom based on God's faithfulness in power and also because it is the Father's to give. All authority belongs to God, and is His to give. All people belong to God. They are His to give. Jesus doesn't take His kingdom by force as Satan, who is a robber. He has been given a kingdom, by right, from the Father. Now we would wonder again, is there a gift that would fit such an atonement? What gift fits perfect righteousness? What gift fits selflessness and perfect humility? The gift of a people.

James Montgomery Boice reflects so eloquently here, "What could be more appropriate for God to give the Son than a people who should be conformed to His own blessed image and He and His brothers and sisters throughout eternity? Nothing we can possibly imagine would be more appropriate to that One who is Himself the Lord of glory than a people of His own" (1251–1252). First Corinthians 15:49, "Just as we have borne the image of the man of dust, we shall also bear the image of the Man of heaven." The gift of a people is given as the fulfillment of a covenant of redemption or, as some call it, the eternal covenant.

THE COVENANTS

To understand redemptive history we actually need to understand the flow of that history as it is revealed in the covenants. We understood that while there are many administrations of that covenant—for example, the Mosaic covenant where we are given the Law, the Davidic covenant where a kingdom is established, the new covenant, often called the New Testament, which is in Christ, the covenant of grace which is the fulfillment of the covenant—we know behind all of these is that covenant which has called itself the covenant of grace. But there seems to be a dimension of that which we often do not explore.

The covenant of grace, as it is presented in Scripture, has as its participants, God the Father and God's people with the mediator, the Lord Jesus Christ. It is through His mediation that grace is then given through the salvation of His people. But there is also what we might call the covenant of redemption which predates the covenant of grace. Some see it as a part of the covenant of grace rather than something distinct. Some see it as being an expression of the covenant of grace where a part of the covenant of grace is expressed toward the people who are saved, and another part is expressed to Christ Himself from God the Father. William G. Shedd, a great systematic theologian, a dogmatic theologian, sees it as a part of the covenant of grace whereas Louis Berkhof, another reform theologian, sees it as a distinct covenant from the covenant of grace.

The covenant of redemption is an agreement before God and His Son, Jesus Christ, a plan of redemption that was struck before there was time. Ephesians 1:4, ". . . even as He chose us in Him before the foundation of the world." There was activity going on regarding the salvation of man and the plan and economy of God before the world was even set upon its foundations. Ephesians 3:11, "This was according to the eternal purpose that he has realized in Christ Jesus our Lord," a purpose that predates time that belonged to the mind of God.

Second Timothy 1:8–9, ". . . for the gospel by the power of God, who saved us and called us to a holy calling, not because of our works but because of His own purpose and grace, which He gave us in Christ Jesus before the ages began. . . ." There was an agreement between the Father and the Son, within the Trinity, that Christ Jesus would fulfill the work of God and in so doing would receive the kingdom, the power and authority over all flesh, and a people in that kingdom whom the Father gives Him.

The Father originates the covenant. The Son executes the terms of the covenant. The Spirit applies the covenant. In the covenant of redemption, Jesus becomes responsible for its legal obligations, the obligations of man before God. He atones for our sins. He fulfills the Law God requires. He becomes the last Adam, our federal representative, of all whom the Father has given Him.

What were the requirements of this covenant of redemption? Jesus would assume human nature and become incarnate with all its present infirmities, though without sin. In Galatians 4:4 and 5, "But when the fullness of time had come, God sent forth His Son, born of woman, born under the Law, to redeem those who were under the Law, so that we might receive adoption as sons." As a second condition of that covenant, or requirement of it, Jesus would put Himself under the Law in order to fulfill the Law and also to pay its penalty. In Matthew 5:17 and 18, "Do not think that I have come to abolish the Law or the Prophets; I have not come to abolish them but to fulfill them. For truly, I say to you, until heaven and earth pass away, not an iota, not a dot, will pass from the Law until all is accomplished."

Many see the emphasis in this verse for the people of God, that we would recognize that Jesus, who Himself was placed under the Law, is not below us in accountability, but we in our union with Him now are also subject to the Law, having it written upon our hearts as the new covenant that is described in Jeremiah 31.

A third requirement of this covenant of Christ—that He would apply the fruits of forgiveness He secured to His own people by the converting power of the Holy Spirit in order that those believers, those followers of Christ, would live lives completely consecrated to the Father. One requirement Jesus owes to the Father is that, in completion of the terms of this covenant of redemption, He would give His people the Holy Spirit for the purpose of their being conformed into His own image that they would glorify God and be consecrated to God the Father in their own life, subjects in the kingdom, glorifying their King. Hebrews 7:25, "Consequently, He is able to save to the uttermost those who draw near to God through Him, since He always lives to make intercession for them."

* * *

Having completed the requirements, the obligations of this covenant, what were the promises given to Christ? We know the promises given to us in the covenant of grace. We know we are told if we will repent and believe, if we will confess with our mouth and believe with our heart that Jesus Christ is Lord, He will save.

But what are the promises given to Christ in the fulfillment of His own obligations to the Father?

1. That God would prepare the Son a body that would be glorified and fit for eternity.

2. That God would anoint Him with the gifts and graces that were needed for His role and task as a Messiah to His people. We see this particularly at His baptism, where he began His ministry and God walked with Him and empowered Him, not only to resist the devil, but also to accomplish through works of miracles and acts of forgiveness and through His teaching all God had designed for Him to accomplish.

3. That God would deliver Him from the power of death, He would not abandon His soul to Sheol, and He would enable Him to defeat Satan and establish the kingdom of God.

4. That God would enable Him to send out the Holy Spirit for the formation of the Spiritual body, which we call the Church. Acts 2:33, "Being therefore exalted at the right hand of God, and having received from the Father the promise of the Holy Spirit . . . ." God promised Him the Holy Spirit. The Holy Spirit was a gift given to Him on completion of the terms of the fulfillment of the covenant obligation. He also promised that He would give Him numerous seed, too many to count.

5. Finally, that God would grant Him all power on heaven and earth for the government of the world and of His Church.

We know now, when we read Hebrews 12:2, what it's referring to when we read, ". . . looking to Jesus, the founder and perfecter of our faith, who for the joy that was set before Him endured the Cross. . . ." The joy of Jesus was in His sure knowledge the Cross would bring to pass the promises of God and secure the salvation of all the Father had given to

Him. Now that's legal. It sounds dry. It sounds as if it's taking place in a courtroom, but I will tell you it's also very personal.

If I'm told my taxes are going to increase arbitrarily, if I'm told next year I'm going to have to pay $2,000 more, and at the sounds of my protests I am assured it's going to a good cause, to needful things, I still have no peace about the fact I'm going to be paying more money. I'm not content to give more money to the government to throw into a big heap of money for them to use as they will.

But if on the other hand I'm told I will have to pay not $2,000, but $4,000, or $5,000, or $10,000 to liberate someone I love, that I will have to give 10 times that amount to secure their life, would I not give it gladly? If I were able to give $20,000 for someone I know and love to save their life, versus $2,000 in taxes drawn arbitrarily by our government, which would I give? Which would I find joy in giving.

Those who would say Christ died for no one in particular, but just simply to make a possibility of salvation are saying Jesus gave His own blood as we would give taxes to the government, just in case someone could make good of it. But those who would say, "Jesus died for those whom the Father has given Him," not only are quoting Scripture, but are saying it's a deeply personal gift of life Christ has given to those whom He has been promised before the foundations of the earth, those whom the Father has given Him. Those are the ones Jesus loves, and , for their salvation Jesus gave His life with joy.

Authority over all flesh—all. We have to explore that just briefly. It's comprehensive in space and time, meaning it's comprehensive everywhere and in every age, past and future. He is the King of kings, He's the Lord of lords, and at His name every knee will bow and every tongue confess that He is Lord. That means those in heaven, that is the spiritual beings, angels, those on earth, all men in all places in all ages, and those under the earth, that is, the fallen angels, devils, demons.

So whether one is Christian, Jew, Muslim, Buddhist, Hindu, a Taoist, whether they're agnostic, atheist, whether they're Presbyterian, Baptist, Pentecostal, Methodist, Roman Catholic, all will know either Christ as Savior or Judge. Angels and the redeemed will acknowledge Jesus as their Lord and Savior with joy and gladness for the salvation that has been given to them. Devils and the damned, even those who are on the earth as damned, will acknowledge Jesus as Lord and judge from whose gaze they cannot escape. They will submit ultimately, but they will be forced on bended knee. They will not take it willingly. His authority is universal, and it is granted He will give eternal life, not to all, but to those whom the Father has given Him. He could give it to all if all were given to Him by the Father. His blood is sufficient to atone for the sin of all men in all places, but not all will be redeemed from the curse of sin.

John 10:25 through 29, the metaphor of the Good Shepherd, also helps us to understand this clearly. In John 10:25 He says, ". . . I told you, and you do not believe. The works that I do in my Father's name bear witness about me, but you do not believe because you are not part of my flock. My sheep hear my voice, and I know them, and they follow me. I give them eternal life, and they will never perish, and no one will snatch them out of my hand. My Father, who has given them to me, is greater than all, and no one is able to snatch them out of the Father's hand. I and the Father are one."

Like Joseph in Egypt, He has a power over all in the land, but a special affection for His brothers. Jesus is supreme and absolute in all the world, but He is head of the Church and we are His body. In the world He rules by providence. In the Church He rules by His testimony.

Here is our comfort. All is put into Christ's hands because He has authority over all flesh. Not a hair on our head is left uncounted. Not a sparrow falls from the sky that is in secret. Not a bullet is fired. Not a devil can stir to change the will of God against the authority of Christ.

We were warned there will be wars and rumors of wars. There will be persecutions and rebellions and yet, even calamity and disasters confirm God is sovereign for we have been warned by God. Though the earth gives way, though the mountains be moved to the heart of the sea, though the waters roar and foam, God is our refuge and strength and we will not fear.

We also know not only that all has been put in Christ's hands and we are secure, but also that we come to Christ as our King and we owe Him our obedience and fidelity. In First John 2:3, "And by this we know that we have come to know Him, if we keep His commandments." It was Christ's joy to go to the Cross, to bring all of human history to this crisis point of redemption. It was His joy to complete all that was necessary for His people and for Him to be established by God as head of the Church and to rule in the kingdom of God. It is our comfort to know our salvation is not secured by our own will, which is fickle, but by the power of God in Christ Jesus, which is sure. He has given us a Holy Spirit that we, who were once far off and dead in our trespasses and sins, are made alive in Christ.

4

Religion Is No Replacement for Theology

(John 17:2–3)

L ET'S RETURN TO THE high priestly prayer of Jesus. There is an intimacy in this discourse as Jesus has completed His teaching to the disciples, and now we are privileged to listen as God the Son addresses in prayer, from His own heart, God the Father.

> John 17:2,3. "Since you have given Him authority over all flesh, to give eternal life to all whom you have given Him. And this is eternal life, that they know You the only true God, and Jesus Christ whom You have sent."

Religion—how do you define religion? An official definition is that religion is *an organized approach to human spirituality.* That definition seems to be descriptive of religion today, suggesting also that America is a religious country. In fact, there is no lack of religion today. Everyone almost to a person, I would say, in America is pursuing religion of one form or another.

But what is theology? Theology is properly defined as *a knowledge of God; a study of God; an understanding of God.* I would submit that while there is plenty of religion even in the Church of Jesus Christ, there is far less theology and even less biblical theology. Biblical theology is a theology that is actually teaching truth about God the Father.

We might ask ourselves, "Well, why does it matter? Why does it matter that we would be concerned with things such as theology when religion and carrying a Bible and reading verses has been so satisfying all of my years and in the days of my walk?" The answer to that is in verse 3. "And this is eternal life, that they know you the only true God, and Jesus

Christ whom you have sent." Now this word *know* can be ambiguous to some people, and we still are seeking a proper definition of Christianity. What is Christianity? The Scotsman, Henry Scougal, defined Christianity as "the life of God in the soul of man." That is as accurate, I suppose, as it is poetic. *The life of God in the soul of man.* But those words minister to the ear of one who already understands what Christianity is. Those words do little to inform an unaided or an untaught ear just what it is to be a Christian.

The apostle John has recorded in Jesus' prayer a description of a Christian. A Christian is "one who has knowledge of God and of His Son, Jesus Christ." So important was this definition in John's thinking that the same description is made in the very last of his teaching as an elder statesman, as an elder apostle and is expressed in the last lines of his series of letters to the church.

> And we know that the Son of God has come and has given us understanding, so that we may know Him who is true; and we are in Him who is true, in His Son Jesus Christ. He is the true God and eternal life. Little children," John says, "keep yourselves from idols. (1 John 5:20–21)

We immediately recognize here that without a true understanding of the one true God, we are prone to idolatry. He exhorts the people in 1 John, "Know the truth about God and in so doing, keep yourselves from idols." In both John 17, and 1 John 5, that word *knowing* is mentioned as something that is essential for salvation. So if the soul of man will have any part in the life of God, then there must be a right and true knowledge of the one true God. We live in a very dangerous and perilous time concerning this.

According to statistics, about 87 percent of the population claims to believe that there is a God. They believe the Scriptures are true. They believe God created the heavens and the earth. There is confusion and ambiguity because evolution has been spun in there resulting in an amalgamation that looks more like a Frankenstein monster of theology than it does anything beautiful and true, but nevertheless, they say they believe these things.

The same people, when asked, "Do you believe that the Jew and the Muslim and the Hindu and the Buddhist and the Christian are all praying to one and the same God?" will answer "Yes." Almost the same percentage who say they believe there is one God, and that they believe the Bible is true, will also say that when the Muslim goes to prayer and when the Jew goes to prayer and when the Hindu goes to prayer, and when the Buddhist goes to prayer, they pray to the one same true God to whom the Christian prays.

How can they believe this? Because they have no knowledge of God. If you have no knowledge of God, then why wouldn't you believe that one entity exists high above the plain of man, and if you bow your head in prayer, it must be that one entity that hears your prayer.

Believing that God exists and having "knowledge" of Him are two different things. Knowledge is not faith, but rather is the cause of faith. We recognize that the Holy Spirit is active in the process of regeneration, but also we see in John 12:50 that , "I know that His commandment is eternal life."

The commandment in and of itself is not eternal life, nor is keeping the commandment the same thing as having eternal life. If so, then grace would be void because for those who could keep the commandment, the law would give life. When Christ says, "The commandment is eternal life," He's not saying the commandment is salvation, but rather the commandment is the principal means of salvation. We would obey Christ as a means to salvation.

A lack of knowledge can lead easily to idolatry. Idolatry in the sense of worshipping pagan idols, perhaps, but more likely in our culture the idolatry of sensuality, the idolatry of materialism, the idolatry of indulgence, of selfism, the worship and the placing before God of anything except God Himself. Also a misunderstanding of use of the word "knowledge" can lead to the ancient heresy we call Gnosticism, a philosophy which claims that knowledge itself saves, which we also declare is not true.

So now, we're left with a question. *How does knowing God equal eternal life?* Thomas Manton, the great commentator and preacher said, "Our Savior understands not naked and inactive speculations concerning God and Christ, or a naked map or model of divine truths. Bare knowledge cannot be sufficient to salvation, but a lively and effectual light" (17:2–3). *A lively and effectual light.* The understanding of saving knowledge can begin with understanding it as a light that illumines the darkness.

In Acts 17:16–17, Paul in Athens, faced a population that was inundated with religions. There was a religion for everybody and everything.

> Now while Paul was waiting for them at Athens, his spirit was
> provoked within him as he saw that the city was full of idols. So he
> reasoned in the synagogue with the Jews and the devout persons,
> and in the marketplace every day. . . .
>
> "Men of Athens, I perceive that in every way you are very reli-
> gious. For as I passed along and observed the objects of your worship,
> I found also an altar with this inscription, 'To the unknown god.'
> What therefore you worship as unknown, this I proclaim to you."
> (Acts 17: 22ff)

George Newton, in the mid 17th century wrote, "I know it's a common fancy that if a man possesses the true religion, if he's been baptized,
if he comes to the assemblies and to hear, and he prays as others do that
he's in good condition. But be assured of this, if he be ignorant of God
and Jesus Christ whom He hath sent, he is in no better shape than a dead
man" (82).

> For this is a people without discernment; therefore He who made
> them will not have compassion on them; He who formed them
> will show them no favor. (Isaiah 27:11)

Religious activity, no matter how active, no matter how committed,
without true knowledge of the living God, is to no avail in matters of
salvation. Our faith must be informed by truth. If it is not, then either
we believe we are saved by some abstract knowledge, or we simply believe
that by believing in something we are saved. In other words, we believe
that we're not saved by the object of our faith, but by faith itself, that by
just simply having faith we are saved, even if our faith is not directed to
the One God who is true.

That is simply false. God expects His people to worship Him in Spirit
and truth. We must know the truth about the God we worship. How can
we truly say we love that which we do not know. Do married folks really
want their spouses to fall in love with them over a misconception? Or do
they want their mates to love them for whom they really are? We cannot
worship in a fantasy world. We have a real God who desires a people who
worship Him in reality, not in some fantasy.

Jesus Himself levels the same charge against the Samaritan woman
in John 4:22. He says to her, "You worship what you do not know; we
worship what we know." Simply going to the mountain as a Jew, as a
Samaritan, and worshipping where Abraham once worshiped was not ad-
equate. Jesus condemns it. He says, "You are worshipping and you believe

you are worshipping the One true God," and in fact, the Samaritans held to the Pentateuch (the first five books of the Bible). So they had documents and yet He says, "The God you worship is not the true God that we worship. You worship one you don't know."

James Montgomery Boice lists four types of knowledge that do not lead to salvation. When we say, "You must know if you are to have eternal life," how do we understand the word *know*? We declare that knowledge itself is not salvation, but neither is ignorance salvation. Neither ignorance nor knowledge of salvation is salvation. How are we to understand knowledge in this sense?

There are four uses of the word "knowledge." The first is knowledge in the sense of just having an awareness of something. This is a sort of general knowledge that one might express when we are talking about the names of those who serve in Congress or about the President. We have an awareness of them, but we don't really know who the person is. We don't have a detailed knowledge of the individual or a personal knowledge. We just have awareness of the individual.

This is a sort of knowledge that's presented in Romans, chapter 1, when it says, "Although they knew God, they did not honor Him as God, and they were claiming to be wise while they became fools." In the 17th century, John Locke argued that the existence of God is the most obvious truth that reason discovers, having an evidence equal to mathematical certainty, but this is not a saving knowledge. Just knowing there is a God, even confessing there is a God, is not a saving knowledge. It is knowledge, but it is not a saving knowledge.

The second type of knowledge is abstract knowledge, a knowledge that goes beyond awareness to include some substantial information. This is the kind of knowledge that can be attained from social networking, from dating services online, from reading and researching a person's life. You get an abstract knowledge of the person because you can read his or her story. You can read about their favorite places to vacation, their college degree, their vocation. You can find out what their favorite color is, the five things they most hated about high school. You can even find out who it is they like to talk to when they're not talking to you. Yet you may never have met or even spoken to them yourself.

So now you have a volume of knowledge in detail, but it's still in the abstract. The danger here is that a student of theology can come to the same sort of knowledge, learning a great deal about God, but never coming to saving knowledge.

The third type of knowledge is an existential knowledge, a knowledge gained by experience. When someone says, for example, "I experience God and I come to know God in the quiet forest or on a smooth lake even on a Sunday morning, or in a thunderstorm, or in a child's laugh, or in a child's cry," they may indeed see evidence of God's wonder and beauty, and it may be profound and moving to them, but it is not the knowledge Jesus is speaking of. It is not a knowledge that results in salvation.

Finally, a fourth would be a knowledge of God alone. So we can acknowledge God and we can learn of God from the Scriptures, but any knowledge of God that does not also by necessary consequence, give us a knowledge of self, still remains incomplete. First Corinthians 13:12 describes the culmination of saving faith as knowing God even as God now knows us, as seeing God face to face. We shall know God and know ourselves and that begins now. That saving knowledge begins now.

What does Jesus mean when He says *knowing*? It's the kind of knowledge that Amos describes in 3:2, "You only have I known of all the families of the earth." Surely we would not say that God in heaven was unaware of all the families of the earth, and yet He says, "You only," speaking to Israel. Here He is talking about a particular knowledge that implies intimacy, an intimate knowledge that is a saving faith.

Again, in Colossians 3:10, "Put on the new self, which is being renewed in knowledge after the image of its Creator." Even as far back as Eden, we find the symbolic trees, one of knowledge and one of eternal life. Ignorance proves to be the great impediment to life as it is said that Eve was unaware, she was ignorant, of that sin which she was about to commit. Ignorance is the impediment to life and it holds men in a state of death. Sin came into the world by a deception, and continues to corrupt through deceitful desire.

Manton points out the force of the new nature is first upon the mind because there is where it takes sin out of the throne.

"Grow in the grace and knowledge of our Lord and Savior Jesus Christ" (II Peter 3:18) They have become callous and have given themselves up to sensuality, greedy to practice every kind of impurity. But that is not the way you learned Christ.

> Assuming that you have heard about Him and were taught in
> Him, as the truth is in Jesus, to put off your old self, which belongs
> to your former manner of life and is corrupt through deceitful
> desires, and to be renewed in the spirit of your minds, and to put
> on the new self, created after the likeness of God in true righteous-
> ness and holiness. (Ephesians 4:19–25)

The Spirit of Christ breathes life into a heart that is dead. Rebirth is a
work of God, not a work of learning, not a work of knowledge. The Spirit
of God breathes life so the mind can then apprehend the truth about God.
That truth is like light in the darkness that leads us on the path. *Thy Word
is a light unto my feet and a lamp unto my path.* The Word of God, which
was light and salvation to men, has now illumined for us the truth about
God showing us our former ignorance when we were lost in sin.

The life of Moses outlines for us a knowledge of God that God's
people have. Moses was born in a God-fearing home and then was raised
in Pharaoh's house. But Moses was taught about God's promise to deliver
the Hebrews from bondage. After stepping up to try to deliver them himself, bringing upon himself an accusation of murder, he fled Egypt. Moses
had became concerned with his own life and his own affairs when he
noticed a burning bush. As he moved closer, he heard the voice of God in
the bush warning him not to proceed because he was on holy ground. Not
until he removed his sandals from his feet did God call Moses forward.
He desired Moses to come to Him, but only after Moses first learned of
God's holiness. Moses understood because he hid his face. He was afraid
to look at God.

Have you been introduced to God's transcendent holiness, His sinless perfection and purity and as a consequence, your own sin? When did
you realize you must ultimately deal with God in whom there is no sin
at all? Do the words of 2 Peter 3:11 concern you? "What sort of people
ought you to be in lives of holiness and godliness?" Or those of 1 Peter
1:16: "Be holy, for I am holy." When you have heard the voice of Christ
calling you, have you been made aware of the holiness that is required of
God's people? Or are you ignorant of that?

What would have happened to Moses if he had not understood the
holiness of God when God called him forward and said, "Remove your
sandals before you proceed any further?" What if Moses, in ignorance,
had continued to stride toward the burning bush? Would he not have
been struck dead for blasphemy against God, for not understanding God's

holiness? The first place of understanding for a Christian, having been made alive by the Spirit is that we serve a holy God, and that we are called to holiness. If you haven't wrestled with your sin before the holiness of God, then you haven't understood the first lesson in coming to a true knowledge of a living God.

The second lesson Moses learned was of God's omniscience or the fact that God knows everything. God told him that He had seen and heard the struggles of the people. He knew their plight. He knew of their oppression by the Egyptians and then God said, "And Moses, I also know you. I know your life and I know your weaknesses." Everything is open before God. Have you ever participated in religious ceremony, even a Christian religious ceremony? Have you ever attended, spoken the words of Christianity, sung the songs of Christianity, recited the creeds of Christianity, but known in your heart that it was far from God? That you, yourself were estranged from God?

Read Hebrews 4:13, "No creature is hidden from His sight, but all are naked and exposed to the eyes of Him to whom we must give account." Hypocrisy may be hidden from men. We may be eloquent in our speech. We might have a soft tongue. We might be one who is able to provide many graces to the people around us. We might be kind in our disposition, but God who knows the heart will know that all the while we have been practicing religion, and we have not had the eternal life that comes from a knowledge of God.

Our first lesson is that God is holy, and our second is that God is omniscient. God knows the hearts of men. Nothing is hidden from Him. The third lesson that Moses learned is that God is sovereign. God commanded Moses to return to Egypt and strive for the release of the Israelites. Moses protested and made excuses. He asked for signs and God gave him signs. Finally, Moses relented before the unyielding will of God. Have you surrendered your will to a sovereign Lord?

To the unconverted, God's holiness, His omniscience, and His sovereignty are threatening. The unconverted want nothing to do with a God that requires of them holiness. They want nothing to do with a God who knows the secret meditations of their hearts and they want nothing to do with a God who is sovereign over their lives and details for them how their lives should be lived. The unconverted are content to dwell in darkness where they believe they do as they please in secret but are working toward their own destruction.

So Jesus provided the only way for us to come to a saving knowledge of God. Jesus, as the incarnate Word, has come as a light to men. "In Him was life, and the life was the light of men" (John 1:4). "No one has ever seen God; the only God, who is at the Father's side, He has made Him known" (John 1:18). Christ has made God known to us. Returning to John 17, see that Jesus prays that God would glorify Him: "Since you have given Him authority over all flesh, to give eternal life to all whom you have given Him."

He says, "Glorify me that is in the ascension, seat me at your right hand and give me authority that I will give eternal life to the elect. And this is eternal life that they know you the only true God and Jesus Christ whom you have sent." He's saying, "Glorify me that I will send to them the Holy Spirit and in sending the Holy Spirit, illumine their minds to show them the Father that they will once again know God and not be estranged."

Jesus prayed, "The hour is come. Father, glorify me in order that I could give eternal life." In other words, "that I can make them to know you and the Christ who is your provision for the satisfaction of your holiness and judgment against sin." We are all born as dead men. If by God's Spirit you are stirred to come to life, the beginning is the pursuit of a holy knowledge of God., "If you seek it like silver and search for it as for hidden treasures, then you will understand the fear of the Lord and find the knowledge of God" (Proverbs 2:4–5).

Jesus is praying to be glorified that He could send the Holy Spirit to give life and light to His own, without which we can never know God. "How long, O simple ones, will you love being simple? How long will scoffers delight in their scoffing and fools hate knowledge? If you turn at my reproof, behold, I will pour out my spirit to you; I will make my words known to you" (Proverbs 1:22).

5

Stick with the Program, Finish What was Begun

(John 17:4–5)

"I glorified you on earth, having accomplished the work that you
gave me to do. And now, Father, glorify me in your presence with
the glory that I had with you before the world existed."
(John 17:4,5)

WHAT IS JESUS SAYING in these two verses? He is saying that He has
glorified God. Where has He glorified God? On earth. And how
has He glorified God? By completing the work God has given Him to do.
Completion: completing the work that God has given Him to do.

In our day, the idea of finishing well, finishing strong, of completing
a task, completing work is not lost upon us, even in secular vocations. At
the beginning of the football season, you will hear talks of finishing well.
Steve Spurrier, the coach of South Carolina, the Gamecocks in Columbia,
had this to say concerning last season. He said, "Last year, we played some
good football, but we didn't finish our games. This year, we intend to
finish the whole game." In other words, play all 60 minutes of football.
He was comparing that to games where they hadn't played the full 60
minutes, and so consequently, no matter how well they played in the first
or the second or even the third quarter, if they did not finish playing the
game, they come up losers.

In sports, injured athletes—I recall highlights from the Olympics—
you'll have a runner who will sometimes sprain an ankle, and still in approaching the finish line, he or she will not quit the race; the runner will
cross whether he/she has to limp, hop or crawl; the race will be completed.
I've seen bikers pushing their bikes after a fall. The bikes would become

broken, and impossible to pedal. They will push their bikes. They will not quit. They want to finish the race.

In basic training, I was volunteered to escort a soldier to psychological counseling—one who was about to be discharged, and was required to have an escort. When I was volunteered, I looked over at my bunk. It was still early in the morning, and my bunk had not been made, and I thought, *You know, this is an opportunity for me to go ahead, and I just won't worry about that this morning because I'm not too big on making up my bed. I've got a job to do. It's a good excuse.* An excuse! So, off I go. When I come back, do you imagine I didn't hear something about my not completing my work that morning? I was counseled severely that I did not complete my work that morning. I left undone that which was supposed to have been done.

We know something about completing work at the end of a semester when the school is finished. Don't we sense the whole concept of completion? Isn't there relief because it is complete? What is the opposite of complete? Incomplete. When you walk across the stage to get your diploma, isn't that simply signifying you have completed the work versus left it incomplete, unfinished, and undone? You have finished the course which you had begun. You have finished the race. You have carried it through to completion.

When I'm training up at Fort Jackson the new soldiers who are coming in, the new chaplains, and they go out for the very first time to run their first PT test—that is, the two-mile trek they have to run—I will tell them each, "It doesn't really matter the first time you run this, how you run the first mile and a half or mile and three quarters. What matters is what I see come across the line. How you finish will trump how you ran the rest because how you finish is character." Anybody here can begin anything. Beginning is nothing. It's the first step, but it's the first step to completion. Completion is where you see the character of the man or the woman or the child. Incomplete is something anyone can accomplish. Completing requires a character.

As Jesus faces Gethsemane, the trials, the Cross, and the tomb, He is testifying that His work is complete, and in reflecting upon that, He is reflecting in joyful expression. He is facing Gethsemane. He is facing betrayal, arrest, scourging, a mock trial, the Cross, and the tomb, and His expression of having completed that which God has called Him to is an expression of joy. The work that God gave to Jesus was God's own work, and it brings Christ joy to have completed God's work. Can anything less be said of the work that we have before us? Is there any work that we undertake that is not ultimately God's work?

Scripture tells us that God gave Him a work to do, this One who was Prince by birth and a Servant by divine decree. George Newton, minister of the 1600's, suggests that "That work which was given is nothing less than work that is ordained" (112). We use the word *ordain* when we talk about life's events, don't we? In response to some event, we say, "Well, it was God's will." We are essentially saying that it was "ordained by God" that that should come to pass. It was God's will. It was God's ordination that that should occur.

We also use the word when we recognize men whom God has called into ministry. We use that word very frequently. We say that he is *ordained* into the ministry. We might think that it is *we* who are giving these individuals their task and work when we ordain them, but in fact, the church is simply acting as God's agent in recognizing the preordained work that God has given to His servant. And the church in ordaining them is in effect submitting to God's will in ordaining that servant in their midst to accomplish God's will, not their own.

Likewise, the work of Jesus was ordained by God. He says, "The work that you gave me to do," that work, given by God, for Christ to accomplish. Jesus' calling was to do this work, and He was locked into accomplishing God's will, not stepping to the left or to the right. "For I have come down from heaven, not to do my own will but the will of Him who sent me" (John 6:38). "We must work the works of Him who sent me while it is day" (John 9:4). It is God's work even though Jesus is the agent who is carrying it out. Jesus makes no distinction between His own work and God's work to that end. In John 10:37, He says, "If I am not doing the works of my Father, then do not believe me." He is saying, "That which I do is actually the works of God." He makes no distinction between His life and the spiritual life.

Regrettably, too many in the Christian community will seek to do that. You'll hear such comments as, "If I were in church, I probably wouldn't say this, but . . ." or, "If I were here or I were there, I might act or be something different." We typically have trouble living lives that are holistically committed to God's will. We live schizophrenic lives, and it's recognized in Scripture because it talks about that war that wages within, being double minded in our own thinking, having a split personality because we have a split devotion, one to God and one to the world. God has a will that He has ordained each of us to accomplish, and we struggle in recognizing and accomplishing that will.

God the Father ordained and ordered the work that Jesus was to do, yet Jesus owns the work Himself because He is the immediate agent who accomplishes the work. So, the work belongs to God, and it belongs to Jesus. "The works that the Father have given me to accomplish, the very works that I am doing" (John 5:36). So, if we keep all this in mind, we can confidently assert that the entirety of Jesus' life was lived in compliance to God's will. From beginning to end, He lived in compliance to God's will perfectly.

Imagine that for just a moment--not one regret, not one misstep, not one "wish I could take that back," not one "I wish I knew then what I know now." This is great evidence for His divinity, isn't it? It's not the absolute proof we would pull from other places in Scriptures, but show me one reliable recorded charge that Jesus Christ, the historical Christ, made a misstep, made a miscalculation, made some error, committed some sin. You cannot find it. Is there any better testimony to His divinity? The work which He was given to do consisted essentially in these two spheres: one of satisfaction and one of application.

Mantan describes it this way: "The quarrel was taken up between justice and mercy. Mercy would pity and justice could not spare. Christ must be sent to satisfy justice, and the Spirit sent to take away unbelief. When God delivered His people out of Babylon, He had to do with creatures. When He delivered them from wrath to come, He had to do with Himself" (170). This is the work of Christ. This is the work of Christ to both satisfy justice and to bring mercy in His body. There was no opportunity for misstep.

You may have heard the word "satisfaction" referred to as the *active and passive obedience of Christ.* William Shedd's *Dogmatic Theology* defines active obedience as "Christ's keeping perfectly the precepts of the law. Without error, without falter, without sin, He kept perfectly the precepts of God's law." As Shedd says, "He . . ." that is Jesus, ". . . obeyed this law in heart and in conduct without a single slip or failure. He was holy, harmless, and undefiled" (720).

The work of Jesus means that He not only suffered for man, but obeyed God's law for Him. That is why in Colossians 1:10, it describes us as complete in Christ. When it talks about being complete, it's not talking about emotional well being—that comes with it, this piece of Christ which surpasses understanding—but when Colossians is referring to us as complete in Christ, it's saying we are not only delivered from wrath, but we are entitled to heaven because of His obedience, because He satisfied the law. And we are now complete, not incomplete. We are completed in Christ.

"For as by the one man's disobedience the many were made sinners, so by the one Man's obedience the many will be made righteous" (Romans 5:19). And the righteous shall inherit the earth. Jesus has fulfilled the law as both precept and penalty. He fulfilled the law's penalty by the Cross. He fulfilled the law's precept by perfect living. This is what Paul is referring to in Romans 8:3 and 4. "For God has done what the law, weakened by the flesh could not do. By sending his own Son in the likeness of sinful flesh and for sin, he condemned sin in the flesh, in order that the righteous requirement of the law might be fulfilled in us, who walk not according to the flesh but according to the Spirit."

This is Jesus' active obedience, the perfect keeping of God's law. When Adam was in the Garden, the condition of his receiving eternal life was, *Obey me. Obey me and you will live.* Adam faltered, and he fell in ignorance and in willful disobedience. Jesus has come and satisfied that simple requirement given by God, Obey me. Obey me and have eternal life. And we who die to self, and are buried with Him in baptism, and raised again in His resurrection, who have died in sin but been raised in Christ by the power and regenerating work of the Holy Spirit, now are in unity with Christ, and His righteousness is counted to our account.

The second type of obedience referred to earlier was passive obedience. Passive obedience is the sum of all that Christ experienced in His humiliation. Everything He suffered in the incarnation is included, everything. Everything He struggled with, every temptation that He faced down, everything that is included in His life was His passive obedience, particularly that time between Gethsemane and the tomb. Yes, the Cross—the Cross is accounted as His passive obedience, that which was done to Him through which he persevered.

God not only told Jesus whom to preach to, but also gave Him the message itself. Isaiah 61 contains the first recorded sermon that Christ preached as He was beginning His ministry. In the first two verses He said, "The Spirit of the Lord God is upon me, because the LORD has anointed me to bring good news to the poor; He has sent me to bind up the brokenhearted, to proclaim liberty to the captives, and the opening of the prison to those who are bound; to proclaim the year of the LORD'S favor, and the day of vengeance of our God; to comfort all who mourn."

The Father told Jesus whom to preach to and what to say. And then, Jesus, when He ascended, sent His Spirit from the Father in the Son. This is the work that Jesus did, and He did it completely—completely. Nothing to be added. Ponder that just a moment. Slow down for just a moment. It is completed. Does that stir you at all as you contemplate your own standing before God, God's justice, His wrath, His law, His requirement for perfect obedience lest you be cast into eternal damnation? Does it give you pause and relieve your anxiety? Does it remove a great weight from your soul that Jesus has completed it? No surprises on judgment day for those who are in Christ. Nothing left undone. No, "if I only knew," or "if I had only." It is completed.

What evidence do we have that this is true? James Montgomery Boice writes, "It is the resurrection that is God's seal upon Christ's work. 'He was delivered up for our trespasses and raised for our justification' (Romans 4:24–25). 'The resurrection is the evidence that the work is completed because Jesus is the first fruits of those who will dwell in eternity" (1265).

Have you ever paid off a long-standing bill? Received that final receipt? I've only been able to pay off one car. They don't seem to last long enough for me to make it that far. I paid off one minivan, and we got the last bill sent off, and received the receipt, and it had some sort of statement that was Chrysler's way of communicating that it was paid in full. It was finished. The bill was settled. There was nothing left to do. No more mailing, no more stamps, no more checks. It was finished. My business with them was complete.

The resurrection is God's declaration that the business is complete. The debt is paid. The application of this gives us a complete confidence in the fulfillment of Christ's completing God's work. It's the height of arrogance and pride to believe our work is added to His, or to present ourselves as any more worthy because of our own works. It's insulting to God to take His gift and declare it inadequate because of our poorly practiced theology. It's also folly for us to imagine our lives are accidental and our work is either casual or optional.

George Newton, a great preacher, said, "If it's so that Jesus was ordered by His Father in the work, why then shouldn't we be ordered by

Him in all the work we do? Shall Christ be in subjection to the Father more than we? What an unreasonable and incongruous thing to say." Newton points out that, "Men do good or men do evil, but in both cases, it is not the work as God has given them to do" (117). He uses Uzziah and Saul as examples from Scripture.

Uzziah used the incense that was prescribed by the law. He used it in the Temple and on the altar just as the law said he should, and he offered it to God, the one true God, just as God had commanded. But there was only one problem. God had not commanded Uzziah to do that. He was not the man who was called to make that offering to God. The same with Saul. Saul offered the right sacrifice, and he offered it to the one true God, but Saul was the wrong man to offer that sacrifice to God.

Each person has been fitted by God to accomplish a particular work for God's glory. As Jesus said to the Father himself, and to none other, "I have finished the work you have given me to do." There are others who engage in work that is not commanded by God or anyone. Their eyes are not on the God that they seek to serve in their life. And they are a rule to themselves. They do whatever whim comes upon them. They follow their own hearts. They hear with their eyes and they think with their heart. Do you imagine that loose living, or gossip, or profaning the Sabbath, or swearing, or living unclean lives, do you believe that these are the works that God has given you to do? Have we deluded ourselves that even if we don't know what God has called us to do, that somehow a God who is holy and just could have called us to perform profane acts? Surely not.

Men do good works, they do bad works, and they can miss God's calling in their lives on both accounts. Our Lord has ordained a work for His people, and it is our goal to complete it. We want to hear what was written in Matthew 25:21, "Well done, good and faithful servant. You have been faithful over a little; I will set you over much. Enter into the joy of your Master." Are you doing the work that God has called you to do? Are you doing that which is contrary to it? Are you simply neglecting that which God has called you to? There is a lesson from this: that we don't serve God begrudgingly. We do so with joy and reflect His own joy when we are accomplishing that work which He has called us to do. Not one person here, not a single person to the youngest among us is without a calling by God to accomplish a work He has given them to do.

As we read in the prophet Haggai, they were a people who were not doing that which God had called them to do. Consequently, their vines did not produce. Their gardens did not have vegetables. They had no fruit in their life. They burned energy. They strove, they worked, and they had nothing. There was essentially God's spiritual embargo on their life. They were not able to grow, and they were not able to prosper because God was seeking to have them turn to Him. And He said, "And though I nearly starved you out, though you had no success in your life, still you would not turn to me. Still you went your own way, even though the track record was abysmal, and you had no success for it, still you followed your own ways and would not turn to Me."

How often do we do the same? We trust ourselves though we have proved ourselves to be utter failures; we'll trust ourselves again tomorrow, and still not turn to God. Jesus said, "I have finished the work you gave me to do." He didn't quit halfway. He didn't begrudge it. He finished it. We say, "We acknowledge the work Jesus has done. We receive His benefits, and we will seek to do the ministry that God has given us to do, and to have the same joy for bringing God glory through our work."

We want our lives to be like the palm tree in David's Psalm 92. There we find a palm tree that is planted in the courtyard of God. And it says that though the tree grows old, it's still green and lush and produces because it flourishes in God's courtyard. It bears fruit even in old age. Is old age something that we believe somehow causes us to fall out of God's will, that we no longer have a calling in God because our years have slipped on past us? If we are planted in the courtyard of God, there is always a work to do. Even if it's only in the mortification of sin in our own bodies, the work must be completed. We want to run the race with endurance. We want to persevere to the end. We want to finish the work God has given us to do, just as Jesus did, in perfecting our salvation.

6

Obedience Follows Certainty, Part 1

(John 17:6–8)

I N TRANSITIONING FROM THE first five verses of this prayer uttered by Christ to His Father, we need to make one more observation. In the first five verses, Jesus has been praying for Himself, but note the manner in which He prayed. "Father, glorify me in order that I may glorify you." The petitions that Jesus made for Himself, were themselves selfless petitions.

> I have manifested your name to the people whom you gave me out of the world. Yours they were, and you gave them to me, and they have kept your Word. Now they know that everything that you have given me is from you. For I have given them the words that you gave me, and they have received them and have come to know in truth that I came from you; and they have believed that you sent me. (John 17:6–8)

Again, Jesus' prayer for Himself is not for His own interests. He doesn't ask for glory so that His reputation will be vindicated or so that others will give Him praise. Jesus has His enemies. He doesn't pray here for their defeat, but rather so that He will be better suited to bring God the Father all glory. His prayer is that His life will be better suited, that He would be fitted, that He will be made more fitting to be a vessel to bring God glory. Even His prayer for Himself is not for His own benefit, and there is really only one petition that He would even make for Himself, while there are four here for others. In first five verses of this chapter, Jesus prays for Himself. In the twenty-one verses that follow, He is praying for His disciples and future believers.

What a weight we burden on ourselves when we carry around a load of self-serving, self-interested petitions in prayers. Think about our own prayer lives. Think about yours as I think about mine. How much of our prayer is occupied with our own interests, our own progress, our own safety, our own development, our own happiness, our own joy, the fulfillment of our own dreams. We may begin a prayer by giving God praise and glory, but in comparison and by weight, if the scales were placed before us, and our prayer petitions for our own selves were placed on one side and that which was a prayer which served to show our subjection to God was placed in the other, I think without exception in almost all Christians' lives, the scales would be bent mightily and quickly to self-serving prayers.

What disappointment we experience when God doesn't make the sun rise and set on us. What disappointment we experience when He doesn't make the sun orbit around us in life. And what ignorance of God we demonstrate when our prayers are more a mantra of our own ambitions than they are a seeking to be servants of God. We ought to model our prayer life after Jesus' own, and pray that our Lord would have His glory magnified in our lives.

In verse 6, Jesus introduces those whom He now has lifted up in prayer. In verse 6, He says, "I have manifested your name to the people whom you gave me out of the world." He is now identifying those for whom He will be praying. He says later on, "I'm not praying for all people. I'm not praying for everyone who is in the world. I'm praying for those whom you have given me." He is praying for those the Father has called out of the world and given to Jesus. The calling of the Christian out of the world and into salvation is a theme repeated throughout Scripture. A benefit of our going through the Scriptures in an expository study is that we learn what God's emphasis is in Scripture.

For example, if we were to take subjects more topically, we might be able to say with integrity that we don't skip the tough subjects. We do preach the doctrines. We might be able to say that we'll preach a doctrine of election, or that we study the Holy Spirit on a particular Sunday. But in this passage, Jesus over and over again makes the same point. There is a people who belong to God whom God has given to the Son, and the Son will not lose one. Just a brief look at those words result in little remembrance. It is worth taking note as God reiterates those points which are essential to our Christian understanding.

If we are to understand God the way God presents Himself, then there must be some call for us to revisit the very things God Himself revisits in His Revelation to us. He revisits here the issue of our being called out of the world and being given to Christ. What is it to be in the world? In Ephesians 2, we find a definition for being in the world, and it's not flattering. To be in the world is to be a son of disobedience, to be dead in trespasses, to be uncircumcised and separated from the promises of God, to be strangers to the covenant, to be a people with no hope, to be far off. In First John, chapter 5, we find that the cause behind all of this is that the world lies in the power of the evil one. It has its king and it has its prince who influences us, but our own hearts influence us even without a prince to take us away.

But for those who are called out of the world, again in Ephesians 2, verses 13 and following, "But now in Christ Jesus you who once were far off have been brought near by the blood of Christ. For He Himself is our peace." Verse 8: "By grace you have been saved through faith." Why does Scripture repeat this theme over and over again? Jesus is bringing this theme before us again so that we do not fail to understand the centrality of this teaching to our calling and the unique calling of a Christian to follow God. It is so central to the character of God and foundational to our understanding of our own salvation that is part of nearly every doctrinal discourse and book of the Scriptures, and yet, how many still do not understand? And how many reject the revelation of God's grace in the doctrine of election?

We only note here again by way of reminder that the text clearly points out that the initiative and result of our salvation is with the Father. John Owen, the great Church father, said, "Christ did not die for any upon condition that if they do believe; He died for all God's elect that they should believe. He did not die to simply say, 'If they happen to believe, then I died for them.' He died to actually save those whom He has called to give to Christ. They belong to the Father from eternity past, and in the fullness of time, Jesus revealed the Father to their opened eyes, and they obeyed God's Word."

God gave Jesus two peoples—two kinds of people. One, the disciples whom He is now praying would be preserved by God as the Spirit will be soon poured upon them. But He also gave Jesus a people like Judas, people who serve for a while, sometimes outwardly in administration, but ultimately remain in the world. There were those who were given who enter into union with Christ, there are those who were given to Him who sometimes serve God's purposes, even sometimes serving for good, and yet they remain outside of the Body of Christ even if they appear to be within.

We see then that Christians are a people who have been called out, separated out, and they are not of the world. Why then are they the special objects of God's affections? What is it about the Christian that warrants such special prayer from Christ? What is it about a Christian that causes a people to be so favored by God among and above their peers as to be saved by the Spirit of Christ? The fact that this is true of Christians has already been clearly established in the passages and chapters before, but when we start thinking about ourselves, and we start thinking about how much like the rest of the world we are, we wonder why does the Lord treat us differently? The answer is nothing in ourselves—nothing.

The premise to the question is a works-based premise. We ask, "What merit is there in me that is so much better than the one whom the Lord overlooks for salvation?" Our whole premise is that we are actually seeking to find *what is there good in me that causes God to love me more?* And the answer is absolutely nothing—nothing! There is nothing in you as you are found in the natural state that causes you to outrank your peers who are lost in the eyes of God. We are given to the Son by the Father, and the fact that there is no intrinsic difference makes the grace that saves all the more amazing.

Five times in the next few verses, Jesus will mention that we are His because the Father has given us to Him. Five times Jesus makes this point. It's not something He simply passes by as a great sentimental thought of the love of God. It's a key and cardinal doctrine truth that the Christian must grasp if the Christian is to understand the God who saves. That is not a misstatement on my part. If we do not understand what Christ is presenting as the cardinal effect and source of our own salvation, then how can we understand truly the God who saves? We can have some notion about God, but what separates us from an unbeliever's notion if we refuse the truth of God? We cannot simply choose what we like and do not like about God and fashion a God in our own image.

D. A. Carson points out that "In a profound sense, they belong to God antecedently to Jesus' ministry" (558). What that means is that before Jesus was incarnate, before Jesus ever began a ministry on earth, God's people whom He has given to Christ already belonged to God in eternity past. Before we were knit together in our mother's womb, God knew us. In John 6:37, Jesus mentions that all the Father gives Him will come to Him. And again, in verse 39, He notes that He will keep them to the last day. In chapter 6:44, Jesus expands on this idea to say that in fact no one will come unless the Father sends him. Do you get the picture? Even though it may offend our human sensibilities, do you get at least what Scripture is presenting—that God has taken a people for Himself, He has removed them from the world, which is the place where the lost will be condemned. He has taken them out just like He took the Hebrews out of Egypt, and He has preserved those people, and then given them to His Son Christ, a gift to Christ that Christ would bring the Father glory through the salvation of their souls in the atonement of the Cross? If you take any piece of that out, how can we truly know God as He has revealed Himself?

In Hebrews 2:13, we see Jesus' affection for us when He says, "Behold, I and the children God has given me." This is Jesus' disposition towards us as He goes to prayer. Imagine if you will in your soul's spirit—spirit's eye—Jesus before the Father, and His role is Mediator, saying to the Father, "Behold, Father, it is I and the children whom you have given me." What favor will there be for those children who are with the beloved Son? We are a special gift given to Him by the Father, and He is as tender toward us as we would be to our own children. In fact, He is tender to us in the perfection, which we lack in our tenderness to our own children.

A Christian then is one whom God has marked out in eternity past, separated out from the world, and given to Christ as the object of redemption. Am I lacking any emphasis on the Christian's response to the gospel? Am I now betraying the fact that yes, there is a calling, an outward calling, and there is a response by people to the call of the gospel? I do not mean to neglect it except that Jesus has no mention of it here in His prayer. We acknowledge that there is a means used by God, the preaching of the gospel, the foolishness of preaching as Paul puts it as he wonders just like we might after reading this, "What purpose then is there in preaching if God has taken a people and has given them unto Christ?" It seems everything has taken place in the eternal realm, in the kingdom of God, in the heavens. What place is there for man to call upon man to repent and to believe?

There is a place in God's economy for that to happen, but it's not the force of argument that changes a man's mind about God. It's the Spirit of

Christ who changes a man's mind about God. And Jesus here is speaking to that. The Great Commission He will give them. He will tell them, "Go and preach the gospel to the very ends of the earth," but here in His conversation with the Father He acknowledges that all those whom are called in the name of Christ have been given to Him by His Father.

So now, we wonder how. How do we know that it has happened? What proof is there that I'm a child of grace rather than a child of wrath? How do I know if it doesn't depend upon a walking of the aisle, or an external profession of faith, or a response at a concert, or at a church service, or at a rally somewhere? If it doesn't depend upon that, how am I to know that I'm saved? How are we to know our children are saved? How will we know that anyone is saved at all if it all depends upon God? If it's not in this realm of human experience, how can we be sure that there are any who are saved at all? These three verses will answer that question.

Notice first of all that Jesus Himself is central. There is no knowledge of God without Jesus. In chapter 14, verse 6, Jesus said, "No one comes to the Father except through me." Jesus is essential, and He repeats this over and over again. Why does He keep repeating it? Because men keep insisting that they can arrive at some knowledge of God apart from Christ. What does Jesus give to us that we may know God? He says very plainly here, "I have manifested your name. . . ." I have shown them your name. "I have manifested your name to the people whom you gave me out of the world." He has manifested His name.

The great preacher H. A. Ironside is in error here when he contends that Jesus here only means that He has shown them a divine paternal relationship of God as their Father, that they would come to know God as Father different from the way they understood God in the Old Testament. It is true that Jesus has shown them a different concept of God as Father from that of the Old Testament, but it's not limited to that. It cannot be limited to that, and most commentators and theologians do not believe that it is so.

Why doesn't Jesus say here, "I just taught them about you" or "I've shown them the true doctrines about yourself, about God"? Because to reveal a name is not any different from glorifying Him on earth. This revelation of God through His name is a fulfillment of Isaiah 52:6 where He said, "Therefore my people will know my name." In the Scripture, a name is connected with character. A name is not to be separated from a man's character. It stands for the perfection of a person and for his strengths. A name tells you what a person really is. When a person in the Bible became an adult, God would change his name—Jacob to Israel for example—to show what their calling in life truly was to be.

When we recommend a business or a person, we might describe that individual as having made a good name for themselves. What we mean is that they have built a business that is trustworthy, that they can do that which they promised to do, that they can be turned to in a time of crisis. Likewise, if someone has behaved badly, we'll say he has really ruined his good name. We understand the idea of name being associated with character, with person, and with life.

George Newton, that great minister of the 1600's, said, "The name of God sometimes imports His nature, sometimes His titles, sometimes His attributes, sometimes His ordinances, and sometimes His works. And the Savior has laid his nature open fully to His apostles and disciples as He professes His Father here. 'I have manifested thy name unto men which thou hast given me out of the world'" (127).

Proverbs 18:10: "The name of the LORD is a strong tower; the righteous man runs into it." Solomon is teaching that we live in a difficult world with problems and with threats, and that our only place of safety is in the name of the Lord, that His name is like a tower which we run into and we are surrounded by that name which represents everything God really is. Let's be careful that we aren't aiding a superstitious mind in thinking or believing that it's the chanting of a name that saves. That is not what is implied in the least. When we say that we run to the Lord and that His name is a tower that we go into, we're saying that everything that name represents about God is what keeps us safe.

In Exodus 6:3, God said, "I appeared to Abraham, to Isaac, and to Jacob, as God Almighty, but by my name Jehovah . . ." or your translation may read "the LORD, Yahweh, ". . . I did not make myself known to them." God is saying that a new chapter of relational history is opening up, and there will be a new intimacy, an increasing intimacy which the people will learn by the revelation of a name. They had known God as *Elohim*, which is strong and mighty One. Now they will know Him as *Yahweh*, or *Jehovah*, the self-existent One, the "I am that I am" showing that He is eternal.

If you were of primitive faith in the first covenants, and you were just learning of the truth of God, you might imagine almost as a superstition that God was a Force. And then you come to understand that God is a personal deity, and that this personal deity is great, and He is mighty, that He created the earth. And now, God continues to expand in His teaching to them and says, "And I am eternally known. I am eternal, and I am self-existent." So, you see progressively God has been demonstrating and showing Himself up to the incarnation of Christ, when the Word became flesh and dwelt among us.

What Jesus said is that by manifesting His name they have come to know God. That is as simply put as we can say it. When Jesus says, "I have manifested your name to the people whom you gave me out of the world," He is saying, "They have come to know you through me. They have come to know the truth of God by me." He didn't just tell them the name of God; He showed them the name of God.

John, chapter 1, verse 18, "No one has ever seen God; the only God, who is at the Father's side, He has made Him known." It doesn't say He has told us about Him. It says, "He has made Him known." Christ Jesus has made God known. In John 14:8–11, "Philip said to Him, 'Lord, show us the Father.'" How will Jesus show them the Father? Hebrews 1:1–3: "God spoke to our fathers by the prophets, but in these last days He has spoken to us by His Son, whom He appointed the Heir of all things." In John 14:9, Jesus said simply, "Whoever has seen me has seen the Father."

So, in Jesus we know Elohim, we know Jehovah Nissi, we know Jehovah Shalom, Jehovah Jireh, El Roi, our Lord, our peace, our provider, the Lord our banner. D. Martyn Lloyd-Jones comments, "What Christ has done in a sense is to let the flood light in, to open them out, and to enable us to grasp them because He has done it in His person "(240). In His person—the living testimony of God. In Jesus we know the God who will heal, the God who protects, the God who leads, the God who conquers, the God who redeems, the God who loves, and the God who will never leave nor forsake us. What Jesus says, He manifested. What Jesus teaches, He shows. He has taken away the veil, and He has made it plain to understand through the incarnation.

So, a Christian is one who is perfectly clear about who Jesus is. That doesn't mean we've attained to all knowledge. It means we are perfectly clear that He is the One of Colossians 2:9. "In Him the whole fullness of deity dwells bodily." Because He is the Son of God, the fullness of God's nature is seen in Him. He is God in the person of the Son. That is why we read in Matthew 1:23, "'They shall call His name Immanuel' (which means, God with us)."

He is not only a representation of God, but the actual manifestation of God. I know that you know what Christ has done, but I would ask you to consider this. Have you known the Father whom Jesus came to show you? I know you know the stories of Christ. I know you know the story of the Cross and atonement and that you have some grasp of some doctrines here and there. But do you actually know Christ who is the manifestation of the Father in flesh? Jesus says, "I came and manifested your name to the people whom You gave Me out of the world. I showed them the Father that they could know the Father through Me." Do you know the Father through Jesus the Son?

7

Obedience Follows Certainty, Part 2

(John 17:6–8)

"I have manifested your name to the people whom you gave me out of the world. Yours they were, and you gave them to me, and they have kept your Word. Now they know that everything that you have given me is from you. For I have given them the words that you gave me, and they have received them and have come to know in truth that I came from you; and they have believed that you sent me."

FOLKLORE HAS IT THAT Abraham Lincoln once asked the question, "If you call the tail of a dog a leg, how many legs does a dog have?" *Five?* "No," he answered, "It still has four. Just calling a tail a leg doesn't make it a leg." Does calling someone a Christian make them one? If we just label someone a Christian, are they a Christian? If we wish it enough, does it make it real? Jesus has been talking about those that the Father has given Him. In verse 9, we will learn that it is those and those only that He is praying for. He makes it very clear by stating it unambiguously that He is not praying for those who remain in the world; He is only praying for those whom the Father has given Him. He is the Divine Mediator, but not for any other except for those who belong to Him by virtue of God's gift.

In verses 6 through 8, as if Jesus wants to ensure to us that there is no question concerning whom those people are, the identity of those who belong to Him, He identifies them in detail. In Revelation 3:1, we have the admonition of John to those in Sardis: "You have a name that you are alive, but you are dead." Dr. Martyn Lloyd-Jones wrote, "Of all the words which are misunderstood in this modern world, there is none which is so misunderstood as the word *Christian*" (256).

So let me ask you a couple of questions. What comes to mind when you hear the word *Christian*? Some imagine great works of social justice, the founding of schools or the running of schools or hospitals, soup kitchens, and the like. Some think of great political agendas—keeping prayer in schools, keeping the commandments in the courtrooms across our land. Some think of a particular personality type, one that is quiet or clean or concerned or joyful. Others believe it is a religious sentiment or feeling that you have as you walk in faith.

We should be clear in our own understanding of what a Christian is rather than leave it to some ambiguous speculation. It has been explained from pulpits day after day and year after year through the ages, but how many people have really listened and absorbed that important truth? How many have ignored the preaching or have turned a deaf ear to the messengers God has sent to preach to them from the Word of God? How many have been blind as well is deaf as the Word has been put out?

Returning to the definition of a Christian, we have the words from Matthew, chapter 7, 21–23.

> "Not everyone who says to me, 'Lord, Lord,' will enter the kingdom of heaven but the one who does the will of My Father who is in heaven. On that day, many will say to Me, 'Lord, Lord, did we not prophesy in Your name and cast out demons in Your name and do mighty works in Your name?' And then I will declare to them, 'I never knew you. Depart from Me, you workers of lawlessness.'"

Attending church and even working for years in a church, do not, in and of themselves, make someone Christian. It doesn't matter the library of Christian books you have. It doesn't matter just how much you talk Christian "speak." None of that makes you a Christian. A lifetime of being born in a Christian household and having a Christian funeral at your death and never missing a Sunday—*that* does not make you a Christian.

> "Enter by the narrow gate. For the gate is wide and the way is easy that leads to destruction, and those who enter by it are many. For the gate is narrow and the way is hard that leads to life, and those who find it are few." (Matthew 7:13)

Again, from Dr. Jones, "It is vital therefore that we should be clear about these things because we finally have no excuse. The revelation has been given, and we shall have to face it and give an account of what we have done in respect to it" (256).

So how do we know? Who are the elect of God? We can tell by a person's response to the gospel. Do they reject it? Do they go part of the way in their obedience, or do they give all of their lives to the gospel of Jesus? Have you given all of your life to Jesus? Jesus says the characteristic of one who is saved is that they obey the Word given to them. It's a person's relation to the truth that shows whether or not they are a genuine disciple of Christ. It is not the sentimental attachment they may have; it is their relationship to the truth which God has revealed in Christ that reveals whether they are in fact a Christian or not.

James Montgomery Boice comments, "According to these verses, the only way to tell whether one is a Christian or not is to see whether he or she believes *and* continues in the words of the Lord Jesus Christ" (1276). While people use the term Christian loosely, we ought to follow the teaching of Scripture that says that we should carefully examine ourselves to ensure our own salvation is resolved with God in Christ.

Verse 8 tells us, "For I have given them the words that you gave me, and they have received them and have come to know in truth that I came from you, and they believe that you sent me." Verse 6 has shown us our salvation from a divine perspective, but in summary, God from all eternity has known His own, and He has known who it is that has belonged to Him. God took those and He gave them to Jesus, and Jesus then revealed God to them so that they in turn might know the Father, and they have received His Word.

Verse 8 now shows us our salvation from our perspective. Jesus gives us truth—the Word, the gospel, in other words. Here, He provides these three explanations for how a Christian can be discovered among all the peoples. The first one is that they have the Word, a correct doctrine, given by God through Christ and through the apostles. The second is that they have a knowledge of them and that they believe them, that is, these doctrines in Scripture that Christ has delivered. They understand, they have a knowledge of these, and they believe that they are true. And thirdly, they know and believe the mission of Christ. That is, that He came from the Father. So Jesus gives us the truth; we can call that the gospel or the Word of God. We received His words, that is, accepting the truths of the gospel and the doctrines of grace, and we believe that Jesus is from God. That is the aspect of the incarnational ministry and mission of Jesus as the Word was made flesh. In doing these, we know and are saved.

The first explanation Jesus gives us the Word of God. In a world that is full of deception, and hearts given to self-deception, only the Word of God can shine the light of truth so brightly as to remove a lie. In a little pamphlet called *The Bleeding of the Evangelical Church*, David Wells writes, "In recovering the church, (which he is saying has been bleeding and dying slowly an anemic death because of a loss of its lifeblood,) the first thing we must do is recover the lost Word of God."

> The problem is not, of course, that the Bible itself has disappeared. There are, in fact, enough Bibles in America to put one in every home. The problem is that we are not hearing the Word of God. It does not rest consequentially upon us. It does not cut. And it is surely one of the great ironies of our time that in the 1970's and 80's so much of our effort was put into defining inspiration and looking at what were the best words to express and protect it. And while all of that work was going on, unnoticed by us, the Church was quietly, unhitching itself from the truth of Scripture in practice.

If we do not recover the sufficiency of the Word of God in our time, if we do not relearn what it means to be sustained by it, nourished by it, disciplined by it, and unless our preachers find the courage again to preach its truth, to allow their sermons to be defined by its truth, we will lose our right to call ourselves Protestants, we will lose our capacity to be the people of God, and we will set ourselves on a path that leads right into the old discredited liberal Protestantism. We have to recover a vivid other worldliness by making ourselves once again captives to the truth of God regardless of the cultural consequences. So that is the first thing." (Wells, 31)

John 1:5, "The light shines in the darkness, and the darkness has not overcome it." This light is Christ. This light *is* the Word of God. In Hebrews 4:12, we learn that the Word of God is ". . . living and active, sharper than a two-edged sword, piercing to the division of soul and spirit, of joints and marrow, and discerning the thoughts and intentions of the heart." What can the words of men do in comparison to the Word of God? Martin Luther said, "We must make a great difference between God's Word and the word of man. And man's word is a little sound that flies into the air and soon vanishes, but the Word of God is greater than heaven and earth, yea, greater than death and hell, for it forms part of the power of God and endures everlastingly" (20).

It was with a word that God created the heavens and the earth. It was with a word that Lazarus was called forth from the grave, and it is by the Word working with the spirit that lifeless hearts are restored and made new.

First Peter 1:23, "You have been born again not of perishable seed but of imperishable through the living and abiding Word of God." The Word is delivered indiscriminately to all. If those who were to be saved were to have a blue stripe painted somewhere on their body, certainly we would walk around lifting up shirts or checking somewhere, wherever they might have that painted across their stomach or on their back, and then we would go straight to them, and we would preach the gospel. But they don't have such a line painted on them, and so we can't limit our preaching of the gospel. We preach the gospel to all people. We don't know who those are that belonged to God, and so we deliver the gospel to all. Romans 1:16, "I am not ashamed of the gospel for it is the power of God to salvation to everyone who believes." This is the power of the Word of God, this Word which Christ has delivered to His people.

The second teaching is that the Christian hears the Word and receives the Word. To receive means to appropriate it to your heart. We first must hear the Word if we are then to receive and appropriate the Word. In Acts 17:11, Paul, debating the Word of God among the people says, "Now these Jews were more noble than those in Thessalonica. They received the Word with all eagerness, examining the Scriptures daily to see if these things were so."

These Bereans listened while Paul was preaching the Word, and then they took what was told with eagerness and went and examined the Scriptures to see if what Paul was telling them was in fact true. They delighted in the preaching of the Word of God and receiving of the doctrines and grace. Why? Because they believed the Word. They believed who Jesus is, and they were not held captive by the lie of the world. The very fact that Jesus mentions both hearing and receiving shows that not all who hear will receive. Not all who read are changed. Not all who travel the walk of Christian faith are those who are walking with Christ. For many, the gospel goes in one ear and out the other.

First Corinthians 2:14, "The natural person does not accept the things of the Spirit of God for they are folly to him, and he is not able to discern them because they are spiritually discerned." In this way, the doctrines of grace act as a sieve, sifting out those whose quest is simply for some sort of an existential religion or a religious feeling or something that is just for them. Our religion is not just for us. Our religion is for the glory of God. Our salvation is to His glory, not our own. Our being a part of the Body of Christ is that we as His bride might anticipate the coming of the Bridegroom.

In addition to hearing, the Word must sink in. As the Word is preached, it must also sink into the mind where it will inform the affections of the heart and give direction to the will. Even though it is the voice of a preacher that brings the Word, it is the work of God that makes the Word penetrate the mind. How many minds, however, are like fortresses, and how many voices are never heard? How much of the gospel falls to the ground just as the seed that was sown on rocky soil? It's not the one who sows or waters that brings growth, but God. Receiving has the effect of causing belief, but even here Jesus is not finished.

In John, chapter 6, after Jesus fed the 5,000, masses of people began coming to Him, professing their belief in Him. They were even called believers, and so Jesus began to reveal Himself to them. He taught them that unless they eat the bread of heaven, unless they take that bread of heaven which is His body, and unless they drink His own blood, they have no life. The crowds left when Jesus said this, and only the disciples remained, saying to Jesus, "Where else can we go, for who else has the words of eternal life?"

The third aspect of verse 8, teaches that knowing follows preaching and receiving. First the Word is delivered. The Word is received, and then God is known by the doctrines that are delivered. This is vitally important for us to understand. Belief—your belief and my belief—has an object, and that object is to be known. It's not to be a mystery or veiled in some sort of a mist or a fog. How can we have an assurance about which we cannot have any clarity? Belief has an object, and the object is to be known. It has been revealed to us in Christ Jesus. *Blind faith* and *leap of faith* are two phrases common in Christian jargon, but such phrases do not appear in the Scriptures to describe Christians.

Biblical faith is a knowing faith. It isn't a sentimental feeling; it's an assurance. The Christian has reasons to believe. Christianity is based on propositional truths—truths such as *I believe in God the Father Almighty, maker of heaven and earth, and in His Son, Jesus Christ our Lord who was conceived of the Virgin Mary* and so on. Propositional truth has been largely lost in the Christian church today. Once during a discussion of worship and communication and preaching, a young lady stood up, and said that a friend of hers had gone to the Far East, and had come across a Buddhist monk who asked her to explain her faith.

The Buddhist monk apparently adept at his own style of apologetics asked her how she experiences God. She asked him for clarity on what he meant. He said, "How is it that you experience God?" I stopped her at that point, and I said, "I reject the point of origin of your question. We are not seeking to answer how we experience God. Our question is, how do we come to know God? It is because God has revealed Himself to us. The whole idea of experiencing God places it in a mystical, hyper-spiritual realm, a sentimental realm, rather than a knowing realm."

But Jesus says, "They know. They know." He doesn't say they simply have an experience of faith; He's saying that they know the truth about God and about Himself. Christians can know. We don't have to wonder and wish. Christians, like apostles, face severe questioning every day. Peter instructs us to always be prepared to give an answer to everyone who asks you to give the reason for the hope that is in you. Can you do that? Can you give a reasonable response because Christianity is not something veiled and hidden from those who have eyes to see? Can you understand? Christians don't know everything, but they do know that Jesus came from God. They know that Jesus was divine and that all He said and did is true. In other words, that Jesus is the way and the truth and the life and that no one can come to the Father except by Him.

There is one last characteristic necessary to a Christian, in verse 6, ". . . and they have kept your Word." They have *kept* your Word. This is really an excellent summary of all three. Do we really know Christ if our living doesn't reflect Him? Can we profess Him to be Lord and yet neglect His instruction in our life? Second Thessalonians 1:8, tells us that Jesus will return, ". . . in flaming fire, inflicting vengeance on those who do not know God and on those who do not obey the gospel of our Lord Jesus Christ." So a good and short description of a Christian might very well be *one who keeps his eye on the truth.*

I was warned as I was learning how to drive that I should never look into the headlights of oncoming traffic because looking into their headlights will cause your car to gradually begin to drift in that direction. The same can be said of staring at a walker or a bike rider or a jogger on the side of the road. If you turn your eyes there and you begin to look, eventually, you'll begin to steer in that direction. When we're in public, we don't want to take our eyes off of our children, especially in crowded places.

There is a mother who had a three-year-old whom she had adopted from Russia, and the child was playing in the sand on Sussex Beach. There were about 800 people, she said, on the beach and a wasp began to buzz her. She was very diligent in watching her child, but as she was swatting after the wasp, she didn't get up. She didn't leave. She was just trying to get the wasp to go away. She turned her head and looked back, and her daughter was gone. Where was she? Was she in the water? Was she stolen? Was she wandering along the beach?

They sought help. They enlisted people to come and help find her. She immediately began looking over the beach. It had only been seconds that she had been working to get rid of the bee. She and her husband both were journalists, and as journalists, they knew full well the depravity of man as the papers report to us every day. They knew the stories about lost children. They did find her, a half-mile away; the three-year-old had wandered along the beach.

What has your attention in life? Where are your eyes trained in life? You cannot keep something unless you have your eyes on it. Send your kids off to college and see if it's not true. Have a child run away from you at the beach, and see if it's not true. If you take your eyes off, you lose that which is most cherished by you. Always, not occasionally, keep your eyes on that which is important to you. Not just in your quiet times, not just on Sunday morning or when you're preparing for a Sunday school lesson or a Bible study, always. Wherever you have your eye will be the direction that you go.

Ephesians 5:1 tells us our direction is that we would be imitators of God. We must have our eye on God at all times and a Christian realizes that nothing in life is as important as the truth of God. He is the one living a life trained by truth. God's people may not all be equal in their understanding. They may not all be equal in their courage. They may not all have the same opportunities to serve, but they have the Word and God gives them the Holy Spirit. If you have kept His Word, He will keep you.

8

Jesus Prays for His Own

(John 17:9–10)

JOHN 17 IS REFERRED to not simply as the prayer of Jesus but as "the high priestly prayer." Jesus in this time of prayer before the Father prays in such a way as to show us that He is indeed our High Priest.

> "I am praying for them. I am not praying for the world but for those whom you have given me, for they are yours. All mine are yours, and yours are mine, and I am glorified in them."
> (John 17:9, 10)

The second portion of Jesus' prayer, from verses 6 through 19, is where Jesus begins to pray for the apostles. In these verses, He not only makes petitions for His disciples, those who were with Him there as His contemporaries, but He tells why He is offering the prayer. Some wonder why they should pray at all if God is all knowing, that is, since God knows all things, since God knows the future, since God knows history before it is even played out and recorded in the history books, why should we even pray? Yet, we see Christ affirming the reasons for His own prayer to the same all-knowing God.

Certainly, God knows the apostles. Certainly, God knows their needs. Certainly, God knows the tribulations they will face in the future, and yet Christ, the only begotten Son of God Himself prays to the Father. As a member of the Trinity Himself, He lifts up His apostles to the Father in prayer. The Westminster Confession of Faith, in chapter 8, the first paragraph is very instructive concerning the role of Christ as High Priest.

It pleased God, in His eternal purpose, to choose and ordain the Lord Jesus, His only begotten Son, to be the Mediator between God and man, the Prophet, Priest, and King, the Head and Savior of His church, the Heir of all things, and Judge of the world: unto whom He did from all eternity give a people, to be His seed, and to be led by Him in time redeemed, called, justified, sanctified, and glorified.

Can you hear the echo of the Scripture we just read in these passages, that He is the Prophet, Priest, and King, the Mediator between God and man, that He is the One who is in possession from all eternity of those whom God has given Him.

Our Westminster Confession helps us to see in summarizing form the high priesthood of Christ. It isn't uncommon for us to think of Jesus as our Mediator, a Mediator standing between God and man as the Guarantor of a covenant of grace. But as Mediator, Jesus does more than simply negotiate a peace. He actually fulfills the term for peace by atoning for sin. That is what is unique about the scriptural language for mediator. The mediator of the Scriptures, in the use of the word *mediator* as it's given to us in Scripture, is more than one who passively or even actively speaks on behalf of another. The mediator of the Scripture is the one who himself has fulfilled the terms of mediation, who has paid the fine required for the establishment of peace.

As Mediator, Jesus serves as our Priest. The priest spoke and acted on behalf of the people in Scripture. "For every high priest chosen from among men is appointed to act on behalf of men in relation to God, to offer gifts and sacrifices for sins" (Hebrews 5:1). To act on behalf of men! What is the action on behalf of men? To offer gifts and sacrifices for sins. This is our Mediator. He is the One who not only stands before God, but who acts before God in offering an atonement for sin.

William Hendriksen points out, "Between the purpose for the atonement and the purpose of Christ's high priestly prayer, there is perfect agreement. Atonement and intercession is the function of our High Priest" (335). We are aware that in the Old Testament, priests sacrificed animals. But they not only sacrificed for the expiation of sin, they also carried the blood into the mercy seat, and they sprinkled it on the mercy seat so that they might have access to God. They never entered into the Holy of Holies without blood. Not only that, but they also carried the incense, and the incense would burn and create a smoke and a cloud, and the cloud would then cover the altar, symbolizing the prayers of God's people going up to the Lord.

Jesus is that High Priest in fulfillment, for He Himself has provided the atoning sacrifice. No longer do we sacrifice bulls or goats or rams on the altar, but Jesus Himself is that atoning sacrifice, and by being that sacrifice, He then also is the High Priest who has taken His own blood into the mercy seat, and now is with the Father. But only by blood are we allowed to be present before the Father. Because of our union with Christ, because we have died with Him and been buried with Him and raised with Him, we are in union with Christ, so, we too, with Christ, are before God, but not displacing Him as our High Priest, for He still intercedes for His people. He prays for His people without ceasing, Scripture tells us.

These verses form a transition into that part of Jesus' prayer in which he would be praying for His disciples. He explains here the nature of that prayer for His disciples, and we begin to see His high priestly work. The two acts of a high priest, remember, are atonement and intercession. In his preface Jesus makes a point to state just who He is praying for and why. "I pray for those whom you have given me. I pray for them, and for none others."

Martyn Lloyd-Jones says, "We must realize that there are only these two big things dealt with here; our Lords puts first the reasons why he prays for these people, and then he gives the requests afterwards" (197). As we see in the Westminster Confession, Jesus asks and God sends the Holy Spirit. That was an act of intercession. The gospel as found in Christ will be preached by the apostles and insofar as they have been raised to life by the Holy Spirit, the kingdom is in them. As the Spirit of Christ has been given to the apostles, they, in possession of that Spirit are also manifesting the kingdom of God among the world, in the world. This makes the final epic of a long exodus for God's people out of the world.

As Jesus hung dying on the Cross, His eyes scanned the faces of the people. He saw the Sadducees and Pharisees, but He did not pray for them. As He looked out at the people, their condition was so much like the sheep described in Ezekiel 34 who were weak and injured because of the shepherds who had not tended to them, but had used them for their own devices that Jesus' heart broke for them. And perhaps even at that moment He was remembering verse 11 of Ezekiel 34, when Jesus promises, "Behold, I, I Myself will search for my sheep and will seek them out." When Peter preached the first Pentecost, wasn't it those Jews in Jerusalem who believed? Jesus on the Cross lifts His eyes, and He sees before Him fields white unto harvest, and He prays for them.

So, in verse 9, Jesus introduces us to Himself as our Mediator. He doesn't pray for those who will not come to faith, but knowing in the omniscient knowledge of God those who belong to God and who are being given to Him, He lifts them up in prayer. Spurgeon said, "A remark that our Lord Jesus pleads for His own people when He puts on His priestly breastplate, 'It is here for the tribes whose names are there.'" You might recall the breastplate that the priests would wear when they were fulfilling an official service, and they would have stones in them, and they would have shoulder boards on them, and there on that breastplate would be the representation of the 12 tribes of Israel for whom the priest was interceding.

Spurgeon relates to that when he says, "The priest put on the breast-plate, and so Christ, in putting on as it were that breastplate is praying for those who belong to the Lord. When He presents the atoning sacrifice, it is Israel whom God hath chosen" (Boice, 1281). In this prayer, and by Jesus' opening remarks, every believer ought to be persuaded of the unique position we have in Christ.

At this very point in our study, we ought to be acknowledging very simply and very plainly that Jesus Christ is the High Priest interceding both in action through the atonement and by word which is in prayer without ceasing that God would supply, that God would protect, that God would save His people. Thus, in 1 John 2:1, we're able to read with confidence "But if anyone does sin, we have an advocate." It is the one who is in Christ who has an advocate, for Jesus says, "I am not praying for the world." Those who are in Christ have an advocate, but not those who are in the world.

Jesus gives three motives for His prayer on behalf of His disciples. These motives are also the three reasons we are assured that they are an-swered. Prayers are answered that Christ utters, first of all, because they, that is the disciples, are His as a gift from the Father. Jesus values them because the Father Himself values them. Have you ever wondered in your own life what makes your children special? Why are we so guarded over our own children? Why is it that even as they go into adulthood, they don't simply become another adult, but they always remain our children?

Why do you love them more than other children even though there is a compassion and a love for other children? Why do you spend so much on their education? Why do you labor so hard that they're able to learn? Why are you willing to be a scout leader or a chaperone at a school dance? Why do you stay up late learning algebra to help them understand, or why do you cry when they're hurt? Why is their future so connected to your own?

You know that since their birth, their lives and their futures, while in the hands of God, was also in some sense in your hands too. You have a stewardship of them. You have a stewardship of their health, their education, their happiness, and their success, and that stewardship becomes a testimony of whether you have been faithful in your own service before God with your children or not.

Jesus was given a stewardship of His disciples. They belonged to God, God gave them to Him, and He was a steward of their learning and growth and faith. And now just as we would pray for our own children, except all the more effectual because it is Christ Himself praying, He enters into intercessory prayer seeking their blessing. Jesus prays because they are important to the Father, because they represent those first fruits of a chosen nation who will receive the Spirit of Christ.

The picture we're given here is much like the picture of the Church which is the Bride of Christ being given to the Son in marriage. The Father anticipates the Bride going away with the Bridegroom into a difficult field of labor. The Bridegroom wants to reassure the Father that all will go well, that He will be faithful to the Bride, that the Bride and He will remain in union together, but even if it goes badly, out of love won't the Father come to the aid of both the Bride and the Groom? Even in human terms, if a father cared not much for the bridegroom, wouldn't he out for love of the bride come to their aid when they were in need? So Jesus prays to the Father, and it's the Father's loving disposition to those who are His own that is the guarantee of an answer to prayer. Christ has secured our favor to the Father by the atonement, and He is asking the Father for blessing for His people, and because of the love of God, it is answered.

The second reason for Jesus' prayer is the bridge which we find between verses 9 and 10. If you look in your Scripture again, "I am not praying for the world but for those whom you have given me, for they are yours. All mine are yours, and yours are mine, and I am glorified in them."

"All mine are yours, and yours are mine. . . ." Everything that belongs to the Son belongs to the Father, and everything that belongs to the Father also belongs to the Son. When a father begins to explain to his son in this life that all of his estate will someday be in hands of his children, when he says, "Son, look at this field," or "Look at this home," or "Look at these accounts," or "Look at this business," and he says, "Someday, my son or my children, this will be left to you," those children upon maturity understand that their father's investment, that all their father has is also theirs, and that the produce and the prosperity of their own father becomes in essence their own prosperity for their own future.

Jesus prays for the disciples not because it's the Father's concern only, not because it's His concern only, but because it is in the interest of the kingdom that the disciples are blessed. The disciples will be the heralds of the gospel to the nations. They will be given the Holy Spirit in union with the Son, and the Father and the Son together have an investment in the kingdom, and the disciples also now are invested in that kingdom. And their work is God's work. Their work is Christ's work, for it's Christ's kingdom that they are being used of God to establish. So, Christ prays for them not only because it's in His own interest and not only because it's in the Father's interest, but because it is in the interest of both, because "All mine are yours, and yours are mine."

That interest is made more clear when you keep in mind our own unity with Christ, because in that unity our concerns and our sufferings are Christ's concerns and Christ's sufferings, and the Father is invested in Christ, and so He is invested in our relief as well.

In trying to understand unity, let's go back to marriage again. Marriage serves us as an illustration to understand unity. In marriage, there is a union between a man and a woman. Traditionally, that is symbolized in her taking her husband's name when she becomes his wife. His concerns then become her concerns. His life becomes her life. The success of her husband becomes her own success. In view of this effect of union, which of them can neglect the needs of the other and still prosper? Can a husband neglect the needs of his wife and expect to prosper? Can a wife neglect the needs of her husband and expect blessing and prosperity?

And so it is that Jesus would not neglect the needs of His disciples and expect their blessing, but rather He enters into prayer for His disciples, and because God is also invested in the kingdom as Christ is invested in the kingdom as the disciples are invested in the kingdom, it is for the mutual benefit of all that the disciples' ministry flourishes to the glory of God.

The third reason, and the final reason, is because He is glorified in us. God is glorified in Christ, and Christ is glorified in His saving work. That saving work is first of all *regeneration*. Regeneration is taking a person who is not only born in sin, who is lost, and who is blind, but is also committed to that sin, who craves that sin and indulges in it. As an animal would crave for food, so a sinner craves after sin. The depth of depravity is such that we could not plummet.

A person who is happy with the way of the world is not inclined to worship God, not inclined to serve Christ, and not inclined to open his own eyes to the gospel. Christ comes and opens a person's eyes. He quickens hearts, illumines minds, and grants people faith leading to repentance and a changed life. It's Christ who does this! It's Christ alone who can save. Man is completely lost without the activity of Christ bringing His Spirit to bear against the dead, cold, lost heart of man to quicken it to life that man would live. This brings Christ glory because His people who were once lost, lift up their voices in praise for now we are saved. Those who truly understand the important and immortal truths of that hymn "Amazing Grace" can truly sing "Amazing Grace," understanding that it is to the glory of Christ that God's work of salvation has been accomplished.

He is glorified in His disciples who were committed to living holy lives. He is glorified through regeneration, and He is glorified through the *sanctification*, that is, the commitment to living holy lives before God. Holiness is the most frequently mentioned attribute of God in the Bible. And we are told by the Scriptures that we also should be holy as our heavenly Father is holy.

How are we made holy? By being transformed in our thinking rather than being conformed to the world. The world has always kicked at the ox goads as it were when it comes to the gospel. The world has always sought to shake off the Scriptures. But look how this ancient text written so long ago by so many authors still stands before God's people, still stands if not proven in the eyes of all men, certainly without being able to be disproved. Still this ancient text confounds the smartest and the most intelligent of men. They still cannot put away ancient writings written in a primitive culture. Not one word can be disproved. While not all may be believers, they certainly cannot disproved.

James Montgomery Boice: "If we live in spiritual adultery, compromising with the values of our society, if the priorities of our non-Christian culture become our priorities, we are not living in a way that glorifies

Him" (1285). But we would add to that, if we order our lives and live as Christ calls us then we do glorify Him.

Jesus is also glorified by our speaking and acting in His *service*. He is glorified by regeneration. He is glorified by the sanctification of the saints by our living, by our being transformed people, because we can't do that of our own power and our own energy and our own intuition, because every instinct we have works against it. He is also glorified through our evangelization of the world, by our speaking and our acting in His service.

When we bear testimony of His grace, and confess Him before the world as our Savior, He is glorified. When we speak of Christ in adoring terms, when we glorify Him by our commitment to Him, He is glorified. When we respond to His grace by obeying the Great Commission, and we labor to advance the estate of our King, to enlarge His kingdom's boundaries by preaching the gospel to the lost, Jesus is glorified. There is no request too large or too small to bring before God by God's people. Philippians 4:6: ". . . by prayer and supplication with thanksgiving let your requests be made known to God."

As you consider this high priestly prayer of Jesus and His motivation and His commitment to you, remember the words of Hebrews 4:14 through 16 that we have a High Priest who stands between us and God and intercedes for us continually. Come to the throne of grace for your High Priest makes continual intercession for you there.

9

Believers Saved by God for Eternity

(John 17:11–12)

JOHN, CHAPTER 17; THIS unique prayer that is given to us. We know
Jesus prayed on many occasions, but we are not given the contents of
those prayers, certainly not to the detail we're given in this prayer as Jesus
is praying to His Father. There is a sense again in which we are standing
upon holy ground because here we are listening not just to Scripture,
which is in itself inspired by God in every word, but here we are listening
to a conversation between God the Son, incarnate in Christ, and God the
Father.

Note the verses in John, chapter 17, verses 11 and 12, for it is God
who speaks to us.

> "And I am no longer in the world, but they are in the world, and I
> am coming to you. Holy Father, keep them in your name, which
> you have given me, that they may be one, even as we are one.
> While I was with them, I kept them in your name, which you
> have given me. I have guarded them, and not one of them has
> been lost except the son of destruction, that the Scripture might
> be fulfilled."

When I think of the word *preserve*, I can't help but think of preserves,
in the sense of preserves that you often eat. I tried my best to get away
from it. I didn't want to use it as any kind of an introduction or an illustration because it just seemed so unsophisticated, but preserves do in fact
provide us an interesting illustration. In this, when you go out to pick a
fruit to make preserves, the fruit you pick must be ripe. If you take it when
it's too green, or if you take it when it is rotted, you won't have preserves

worth preserving. You gather the fruit at the appointed time, and then you prepare it through boiling or cooking in some way, then putting it in a jar. The lid goes on tight, the air is removed, or the wax is put on, and there it remains until it is brought out to be enjoyed.

Now, how do I relate this at all to us? God has called us out of the world, and we cannot remain. If we remain, it's essentially the same as when fruit remains on the tree. It will have a deteriorating effect, not a life-giving effect. But in removing us from the tree, we're not then left to die and to rot. God preserves us and He keeps us much like we might do in preserves.

Christ is praying that God would preserve the disciples, that He would keep the disciples. In many respects, this whole chapter of John 17 is a summary of Jesus' teaching in the entire Gospel. And we find here the calling out of God's people, and we find here the preservation of God's people in the prayer which Jesus now offers. We found in the very first petition the incarnation story once again related, and the glorifying of Christ on earth, and the glorifying of Christ after the resurrection and ascension in heaven as He sits at the right hand of God the Father.

Jesus begins by addressing God in this passage as "Holy Father—Holy Father." This address is found only in the Gospel of John—only in the Gospel of John is He addressed as *"Holy Father"* by Christ. He presents God as transcendent. When we hear the word *holy*, we recognize in that word something that is removed, set apart, something that is not like what we are except as we are found in Christ. But we're not naturally a holy people. We are naturally a people of flesh and of this world. Only as we are called out and preserved, if you will, are we made holy, but God is by His very nature holy.

Jesus prays, "Holy Father," presenting to us this transcendence of God, that God is above all, that God is high, and yet it also preserves the sense of relationship and immanence, because He says "Father," a familial term. *"Holy"* communicating transcendence; *"Father"* communicating a familial intimacy or immanence of God.

We find in this title given to God really our first point, which is a point of contrast. A wicked world is contrasted with the holy Father. This title also sets the stage for the theme of consecration and sanctification in verses 17 through 19, which we'll be studying in the future. Consecration is a word we often misuse. That word *consecration* comes from a Greek root meaning *to make holy*. If we consecrate something, we are making it holy, not because we have the power to infuse holiness into anything, but by taking it and consecrating it, that is setting it apart, appointing it to a particular use, we are in fact making it holy. Both Jesus and His disciples are to be consecrated to the Father. That consecration is to reflect nothing arbitrary. It's to reflect nothing that man can imagine. Only the very character of God is the definition of holiness. We are to be made holy, consecrated, sanctified—to be made holy.

There is a good bit of evidence that prayers of various sorts were often associated with farewell addresses, so it would have been good, and it would have been instructive for the disciples understanding Jesus going into prayer at this point. It would have helped them to understand that what He was giving them now was a farewell discourse. It was the end. It was the conclusion of His ministry. So, in that sense, the prayer is recognizable in helping the disciples to understand the events that are unfolding. It's the content of that prayer that makes it unique, however.

D. A. Carson, a great commentator, remarks, "He is the incarnate Son of God, and He is returning to His Father by the route of a desperately shameful and painful death. He prays that the course on which He has embarked will bring glory to His Father, and that His followers in consequence of His own death and exaltation will be preserved from evil and for the priceless privilege of seeing Jesus' glory" (551). Jesus' motivation for lifting them up in prayer was that with His departure the disciples now become vulnerable. There is always a physical danger for those who follow Christ. We know that. There have been martyrs through the centuries, but Jesus' concern here is not so much for the physical danger as for the spiritual. The spiritual danger is the greater danger in Jesus' view.

It's interesting that in Zechariah that we find this very characteristic of God listed as what God does with His people. He says that if anyone messes with God's people—to paraphrase in today's street talk—they are messing with the apple of His eye. He says, "I will be like a flaming wall around you to protect you." Hasn't that been a characteristic of God? Hasn't that been a characteristic of God's relationship and association with His people that we have anticipated, that God would preserve and protect His people?

So, we only ask, "What kind of protection? What is it that we are to expect as God protects His people?" In this second petition of the high priestly prayer, we see Jesus praying specifically for the spiritual protection of His disciples. The first petition was Jesus' prayer that God would glorify

Him now that He had finished the work the Father had given Him to do. This is the second petition—that the Father will protect the disciples.

Now, where is Jesus going in His prayer? The third petition, which is verse 17, will be a prayer for their sanctification. The fourth petition, verses 20 through 21, will be a prayer for their unity, a unity in faith in the Body of Christ. And the fifth petition, verse 24, will be for their ultimate gathering with Him in heaven. He wants God to glorify Him on earth, then He prays that God would protect, sanctify, unify, and then eventually gather the disciples with Him.

Jesus, addressing the holy Father, says, "I am coming to you. I am coming to you." That means that the work and calling of the disciples in the world will be contingent upon Jesus going to the Father. What they will do afterwards is contingent on Jesus' leaving. Again, this is simply a summary statement of what He has already told us, that the Spirit cannot be delivered unto them until Christ Himself has ascended. And with the coming of the Holy Spirit comes the opening of the entire frontier of the New Testament mission, the gospel mission. The evangelistic mission goes out with the outpouring of the Holy Spirit. Jesus now says, "I'm at the threshold of coming to the Father. Their mission, their work, which I'm now praying you would protect them to do is contingent upon my going to the Father."

It's important to note that the prayers of Jesus for the disciples are for their spiritual good and progress. The request is that the Father will keep them in His own name—in His name. That means to keep them in that revelation of Christian understanding as Jesus has revealed the Father's name to them and to keep them grounded in that faith and understanding.

Jesus requests that God would preserve their fidelity to that name which was revealed to them, and in that name that they would have unity. There can be no unity without agreement and preservation of that name which was shown to them. Where else will there be unity except in social function?

Again, D. A. Carson, when speaking to that point says, "The persistence in the truth is the prerequisite to participation in Jesus' sanctification" (563). Sanctification is growth in Christ, perfection of Christian character in the individual. We will not be perfected in this life because sin will always beleaguer us, but we are being perfected, we are being worked day after day after day until the end of our days when God will perfect it at the glorification and the resurrection. Until that time there is progress, and there is growth, and there is a mortification of the sin which is in our own bodies, and the war that wages within us as we are a double-minded people begins to be won, and victory begins to be had by that which is true in Christ. That is sanctification.

Our justification happens only once. We are declared saved in Christ, and His blood has bought our pardon. Following that is a lifetime of work in the Spirit of Christ, not in the flesh. We are not sanctified because of our own labors regardless of how much Christian work we might be involved in. It is the Spirit who works sanctification in us. But we are in fact active because of the Spirit in that lifetime work of being sanctified. Jesus is praying that they will be one in love and in defense of the truth against an evil and apostate world.

Being able to make a defense for your faith—why would that seem to be important? Because you can't defend what you do not know. You have nothing to say if you do not understand. So, in being able to make a defense for your faith, the implication is that you know truth, and you're defending truth because Christ Himself is the Way, the Truth, and the Life. And in defending truth, you are defending Christ. Not that Christ needs defense, but we defend the faith that the gospel of Jesus Christ might be proclaimed and that our own soundness of the faith can be established. And in doing that we're honoring Christ the Lord as holy.

> "In your hearts honor Christ the Lord as holy . . . always being prepared to make a defense to anyone who asks you for a reason for the hope that is in you; yet do it with gentleness and respect" (1 Peter 3:15).

James Boice points out that another great 19th century preacher Marcus Rainsford said, "The Lord does not ask for riches for them, or honors, or worldly influence, or great preferments, but He does most earnestly pray that they may be kept from evil, separated from the world, qualified for duty, and brought home safely to heaven" (Rainsford 173). Listen to this: "Soul prosperity is the best prosperity, and in truth, all temporal prosperity as it is so called is only real when it is in proportion to the prosperity of the soul." He quotes from 3 John, verse 2. "Beloved, I pray that all may go well with you and that you may be in good health, as it goes well with your soul."

What is it that we're speaking of? Rainsford concludes, "Soul prosperity is the index of true prosperity" (173). And the food of the soul that brings it health is truth. Truth is the food of the soul, and without truth, the spiritual life of any individual becomes anemic and withers on the vine.

When you want to give a flower to someone in your own life, you cut the flower, you put it in a vase, and it looks alive for some time, but the moment you cut it, you have severed it from that which gives it life. And so, it only takes time for the decay and the rot of death to begin to set in, even on the most beautiful flower. And so it is with people. When people are severed from truth, their spirit will begin to wither. They may clamor, they may panic, they may begin to grasp and seek ways to be fed again, but because they have either an aversion to or cannot hear and understand truth, they do not receive.

Jesus has a true and sincere concern for the spiritual safety of His disciples, and He wants the prosperity of their spirit to be real, even as they are left to dwell in an evil and an apostate world. Another great minister, Thomas Manton says, "As a father when he is about to die commends his children to the care and tutelage to a near friend, so does Christ commend His disciples to God" (269).

What an apt picture! A father who dearly loves his children but is on death's bed wants his children to survive, to be protected, to thrive, to be fed, to be given opportunity and a future. And so, he doesn't leave them unattended. He turns to his most trusted friend, and he says, "Will you take my children? Will you care for them? Will you adopt them as your own? Will you protect my children?" A beautiful picture of what Christ in this prayer is doing. He is begging of the Father, "Take these disciples. I have protected them while I was here, but I am leaving to come to you. And now I'm praying, God Father, will you protect these disciples?" Jesus' concern is the danger the disciples are in because while He is leaving, they remain in the world.

There has been a recurring theme of the blessedness of Jesus' departure, of His sitting at the right hand, and of all the blessings that come with that as He is once again glorified with the glory He had before, but the disciples are remaining behind. So now, Jesus moves beyond encouraging their patience for His return to point out the dangers of their remaining in the world, because no longer are they a part of the world. They have been removed from the world. They have been picked from the vine. They are no longer of the world, and so, just like the body's immune system—when a germ comes in, the immune system attacks to drive that germ or that virus out. The world will desperately want them out of its midst. They cannot bear to hear the truth that comes from the disciples' mouths. If it means anything to them at all, it only means something to drive their hatred, like fanning the flames of a fire.

Jesus had experienced the world's rejection and persecution, and so would they. In John 15, verses 20 to 21, Jesus said clearly,

> "Remember the word that I said to you: 'A servant is not greater than his master.' If they persecuted me, they will also persecute you. If they kept my word, they will also keep yours. But all these things they will do to you on account of my name, because they do not know Him who sent me."

But the danger is really not just physical; it's spiritual as well. While some will be called upon to die for the faith, the danger is more than that. It's because the One who has left them also leaves them in this world which is still full of darkness. Already one has left the body. One has left the disciples and gone out into the darkness to betray Christ.

The title "son of perdition" is found another time in Scripture, 2 Thessalonians 2:3. There it refers to the one we call the "man of sin" or the Antichrist. Judas is of the same ilk as the Antichrist, this "son of perdition." Jesus had also been approached by the tempter, and He was tempted to sin, but Jesus withstood it, and so He knows temptation will come to the disciples. Jesus prays that God will preserve the disciples through these trials and tribulations and temptations, that He will preserve them both in body and spirit. While the trials to the body are real and historic, trials to the spirit are issues of belief and fidelity.

While in the flesh, Jesus kept all those the Lord had given Him and none were lost, except Judas, who shows what happens to an unregenerate person no matter how long they appear to be religious. And this also was an answer to prophecies of Scripture, as Jesus says in the passage today. He says that "not one of them has been lost except the son of destruction, that the Scripture might be fulfilled." The Scripture had prophesied that Judas would be lost. Now Jesus returns the remaining disciples to the Father's care.

How does Jesus commend us into that care, and how does God care for His people? The same way in which He has always cared for His people. God has given them truth. The truth was incarnate in Christ, and it is now the revelation of God's will in Scripture, and it comes to us because of our possession of the Holy Spirit. It is truth that gives life. While Jesus was with them, He kept them through the teaching and through miracles. He kept them in the truth by constantly teaching them and keeping it before them in teaching them all that He heard from the Father.

He protected them against apostasy by correcting wrong belief and wrong conclusions all along the way because Jesus was God's Word made flesh. Now God still keeps us by His Word. "All Scripture is breathed out by God and profitable for teaching, for reproof, for correction, and for training in righteousness" (2 Timothy 3:16). In other words, Scripture preserves us against error, and it works for our consecration and sanctification.

We can understand the protective power of God because it has been explained and given to us almost pictorially through the words of Scripture all throughout the Old Testament. Psalm 121 presents God as a protector, using the words "watch over" or "watches" five times in that one psalm. In Ezekiel 34:11 and following, God had spoken about the bad shepherds in Israel, and He promises, "I myself will be a shepherd over them." In Isaiah 27, God is compared to a vine keeper, keeping a fruitful vine. It says, "I the Lord watch over it. I water it continually. I guard it day and night so that no one may harm it."

These are the pictures that should come to our mind whenever we think of God's protecting and keeping power. The keeping power of God is commonly called in our own understanding and theology the *perseverance of the saints.* The perseverance of the saints is just another form of the expression, *once saved, always saved,* or sometimes *eternal security.* It means that apostasy is never the final lot of any true child of God, that we will be preserved, and we will not finally and ultimately fall in apostasy.

Our Confession of Faith affirms that same teaching of Scripture, saying, "They, whom God has accepted in His Beloved, effectually called, and sanctified by His Spirit, can neither totally nor finally fall away from the state of grace, but shall certainly persevere therein to the end, and be eternally saved." When the Confession says that "none can totally or finally fall away from the state of grace," the word *can* there is talking about ability. We do not have the ability to wrench ourselves out of God's hand. What God has held firmly cannot escape His grasp. While it is possible for believers to fall into deep sin, such as David did or Peter when he denied

Christ, the Confession recognizes that Scripture teaches the permanence of the change that is in man when he is regenerated, because we are not preserved by our own will, but by the keeping power of God.

God's purposes to save His elect aren't going to be frustrated by our frailty or our weaknesses. In fact, it is in our weaknesses that the power and grace of God are made most abundantly clear. Paul refers to the active involvement of God in Philippians 1:3 through 6. He says, "I thank my God upon every remembrance of you, always in every prayer of mine making request for you all with joy, for your fellowship in the gospel from the first day until now, being confident of this very thing, that He who has begun a good work in you will complete it until the day of Jesus Christ."

We are God's handiwork, and it is God who is the perfecter of our salvation in Christ, and it is God who is at work to preserve us to the end that we become His handiwork, for we're not just a project or work of God, but God also loves us and calls us His very own.

> What then shall we say to these things? If God is for us, who can be against us? He who did not spare His own Son but gave Him up for us all, how will He not also with Him graciously give us all things? Who shall bring any charge against God's elect? It is God who justifies. Who is to condemn? Christ Jesus is the one who died—more than that, who was raised—who is at the right hand of God, who indeed is interceding for us. Who shall separate us from the love of Christ? Shall tribulation, or distress, or persecution, or famine, or nakedness, or danger, or sword? As it is written, "For your sake we are being killed all the day long; we are regarded as sheep to be slaughtered." (Romans 8:31–36)

Nothing can separate us from the love of God in Christ. Paul lists any number of conditions that might draw men away from God, but he affirms none of these will do so, because we are held not by our own desire, not by our own will, not by our own power or spiritual prowess, but by the love of God. There'll be many who come up against us, but God is for us, and we're kept by His name.

To be kept in His name implies that we are the benefactors of His sovereignty, holiness, and compassion. "The name of the LORD is a strong tower; the righteous man runs into it and is safe" (Proverbs 18:10). "God is our refuge and strength, A very present help in trouble. . . . The LORD of hosts is with us; The God of Jacob is our stronghold" (Psalm 46). That was the inspiration for Luther who sang, "A mighty fortress is our God, a bulwark never failing." What would be your response to the preserving and the protecting power of God? Should we, as Paul asked, live in sin "that grace might abound"? Should we live carelessly? Like Paul, we would say, May it never be! No, we must keep in mind why we are to depend upon God to preserve us. It's because we are a weak people, and we live in a hostile world. Knowing that God preserves us should cause us to persevere all the more.

He preserves us in times of discouragement. He preserves us in times of persecution. He preserves us in our work, and in our study, and in our prayers, and in our family living. In all ways, God preserves us, because it is God who sees us through to the end. This was the prayer of Christ for us, that we would be preserved in all ways and in all places, that our spirits would reflect the glory of God. We are God's workmanship, and Christ has prayed that God would protect His own people, which He has done by giving us His word, by granting to us the Holy Spirit, and as we hold fast to the truth, it has its preserving effect upon our lives, that we would walk as God has called us to walk.

Therein, is our perseverance, that we would walk the path which God has set before us, which He has illumined by His Word, and in so doing, and not straying, we will not fall prey to the lion that is waiting to see on whom he may pounce. But by staying to the path, illumined by the light of God's Word, we will be preserved to the end.

10

Resident Aliens

(John 17:12–16)

"While I was with them, I kept them in your name, which you have given me. I have guarded them, and not one of them has been lost except the son of destruction, that the Scripture might be fulfilled. But now I am coming to you, and these things I speak in the world, that they may have my joy fulfilled in themselves. I have given them your Word, and the world has hated them because they are not of the world, just as I am not of the world. I do not ask that you take them out of the world, but that you keep them from the evil one. They are not of the world, just as I am not of the world." (John 17:12–16)

WHEN YOU THINK OF the church, what is it that you think of? What is your default definition of the church? Do you think of worship? Do you think of fellowship? Do you think of Bible study? Perhaps you think of missions. Maybe you think of friends. Maybe you think of your own history in the church or an old Sunday School teacher. Maybe you think of outreach or events. Maybe you think of different organizations within the church. What is it that you think of when you think of church? A building. A people.

What if I asked you to describe the character of the church? Now be careful here because Christians populate the church and become the public expression of the character of a church, and it is by that expression that we can often distinguish a true church from a false church, so if you are going to describe the character of a church, you have to describe the character of the church by the population of the people who are in the church, and in describing the character of the people who are in the church, it is there that we can discern whether the church we are describing is a true church or not.

Beginning in verse 13, Jesus begins to list several vital characteristics of the church. The first one, presented in verse 13, is joy. In verse 17, truth. In verse 18, mission. In verses 21–23, unity, and then in verse 26, love. These are the characteristics of a true church—joy, holiness, truth, mission, unity, and love. These are the manifestations of a true church as it projects its image, which is not its own image, but it is testimony of the gospel of Jesus Christ into the world from which it is called out. The church too often reflects the world instead of Christ.

The church too often acts as a mirror of the world, presenting a slightly sanctified view of the world by eliminating some of the coarse language. We don't perform some of the activities which might be considered distasteful, but we recreate among ourselves, just as the world does. We sometimes dress or carry on or organize in our church government the same as the world.

We look sometimes even to our leaders, our elders and our deacons, as if they were somehow elected politicians and we are their constituency, and so they are supposed to represent us on some board here or there, when, in fact, they represent God to the people, and so we form lobbying groups within the church, just as they do in secular government and in the world. So often we in the church reflect more of the world than we do Christ.

There is an interesting dynamic in verse 14. We, the church, are to possess all six of these character traits in a world that hates us, in a world to which we do not belong, a world in which we are residents, and yet we are aliens. We are pilgrims, sojourners, a people on a journey, a people that are not settled with this place as the source of our joy or our character, a people who will always be foreigners, even as we pursue the same delights that the worldly people pursue.

In Philippians, Paul instructs the church to "have this mind among yourselves, which was in Christ Jesus," and reminds them that their citizenship is not here, but it is in heaven. Paul calls the Philippians to a spiritual journey.

In their book *Resident Aliens*, Hauerwas and Willimon describe our life as a journey, which is to live and to die like Christ, to model our lives so closely upon Christ that we can bear within ourselves the very mind of

Christ. The fulfillment of that journey will be our joy, but here our journey is not yet complete. Our joy is challenged by the world. If having the mind of Christ is what brings us joy, that joy is being dampened, it seems, by the world as the world finds us to be an intolerable part of society.

Too many of us are backing into heaven with our eyes on all that we think we must forfeit for Christ and Crown rather than looking forward and counting whatever we lose in this world as all joy for the reward that is set before us. That is, we have more of an eye to the things which we believe we sacrifice for Christ than we do for that which we gain for Christ. We are so concerned about all the things we can't do because "good Christians do not do them," that we miss out on the joy of shedding those as encumbrances on our journey to be like Christ.

Maybe when you were growing up, your parents, or maybe you yourself had one of those station wagons with the back seat that was facing out the back window and you could see all the things after you missed them instead of before you reached them. Thank goodness the driver knew where he or she was going and had an eye to that, because all we could see were all the places we wished they had stopped along the way.

How many of us live our Christian lives in just the same way? We are so consumed with what we think we have missed, all the fun we could have had, that we don't see where we're going and so we do not grasp the joy of our destination.

Let us remember this: We are not at home in this world. Our citizenship is in heaven. We, who are the church, are a colony of heaven. Our example is that of the Jews who are in the dispersion. When they were taken away from their home in Israel, the Promised Land, the Holy Land, the City of God, the City set up on a hill, the Zion of God; when they were taken into Assyria, Babylonia, when they were dispersed into places that were foreign to them, they lived as strangers in a strange land.

As strangers, they gathered together to tell the stories of God, to sing songs about God. Many of our Psalms were sung by the people who were dispersed, away from their own land, living in foreign lands, and they passed those songs along to their children in the hope of their eventual arrival in the land of promise.

Are we so unlike them, the Jews of the dispersion? We, too, are a people removed from our true home, which is heaven, and we are a people who are dispersed in a foreign and hostile place, and we gather together to tell the story, to be reminded of the gospel, to sing the songs of our faith, to have hope that is renewed until we finally do arrive in the place of promise, a place of rest. Until then, Willimon calls us "a colony, a beach-head, an outpost, an island of one culture in the middle of another."

Using those terms for the church today is just as appropriate I believe. Those who are aliens in a foreign culture are typically isolated and alone, but God has given us brethren, and He has given us His Church. There are many who are flung out in far reaching places around this world that do belong to Christ and they are alone, and they are left alone to strive for godliness, to strive to have the mind of Christ because there are none around them who believe and follow Christ.

We are blessed. We are a blessed people. We come together week in and week out, and we are reminded again that we do not walk the path alone. There are brothers and sisters in Christ who are, or ought to be, striving with us to be like Christ. We are a people who are most blessed with people, friends of kindred spirit in a hostile world. We are people gathered together in the name of our Savior, Jesus Christ.

Teacher Bonhoeffer said this, "It is true, of course, that what is an unspeakable gift of God for the lonely individual is easily disregarded and trodden under foot by those who have the gift every day. It is easily forgotten that the fellowship of Christian brethren is a gift of grace, a gift of the kingdom of God, that any day may be taken from us, that the time which separates us from utter loneliness may be brief indeed. Therefore, let him who until now has had the privilege of living a common Christian life with other Christians praise God's grace from the bottom of his heart. Let him thank God on his knees and declare: It is grace, nothing but grace that we are allowed to live in community with Christian brethren" (18). The church is a gift to God's people, a place of refuge for those who are called out of the world.

The great commentator and preacher, Martyn Lloyd-Jones, said that if all Christians simply began to function as the New Testament would have us do, there would be no problem of evangelism confronting the church. Is it rather a matter of will or understanding that we don't?

If we all possessed those characteristics, which Christ lays out for us in John chapter 17, and that is what the church was known for, we would not have to knock on a single door. We would not have to hand out a single flyer. We would not have to mail a single letter, place an ad in a single newspaper, because there would be an acknowledgement that this is a light set upon a hill that cannot be extinguished and that Christ resides here and those who belong to Christ would be drawn to where they can receive the purity of God's Word from a people who have actually been changed by God's Word.

That would be our testimony, and that would be the attraction to Christ. Why do we not? It is either will or understanding. Either we do not understand what it is that Jesus is teaching or it is our will where we have placed our affection on something other than Christ.

Given the preciousness of Christ's church, Jesus prays for those who are gathered to her. He prays for us. He prays for His disciples that they will possess a character that builds and preserves rather than distracts and destroys, that they will obey rather than neglect and be protected rather than perish.

The first of the qualities Jesus describes is joy. He says to them in verse 13, "But now I am coming to you," speaking here of the Father. He is talking, remember, in prayer to God the Father. He says, "Now God, my heavenly Father, I am coming to you and these things I speak in the world that they may have my joy fulfilled in themselves."

Jesus prays not only for our safety and perseverance in a hostile world, but also prays that we would be a joyful people. As the great pastor, Marcus Rainsford, put it, "He would have us go on our way through the pilgrimage of life, not only secure, but singing, fully realizing that He is all, has done all, and that He has said all that is necessary for our comfort, as well as our safety, for our joy, as well as our salvation" (273).

The angel that appeared to the shepherds in the field announced, "I bring you good news of great joy, which will be for all people" (Luke 2:10). At the very announcement of the gospel was this idea of joy, this joy that was announced as having arrived. The angel did not say to them, "I bring you good news so you might be of great joy." The angel said, "I bring you good news of great joy that will be [as a gift to] all people."

When Jesus taught the disciples, He ended by saying, "I have told you this so that my joy may be in you" (John 15:11). That His joy, the joy of Christ would be in them and that this joy may be complete. How often do we prevent people from coming to Christ simply by going about with long worried faces as if we have nothing in which to rejoice.

Throughout Scripture, joy is not just a goal of the Christian, but a characteristic of God's people. We cannot say, "I just do not feel joyful right now," because joy is something that is given to us. It is not something we conjure up within ourselves. It is a part of the new man, not a mood that we have.

Along our pilgrimage, we pass through dark valleys, dangerous plains, but Jesus not only holds out to us a future joy, but also gives us our present joy that is a healing balm for the wounds which the world would inflict upon us. So we note in Scripture, and in Jesus' prayer, joy is simply not an option for the Christian. It is a part of the character of Christ.

Now that does not mean that there isn't sobriety in the Christian Life. I am not talking about a silliness or laughing your way through the Christian Life. Christian joy is not like the world's joy, which is based usually on some sensual pleasure, either visually or of the flesh or indulgence in one thing or another. I am not talking about a momentary pleasure or happiness which you only enjoy until some activity is over. That is worldly joy, consumer joy and is not the type of joy Christ is talking about. His joy that is based upon a vision of the future that brings a deep, satisfying joy, is Christ's joy, the same joy He had even as the Cross was set before Him.

So let us simply ask, Is the church joyful? Is our church joyful? Are Christians joyful? Are you joyful? In Nehemiah 8:10, we learn "the joy of the Lord is the strength of His people." Jesus said, "My joy will be in you."

Joy is given to us by God. It is not manufactured and it is not whipped up by us, and it cannot be taken away by another. You cannot legitimately say when it comes to the Christian characteristic of joy, which is part of the new man, the new creation, you cannot say, "I have no joy because of this man or that woman." You cannot say, "I had joy, but when this person came into my life, they took it away." It is not legitimate to blame our lack of Christ-like character on someone else's existence or behavior. That is an out. That is an excuse. That is sin.

Joy which Christ gives us, another will not take away. That does not mean that we are not challenged in life. It does not mean that we are not disappointed at the way things turn out, but those cannot steal away the joy which Christ gives unless it also takes away the hope of the Cross, or our hope for eternal salvation and arrival into heaven. If those are gone, then, yes, indeed, we have allowed the world to remove that from us, and so our long faces and our downcast eyes come from some other source because it cannot be that the joy of Christ can be removed by the hand or the action or of another individual. We wonder, is the reason the church seems so weak today because we lack Christian joy. Do you have joy when God's Word is read?

The reading of God's Word should be a joyful sound in the ears of a person. When people in the church sit in the pew with long faces, have they taken their eyes off the gospel? Or are they simply trying, as the Pharisees, to manipulate others by giving out some air of brave and serious concern?

Are they trying to present themselves just as those who would starve themselves and not shave before entering into the temple to pray so that they could show how seriously they took their religion? Jesus said, "Cut it out. Stop that. Pray in your closet. Do not pray to be seen before men. Shave before you come out. Eat. Do not present yourself as if you are dying when you should be full of joy in your service to Christ." Have we taken our eyes off the gospel, or perhaps we must ask the question, was there never really a grasping of the gospel to begin with?

Martyn Lloyd-Jones said, "Some Christians are in this condition because they never really understood the great central doctrine of justification by faith alone" (37).

You will recall the story of the blind man in Mark 8:22–26. Jesus lead him out of town. He spit on his eyes and he put his hands on them and then he asked the man if he could anything and the man said, "I see men walking, and they are as trees before me" (Mark 8:24). The man is no longer blind, and yet he really does not see either. Jesus again spits on his eyes and he asks him the same question, and the man answers, "Yes, I do see." How many are like the man who saw men as trees, walking. They've heard of the things of Christ, and yet they do not quite fully comprehend them.

On another occasion the disciples were in a boat with Jesus. Jesus was talking to them about the leaven of the Pharisees, and that reminded them that they only had one loaf of bread in the boat, and so they began to despair that there was not going to be enough food to eat. Jesus, having just fed the 5,000, looked at them because they were worried. He asked them, "What is it that you do not understand?" Jesus said to them, "I am here. I am here. I just fed 5,000 people. How can you still not understand?"

Are there those who have taken a step of faith, who have walked, and yet have still remained uncertain about the realities of the Scripture? Jesus says in John 17, "These things I said." What things? He has already told us that He revealed God's name to us, the character of God, that we would know God fully. Without a knowledge of God, without understanding the character of God, would not we be an insecure people?

There are many, as Dr. Jones says, who simply have never really understood the cardinal doctrine of justification by faith alone.

> "He saved us, not because of works done by us in righteousness, but according to His own mercy, by the washing of regeneration and renewal of the Holy Spirit" (Titus 3:5, 7). For our sake, He made Him to be sin who knew no sin, that in Him we might become the righteousness of God." (2 Corinthians 5:21)

"And to the one who does not work, but believes in Him who justifies the ungodly, His faith is counted as righteousness, just as David also speaks of the blessing of the one to whom God counts righteousness apart from works: 'Blessed are those whose lawless deeds are forgiven, and whose sins are covered; blessed is the man against whom the Lord will not count his sin.'" (Romans 4:5–8)

And finally Romans 5:1: "Therefore, since we have been justified by faith, we have peace with God through our Lord Jesus Christ."

What does this mean? How does this clarify the issue of joy? We are saved despite ourselves. Despite the depth of our sin, despite our imperfections, despite other people's opinion of us, despite our daily transgression of the law of God, we are saved if we are held by faith in Christ's hands. We are clothed with his righteousness.

As we read in Zechariah, the high priest stood in filthy rags and the Lord said to take off those and put on a clean robe. We are clothed with the righteousness of Christ. No person, no tragedy can take away a joy which finds its supply in Christ and our justification by faith alone, but we can forfeit our joy by keeping and pursuing wrong living and wrong priorities in our ignorance of the things of God.

Boice relates a story of a man in a church in Scotland who had become bored with the sermon, and he started doodling on his bulletin. He doodled these words:

> To dwell with the saints I love,
> Ay! That would be glory.
> To dwell below with saints I know;
> Now, that's a different story!

We have plenty of people who know something about Jesus. We need more of those who know something about Jesus to possess the joy that comes from Jesus and then to be the Church. What is the remedy for our conflicted witness as we do not have, or lack, these characters that we are to possess as testimony of Christ? We say we know, but we look and act as if we are full of dread and helplessness all the time. Why do we struggle with joy when our souls have been redeemed by a Savior?

Again, Martyn-Jones suggests several issues that relate to these words, "These things I speak in the world." Jesus says that His teaching is the foundation of our joy. We do not have joy because we simply find some way to manipulate our own emotions and get it pumped up for a Sunday. Our joy comes from without because of the teaching of truth which we have received with understanding concerning the gospel of Jesus Christ, but we know so little of that teaching that sometimes we miss the joy.

Jones describes it as people who know enough about Christianity to spoil their enjoyment of the world, and yet they do not know enough to feel happy about themselves, so they are neither hot nor cold. The gospel becomes not a source of joy, but a source of confinement for these. For they only see the gospel robbing them of all that they enjoy, which is of a dying world, and they do not receive the promises, which the gospel gives, that bring the great joy.

There was a time when they were perfectly satisfied with themselves in the world, but as they grasp a little Christian doctrine, they realize that something is wrong and all they learn is what they can't do, and the joy of the gift of salvation eludes them. They wrongly believe that the source of their discontent is the teaching itself, the teaching of Christian doctrine, that it is that doctrine that has taken away their joy, when, in fact, doctrine has acted like an x-ray to show them an undiscovered tumor of cultural Christian apathy.

So we learn that the first remedy to long faces, to discouragement, and Christian cynicism is Christ's teaching, that is, to put it in our modern terminology, Christian doctrine. David said, "The precepts of the Lord are right, giving joy to the heart" (Psalm 19:8). "I will rejoice in following your statutes as one rejoices in great riches" (Psalm 119:14). But many have an aversion to Christian doctrine. Sometimes people contrast a spiritual reading of the scriptures with doctrinal teaching. As Dr. Jones asks, "What is the purpose of the Bible except to present truth, and what is presenting truth except to teach doctrine, and what is doctrine then except the teaching of Christ."

Why is there an aversion to this doctrine? I love Jones' answer to that: It is the doctrine that hurts. It is the doctrine that focuses things. Doctrine speaks to us. It insists upon a decision. This is truth and it examines us. It tries us and forces us to examine ourselves. We are much more comfortable with ambiguity and sentiment and feeling and intentions. Doctrine dispels all of those things and says, "Thus saith the Lord," and we are forced to deal with that.

It clarifies our position in Christ and leads us to not only spiritual rest, but psychological peace, because when we are unsettled about our life in Christ, we remain in some quagmire of doubt, unable to live peaceably in the world or in the church. We come to know God as He is presented in all the Bible, however, and our doubts about His love, His providential care, His sovereign Hand, and our own life, and His provision in Christ, all those doubts are removed and we are able to live life, knowing that all things are working together for good, for those who are called according to His purpose.

If the first reason for our lack of joy is an aversion to teaching, the second one is a lack of fellowship. There are two kinds of fellowship, one that is vertical and one that is horizontal. Our fellowship with the Lord and our fellowship with one another. Jesus is not suggesting an attitude of joy except that we would enter into His joy. "That they may have my joy fulfilled in them." That is certainly a future joy, of course, but it is also a present joy experienced in the unity and fellowship that we have with Christ.

As we live moment by moment, praying without ceasing as children of the faith, we have a joy that is an unbroken communion with Christ. We also have a joy as we fellowship with other Christians. "That which we have seen and heard we proclaim also to you, so that you too may have fellowship with us; and indeed our fellowship is with the Father and with His Son Jesus Christ. And we are writing these things so that our joy may be complete" (1 John 1).

First John 1 also indicates to us that fellowship with the Father and other Christians goes together. If you have fellowship with God through Christ, you have fellowship with one another, and if you cut yourself off from either one, your joy will be lost. If you lack fellowship with one, you will lack fellowship with the other, and losing that fellowship with the other, your joy is lost.

So here is the conclusion of it all: Our joy is found in our faith in Christ, in His love for us. He is the link between ourselves and the Father. We have ample reason for joy and God has supplied ample means to attain it by giving us the words of Christ.

"Oh, may we henceforth in His strength resolve to deal more with God's Word, to wrap our souls in God's promises, to lie down in the green pastures and by the still waters, and then joy, and peace, and rest, which the world cannot give, and which the world cannot take away, will flow deeply into our souls as we trust Him" (Rainsford 254).

11

Resident Aliens: Keepers of a Sacred Trust

(John 17:12–16)

"While I was with them, I kept them in your name, which you have given me. I have guarded them, and not one of them has been lost except the son of destruction, that the Scripture might be fulfilled.

"But now I am coming to you, and these things I speak in the world, that they may have my joy fulfilled in themselves. I have given them your word, and the world has hated them because they are not of the world, just as I am not of the world. I do not ask that you take them out of the world, but that you keep them from the evil one. They are not of the world, just as I am not of the world. Sanctify them in the truth; your word is truth."

I ENJOY LOOKING AT bumper stickers. It is a little distracting, probably worse than texting and driving at times. But I still enjoy looking and reading because I find short philosophies of people's worldviews and their lives. You find some interesting things as people narrow down their philosophy to a short phrase.

Sometimes, of course, you have those who have too much to say, and they cover the back of their car from top to bottom. Those are folks who do not know how to carry on a shorter, idle conversation. I believe they simply have too many opinions in too many areas that they want to advertise. But nevertheless, those who have one or two that you actually have time to read from a moving vehicle often have bumper stickers that do present their views or their beliefs.

I've seen one related to the health care debate that our nation is involved in that simply says, "Abortion is not health care." Regardless of your views, I think that is a very profound and a very clear and articulate statement of this individual's view. There wouldn't be any doubt in your mind as to where this person stands on probably two issues—one being whether or not we should have a nationalized health care and the other being his or her views on abortion.

Another popular one that I enjoy says, "My kid beat up your honor roll kid." I find that probably says a whole lot more than the people who bought the bumper sticker intended to say about themselves and their view of their kid's academic performance and perhaps their kid themselves and maybe even their parenting skills.

Another one that begins to take us in the direction that we will actually be moving in this chapter: "Guns don't kill people; people kill people." I find that one to be a startling admission of the depravity of man. I know the person who put it on the car probably is simply talking about the second amendment right, which I obviously would support. Protecting their right to bear arms is an admirable thing to do.

But the sticker itself, "Guns don't kill people; people kill people" is a startling admission of the depravity and the evil of man. We know if it weren't guns, it would be clubs (and was before there were guns) or sticks or bows and arrows or spears or whatever. Man will find a way to kill other men. But we live in a day where people don't want to believe in the evil and the depravity of man.

So we have people like our past (sometime now past) Surgeon General who said, "What we need is safer bullets in our gun. After all, it is guns that are killing people. So we need to limit the power of a gun to kill." We find phrases like alcohol kills, but does alcohol on a shelf actually kill, or is it people who kill themselves with alcohol? On the news, you will hear of an SUV that kills people. Anytime there is a car accident that involves an SUV, it's not the individual who wrecked the car. The SUV killed the person who was in the car or the person who was a victim of the SUV that ran over them. So we need smaller cars that are less lethal than SUVs.

We work very hard to phrase things in such a way as to get around the absolute depravity of man. We change our philosophy of living in denial of what our eyes and ears and the newspapers testify. Even our bumper stickers tell us the simple truth that man is born for trouble. "As the sparks fly upward from a fire, so is every intent of man's heart set on evil continually." Continually! How bad is man without Christ? There is no way to plumb the depths of man's depravity, the evil that man would go to.

We're told in the Scriptures that when God finally does remove the restraint there will be no limit to man's evil behavior. There is much debate about what the restraint is, but whatever it is, when that is removed, then that which restrains men's evil behavior will be gone, and there will be no limit to man's imagination in being evil. No limit to how low men will reach.

In September of 2001, I sat in my office in a rural church in New Jersey. There wasn't anything unique on my schedule. Just some phone calls to make, a shut-in visitation or two, a counseling appointment that afternoon and, of course, the work on the bulletin. As I sat there going through papers, the secretary called out. She said, "Are you listening to the radio?" I didn't listen to the radio usually in my office. I said, "No!" She said, "Well, there has been an accident in Manhattan. A plane has hit the World Trade Center." I said, "Oh that's terrible!"

She began to tell me about when planes have hit buildings in the past, and we had an interesting conversation. We said, "Well, I hope no one is injured by that. Maybe it just hit the side. I know the people in the plane are, but I hope that all will be well." We just simply got back to work. Then she came in, and she said, "I think you need to turn on the radio because a second plane has hit the other World Trade Center." When she said that, you could tell by the blank expression on her face that she really didn't even know what to say after that. There wasn't really an explanation that could be given. There was no follow-up comment.

I said, "Well, let me check that out." I turned on the radio, and of course there was a great deal of conversation about it. We immediately started thinking about the people whom we knew in our church who were in that area. We had a man who worked directly in that area. We began to wonder about him, and we prayed about him. Then we started listening, wondering what was going on and hoping against hope that this wasn't really what it seemed to be.

Then the Pentagon was hit, and any doubt we had was removed. We realized there were people who were deliberately crashing airplanes into the facilities—the World Trade Center and the Pentagon—in the United States. Planes didn't murder people that day; people murdered people. Politics didn't murder people that day. People murdered people. Why?

Why? In the days that followed, the names and the faces of those who were killed, those who were murdered, played on our television screens.

The dead came from so many different backgrounds, so many different faith groups, so many different countries. Why did those men kill people they didn't know? Why did those men kill those folks who had done them no harm, and those who, in some cases, even shared the same faith they did? The answer we have to give is unsatisfactory to our ears. They had no real issue with any individual who was there as far as we know even to this day.

Those people were killed simply because of their identity as Americans, their identity as a people who were participating in a democracy, as a people who were advocates and participants in freedom and freedom's cause, as people who had opportunity set before them and opportunities that were provided for them. Yes, for all of these reasons, but I would submit to you there is an even greater, overarching reason that has been historically true that even pre-dates America and her Constitution and her freedoms. That is Christ. Christ. Christ has been the flashpoint for violence. Christ has been the flashpoint for murder.

First John 3:12, "We should not be like Cain, who was of the evil one and murdered his brother. And why did he murder him?" the Scripture asks rhetorically (I John 3:12). "Because his own deeds were evil and his brother's righteous. Do not be surprised, brothers, that the world hates you." Do you ponder this very much? Do you mull over this very much? Do you realize you are being marked out by the world for its hatred? Whom does the Church bother? Whom does the Church encroach upon really? Isn't the Church always having its place eroded in culture? Aren't the laws normally written antagonistic these days to the Church?

Why is the Church such an object of people's disdain, and why are they so uncomfortable that the Church even exists or the Church preaches the gospel? If it doesn't matter, then why be so preoccupied with it? Because it's truth, and it's light. The darkness cannot stand the light and seeks to extinguish it. All the hatred and violence of the world toward any that are known by the name of Christ, any plotting that is against them, any distress that is caused to them, is because the god of this world hates Christ.

So a strike at those who are in union with Christ, the Body of Christ, the Church, is a strike against Christ Himself. This is exactly what we should expect. "Do not be surprised, brothers, (1 John reminds us) that the world hates you." Their deeds are evil, and we are declared righteous in Christ. We are a changed people. We are light in the world, and the darkness intuitively and naturally hates the light.

Paul in Acts, Chapter 20, calls the elders of Ephesus to come together. He wants to speak with them. He mentions his trials in surviving the plots the Jews had made against him all along. He tells them the Spirit has shown him in every city that chains and afflictions await him in Jerusalem, and he will never see them again. Yet Paul is hastening to Jerusalem. He warns them there will be fierce wolves who will come into their churches to attack their flocks. He calls the elders to arms. He calls the elders to be vigilant against these attacks.

Here is the message. This life is full of conflict. This life is full of trials, tribulations, temptations, and yes, ultimately termination. We're in the midst of a battle such that Paul exhorts us to wear the gospel as our full armor of God. That is our only spiritual defense as we put the gospel on against the world which would try to destroy us. Tragedies will be all along the road we travel. Adversaries will greet us with every sunrise and every sunset. First Peter 5:8 teaches us to, "Be sober-minded; be watchful. Your adversary the devil prowls around like a roaring lion, seeking someone to devour."

In the face of all of this, we might echo David in Psalm 22 who says, "My God, my God, why have you forsaken me? Why are you so far from saving me, from the words of my groaning?" Listen again to Jesus in the passage, however, as He prays for us. He said, "I do not ask that you take them out of the world, but that you keep them from the evil one." How should we take His request in light of all the troubles we have in this life?

In light of all the tragedies, all the trials, all the tribulations, even the fact that death still is before us, and we must face it either prematurely or after living many years, do we say God does not hear His prayer? Do we say God did not answer His prayer as He prayed we would be preserved from the evil one? Was it simply a nice platitude which He meant as an encouragement that one day evil would be removed? Or is there a very literal sense in which Jesus asks the Father that we are even now preserved from the evil one?

"Keep them from evil" is the theme of Jesus' prayer. In verse 11, He says, "Holy Father, keep them in your name." He said, "While I was with them, I kept them in your name. Father, I'm coming to you now to my glory to be glorified in heaven and sit at your right hand. Now you,

Father, you keep them in your own name." Verse 15, Jesus says, ". . . keep them from the evil one." There is a danger because of the world's hatred, and it's focused on them, the apostles, because of their relationship with Christ and His mission.

What does it mean by *world*? If we're going to understand this, we first need to listen to Jesus' words when He says, "I am not asking you to take them out of the world." We've already established that the world is the enemy of Christ. What do we mean by *world*? Simply that which is contrary to Christ's kingdom. That which is fallen. That which is natural. That which is dying. That which is lost.

As Thomas Manton describes it, "Sometimes they are called the kingdom of darkness because the devil is their head and chief. Sometimes the world because that is their aim. They are guided by the malicious spirit of Satan enacted by their own ends and interests" (364). We can contrast Jesus' description of those religious leaders, which He gives in John 8:44 when He said, "You are of your father the devil, and your will is to do your father's desires," with Paul's description of Christ's own people in 1 Corinthians 2:12 when he said, "Now we have received not the spirit of the world, but the Spirit who is from God, that we might understand the things freely given us by God."

As such because we are not of the world and we are of God, we live differently. It's that living differently that antagonizes the world. It's that living to a higher calling that so confounds and exacerbates the world's anger. They hate it. It's not enough for us to do it privately. It's not enough for us to do it because we are bound by our own conscience. We must cease, or they will not be happy. They will not be satisfied until our own lives no longer bear testimony to the judgment of God against them.

"With respect to this they are surprised when you do not join them in the same flood of debauchery, and they malign you" (First Peter 4:4). The world begins by offering you an invitation. It might sound something like this depending on your age and your station of life. "What are you doing this weekend? Oh no, no. We're going to go out! We're having fun! We're going to have a party. We're going out to meet some people. We're going to go travel here. We're going to travel there. What? You've never done that? You're so oppressed! You're so put upon. I can't believe you're from the sticks! You have to get out a little bit. You have to live a little bit!"

They invite you to participate in their debauchery. For those who say "no," do you think they don't care? Do you think they just go, "Well, suit yourself. To each his own. It doesn't matter." They begin first with ridicule. Then they begin by trying to entice you by making you feel that you're really, really missing out. You don't know what you're missing out. Then they judge your views. If all that fails, they condemn you. They spite you, and they hate you.

You don't think it's true? If you have a friend or two who has drawn you into that, why don't you turn the corner and see what their reaction is. Why don't you say to them, "You know, I don't think that's really the right way to live." See what they do. They will come at you with their teeth bared. They will not look like the people you think you know.

This is why we are called to live contrary to the world. "If the world hates you, know that it has hated me before it hated you. If you were of the world, the world would love you as its own; but because you are not of the world, but I chose you out of the world, therefore the world hates you" (John 15:18–19). We who are in Christ live contrary to the world. The world calls it *backwards*; we call it *righteous* and *holy*. We call it *obedient*; they call it *naïve*. We have contrary hopes because we live for things that are eternal versus just a living for that which is temporal.

We have a contrary standard because our rule is the righteousness of Christ, whereas they see themselves as bound only by civil law and only when they get caught. We have a contrary disposition because we are appointed as lights in the world. We don't abide by the spirit of the world. We abide by the Spirit of Christ. We have a contrary purpose. We have a purpose that is to serve Christ. The difference and the estrangement to the world is provocative to the world. No, they're not indifferent. They will not tolerate our refusal to living according to the world.

So Jesus pleads with His Father for His own people. Yes, the Father has heard, and yes the Father has answered Jesus. Jesus says to them, "I do not pray that you would remove them from the world, but that you would keep them from the evil one." Some translations don't say *the evil one*. They just simply say *evil*. Without going into the particular language, know this. The word *evil* and *evil one* as they are translated can be taken in the neuter, which simply means *to protect them* or *to save them from evil*. That would be something like you might read when it says, "to save them from the world." The same language construction is used there.

But we in translating it "the evil one," we're taking our cues from the same language that is used by John in 1 John, chapter 2.

> "I am writing to you, fathers, because you know him who is from the beginning. I am writing to you, young men, because you have overcome the evil one. I write to you, children, because you know the Father. I write to you, fathers, because you know him who is from the beginning. I write to you, young men, because you are strong, and the Word of God abides in you, and you have overcome the evil one." (John 2:13–14)

The same phrase is in First John 3:12, in First John 5:18 and 19. Thus we can accept the usage of the evil one, which is a personification of evil, Satan, the devil. But is that really contrary to saying evil, too, because the world is under the reign of the devil? If the devil is the evil one, then his reign is evil, and the world itself can be classified as evil. So I would be satisfied actually with either translation because in both cases, by God we are being extracted from that which is evil, preserved from either the particular power and hand of the evil one or from the effects of his rule, which is the evil in the world.

In either case, God is answering the prayer of Jesus. In these verses, we note Jesus also says we are to remain in the world although we are not to be of the world. Commentator Marcus Rainsford describes our presence here. "To learn [our] own great need, [our] indescribable weakness and emptiness; to learn the strength of the foes with which we have to do battle and to learn our Father's loving, tender, and keeping care" (282). We're left here so we can know our need of Christ. That's one reason.

We're left here because, in ourselves, we are not sufficient for the day. We are not righteous, and we are not strong enough to take on the strong man and cast him out of his own house. Only Christ can do that. We cannot raise ourselves from the grave, nor can we cause ourselves to persevere to the end of ages. The promise of Psalm 121 (which is a hymn of thanksgiving), verse 7, is this: "The Lord will keep you from all evil; He will keep your life." Second Thessalonians 3:3 echoes the Psalm: "The Lord is faithful. He will establish you and guard you against the evil one."

So we wonder then, if in fact Jesus' prayer is answered and all of this is still going on around us, then how is it answered? Again Rainsford points out the experience of the Church is that while we are kept from the evil one, we are not kept from spiritual conflict. As we have already mentioned, Paul teaches that we are to face this spiritual conflict from behind the armor of God

> "Put on the whole armor of God, that you may be able to stand against the schemes of the devil. For we do not wrestle against flesh and blood, but against the rulers, against the authorities, against the cosmic powers over this present darkness, against the spiritual forces of evil in the heavenly places."

The Scriptures on the one hand tell us Christ is praying that we'll be preserved from the evil one. But then on the other hand, it teaches that we will be engaged in battle with the spiritual forces of this present darkness. We will not do so under our own strength, but we will do so in the strength of Christ as we are clothed with His righteousness and armed with the gospel, our spiritual armor.

We are not preserved from spiritual conflict, nor are we exempted from temptations or trials. The result from both the malice of the devil and the weakness within ourselves is to seek to draw us into various temptations and lusts of the flesh. But the Lord prayed, "Keep them from evil." Neither are we exempted from bodily suffering or death. Not even sadness or the loss of the means for living. Yet Jesus prayed, "Keep them from evil." We're not preserved against our own sinning, and not even against the burden of our own sin. In Isaiah 53:6 we read confirming this, "All we like sheep have gone astray; we have turned *everyone* to his own way." Still Jesus prays, "Keep them from evil."

"In the face of all this," Rainsford concludes, "not one of these nor all of them together constitute evil to the people of God." Not the spiritual warfare in which we are engaged, not the temptations or the trials or the tribulations or even facing physical death. None of these qualify as the evil which Christ is here speaking of in His prayer to the Father. "Or if evil in themselves our Lord Jesus Christ's prayer secures that good shall be brought out of the evil, and that all these things shall work together for good, to them that love the Lord" (285).

In the final analysis, there is nothing that is truly evil, but that which can separate us from the love of God. That's what Jesus addresses. It's not to say we won't encounter evil. But there is nothing that can inflict itself upon us as evil except those things which might sever us from the love of God. We know nothing can sever us from the love of God. Why? Because we are kept in the name of God as Jesus has prayed.

So if a murdering terrorist or if suffering or if temptations and death are not kept from us, what is Jesus praying for and how was it answered? In Psalm 121:5, "The Lord is your keeper." Verse 7 of Psalm 121, "The Lord will keep you from all evil; He will keep your life." That which happens to us is only evil to us if it can injure our soul. I'm not talking about misfortune. I'm not talking about the effects of a fallen world. I'm not talking about the natural consequences of sin, which is death ultimately. I'm not talking about the brokenness of man. I'm talking about evil, which is that which Satan would inflict upon Christ as they judged Christ and put Him on the Cross.

But we cannot be severed from the love of Christ. What will separate us from the love of God? Neither height nor depth nor principalities nor forces above nor forces below. Nothing can separate us from the love of Christ. Nothing! As Christ prayed, "Keep them from the evil one." We are the possession of Christ. Keeping us from the evil one doesn't mean keep us from all suffering because Christ Himself said, "You will endure much suffering." Keep us from the evil one means keep us out of the possession of Satan. That which happens to us is evil only as it can injure the soul.

The very God who kept Daniel in the lions' den with the lions mouths shut up is the same God who preserves us in the world of lions in which we now live. Temptations come and show us who we are. They reveal our character. Will we stand? Will we fall? Failures show us our finiteness and our weakness. Sickness shows us our frailty. But none of these things can take us away from Christ. None of these things can remove us from the hand of our Savior.

These comforting words of Psalm 91 beginning at verse 9, "Because you have made the Lord your dwelling place *the Most High, who is my refuge,* no evil shall be allowed to befall you, no plague come near your tent. For He will command His angels concerning you to guard you in all your ways. On their hands they will bear you up, lest you strike your foot against a stone. Because he holds fast to me in love, I will deliver him; I will protect him, because he knows my name."

Jesus prayed, "Keep them in your name." Do you know God's name? Are you kept in the name of God? Are you preserved from the evil one? Are you kept from the evil one? In preserving us from any evil that might destroy our soul, God is sanctifying our soul. He sanctifies our soul in truth. As we reflect upon these passages, I hope we realize a couple of truths.

1. *We live in a hostile environment.* This is not our world. Yes, the world belongs to God, but its destiny is to be destroyed. There will be a new heaven and a new earth.

2. *Those encounters with tragedy which befall us, even the ones who ultimately end up in our own death, none of those can tear us away from the hand of God.* Though we may stray, though we may, as it were, backslide, though we may live a season of our lives in rebellion against God, if we belong to Him in Christ, nothing—not even our own strength—can tear us away from Christ.

We can choose to live miserably in rebellion against the truth which we know, but nothing can separate us from the love of God if He has put His love upon us. Jesus has prayed, "Keep them in your name, and keep them from the evil one." Our assurance is Christ continually prays for us at all times, every day, every moment of the day. He is praying, "Keep them from the evil one. Keep them. Keep them. Keep them."

12

Resident Aliens: Sanctified and Holy

(John 17:12–16)

"While I was with them, I kept them in your name, which you have given me. I have guarded them, and not one of them has been lost except the son of destruction, that the Scripture might be fulfilled. But now I am coming to you, and these things I speak in the world, that they may have My joy fulfilled in themselves. I have given them your Word, and the world has hated them because they are not of the world, just as I am not of the world. I do not ask that you take them out of the world, but that you keep them from the evil one. They are not of the world, just as I am not of the world. Sanctify them in the truth; your Word is truth."

PERHAPS YOU HAVE IN your own home a plaque hanging over the door or above the fireplace or somewhere that says, "As for me and my house, we will serve the Lord." Perhaps you have that hanging somewhere prominently, so any one who comes in may see that plaque hanging there, as you have declared, "This is a house where God's Word is the rule, where God's Word sets before the people who live there the path they are to walk."

It might surprise us, if we think about that for just a moment, to realize that we are taking an actual oath. It's not just beautiful Christian poetry. It's an actual oath we are giving our word to, especially as we proclaim it to other people. However, what people usually mean is, "As for me and my house, we will *usually* serve the Lord, rather than we *will* serve the Lord."

We would ask them, "How is it that you are serving the Lord with your whole house, with your whole lives? And they might say, "Well I'm serving the Lord by doing this," or "I'm serving the Lord by doing that. I'm serving the church in this way, and I'm giving my life to ministry in this or that way." But really, as we look at it, we can equate that to people dropping change in a red kettle and feeling they have made a tremendous difference in giving themselves to the ministry of charity. As we declare that for us and for our house, we serve the Lord, are we essentially dropping small change into a red kettle and calling that giving our whole lives to the Lord?

We are a people who are on a mission. I'm not talking here about the Great Commission which is certainly a mission that we are on, but that Great Commission will not be possible unless we first accomplish this mission: transformation. Our mission, our work, is transformation, the transformation of our culture and society? Not directly. All we can affect in our culture and society is the passing of law. The passing of law simply serves to restrict people. The gospel is what sets them free. The law shows them their sin and their error, but they rebel against that, don't they? There should be good laws that reflect Christian virtue because it is the law of God, but those should not be positioned above people in such a way as the people without salvation are thought to be Christian in conduct, simply because the law restricts their behavior.

To understand this petition which Jesus gives, look again at verse 17. Asking of the Father, Jesus says, "Sanctify them in the truth; Your Word is truth." If we are going to understand this petition in the Lord's prayer to His Father, we need to quickly again touch on the context of it as a prayer that is spoken on the eve of Jesus' crucifixion, His death on the Cross. We are so near to that, that it would be the only thing we would be able to think of in our fleshly humanity, our own demise. Jesus is fully aware of the suffering that is before Him. He is also fully involved in His thoughts and the realization of the glory that will be restored to Him as He is glorified again with the Father, and so Jesus is aware that He is leaving His disciples, and that they will remain.

While Jesus is with them He says, "I have guarded them . . . I kept them in Your name," speaking again to the Father. And He asks now as He departs, that the Father would "keep them from the evil one," to continue that same spiritual safeguarding, to protect them from the pollution of the world, especially the evil one. He prays that they will be a people of joy—joy because of their convictions and faith and the reality of their adoption as sons of God. And He asks and expects that joy will radiate as a light does in the darkness from the children of God who remain in the world, for the glory of God is an extension of His kingdom in the lives of His people.

Verse 17 brings us to another petition in the Lord's prayer. Jesus prays that we will be sanctified in truth. For our understanding, we need to read it like this: "Father, sanctify them and that in accordance with the truth as revealed in your Word," or perhaps we might understand it as "Father, seal them up in your truth."

We need to be reminded of a common reply which people give as they seek to justify sin or habitual vices in their lives. When we confront people with the way they live, when we confront folks that they are not living according to the teachings or the precepts of Scripture, they make excuses: "You know, that's just something I enjoy doing. That's just something I've always done. It's just a small thing I don't think it's going to change the whole world. It doesn't mean I don't believe; it's just a little vice that I have," whether they're talking about their drinking, their flirtatiousness, their cussing, their gambling, or their smoking. Whether it's talking about desecrating the Sabbath or about being gossips, whatever it might be, it's just a little something they enjoy doing, and they are fine and content to hold that in their own heart, even while their mission is to be transformed into Christ's likeness.

Jesus' great hope is that His people will be protected and prosper, yet He asks specifically that they not be removed from a world full of temptations, troubles, and tribulations. We would expect that if Jesus is going to show His love for His people, that He would say, "And Father, I am leaving them, and Lord God, I would pray that you would quickly bring them to Me. That they would not be left to suffer and to anguish, but Lord bring them out of that place of evil and remove them from the evil one that they could be preserved, here with me, and I can continue to safeguard and watch over them." But He prays the opposite. He says, "Lord God, I don't want you to take them out." He didn't just leave it open, He actually says, "Don't remove them. I'm not praying that they would be taken away; I'm praying that you would keep them in your Word."

We are kept by God by being sanctified. Sanctification then is not evacuation. It's not getting everybody out. Sanctification is not monasticism. It's not hunkering down into little holy clusters and avoiding contact with the world so that we won't be stained by sin. Sanctification is consecration and transformation. We aren't called to quit life, nor are we called to be like the world. We are called to be salt and light. Foreigners in the world, we are to be preserved by God in that work of mission which we are called to do. Then we ask, *But how? How?* We are weak. We are prone to sin because, frankly, we like it. We enjoy those things which we are caught doing that we shouldn't be doing. That's why we're doing them. We're double-minded. We're drawn to it like a moth to a flame.

So how are we going to be preserved? How are we going to be transformed when we really don't want to most of the time? We want to when we're thinking about it, but we don't think about it much? Truth be told, we're not puzzled over it. We don't ponder it. We're not wrestling with it when we wake up in the morning, about our living lives that are holy and consecrated to the Lord. We look at our calendar. We look at the schedule. We begin with our list of disappointments and the people who are failing us each and every day, and then we get about our business of the day to try to earn the almighty buck, so we can buy things that we like. We don't trouble ourselves with our primary vocational calling, which is to be made like Christ.

J. C. Ryle says,

> He who supposes that Jesus Christ only lived and died and rose again in order to provide justification and forgiveness of sins for His people, has yet much to learn. Whether he knows it or not, he is dishonoring our blessed Lord and making Him only a half savior. The Lord Jesus has undertaken everything that His people's souls require, not only to deliver them from the guilt of their sins by His atoning death, but from the dominion of their sins by placing in their hearts the Holy Spirit, not only to justify them, but to sanctify them. (11)

This is why Ryle begins his chapter on sanctification in a book simply titled *Holiness* with this statement. "It is a subject," speaking of sanctification, "of the utmost importance to our souls; if the Bible be true, it is certain that unless we are sanctified, we shall not be saved" (10).

Does that bear repeating? "It is a subject of the utmost importance to our souls; if the Bible be true, it is certain that unless we are sanctified, we shall not be saved." If sanctification is that vital to our salvation—and it is, and if it is not a doctrine well understood by the Church—and it isn't, then we need to take a moment to look at it as it is contained here in Jesus' prayer and as it pertains particularly to us.

So what does Jesus mean when He prays "Sanctify them in the truth"? We're on the eve of the crucifixion. Jesus is summarizing the cardinal doctrines, as He prays to the Father, that are essential in the understanding of our own salvation in living in Him, and He says, "Sanctify them in the truth." We need to define this word *sanctification* because the same word is going to be used by Jesus in verse 19 about Himself. He says in verse 19, "And for their sake I consecrate myself, that they also may be sanctified in truth."

Consecrate? Is that the same word? It certainly is. In the original language it's exactly the same word. The interpreters, or the translators of Scripture as it were, were correct in using the word *consecrate*, instead of *sanctify* because that is the sense in which the word is used. *Consecration* is the same word as *sanctification*. There are two senses in which the word *sanctification* is employed, and one of them is the same as *consecration* which Jesus uses to describe His own work. Most understand the two senses of *sanctify* that are used throughout the Bible, but the sense most commonly used is simply *to set apart*. That's why the ESV (English Standard Version) and other translations make that distinction in verse 19 by using the word *consecrate*. To consecrate something is to set it apart.

In the Bible, *sanctify* is not just used of men, however. It is used of mountains; it is used particularly of Mt. Sinai. It's used of Jerusalem. In Psalm 48:1 we read, "His holy mountain, beautiful in elevation, is the joy of all the earth." That word *holy* means something that is set apart, something that is different. Mt. Sinai was set apart because God used Mt. Sinai as the place where He revealed His law. Jerusalem was set apart from all the other cities as the place where God's people, who live according to His law, would gather. It's the place where God is revealed through the tabernacle, through the temple, through the lives of His people. In the scripture, even buildings or instruments and other various items that are found in the temple and tabernacle are all set aside for service to God. They are *sanctified* in the sense of *consecrated* or dedicated to a purpose.

One of the simplest examples that I have was given by a seminary professor who took a pen, and he said, "If I would like to sanctify this pen, I would use it only for writing. If I use it for doing anything else, if I use it as a page holder or a bookmark, if I use it to scratch something off of the desk, if I use it to do anything other than write, I'm not sanctifying that pen. I'm using it for something it wasn't designed to be used for." Could God say the same thing about us? Are we designed for a particular purpose? And to use our own bodies and time God has given us in our lives for something else, is that to not be sanctified in our lives and in our living?

When Jesus entered the courts of the temple and turned over the tables of commerce, He yelled at them, "This is My Father's house. This is a house of prayer, but you have made it into a den of thieves." Can the house of God be said to be consecrated to a particular purpose?

I know that we certainly have striven, even in our own imperfect understanding, to make sure our sanctuaries are consecrated to a particular purpose. We don't use the sanctuary for anything other than the celebration of God the Father, of the gospel of Jesus Christ. It's what we come to church to do. It has been sanctified, set apart, for that purpose. We don't use it for civic meetings of outside organizations, or clubs, or at least we shouldn't. We don't use it for other gatherings of different sorts of celebrations or understandings. We don't exalt man here in the place where God is exalted. It is singularly set aside and sanctified, a place consecrated for the worship of one: God. And God alone. That's what it is consecrated for.

When Jesus went into the temple courtyard, did he find people selling trinkets? No. They were selling sacrifices for people to use in worship. They may have been able to make a case that they were providing what people couldn't bring themselves. They were giving them something they had to have. Shouldn't they make their own living from this as well? They were giving them, I'm sure, a deal. And Jesus said, "That's not the purpose of this place. Sacrifices are necessary, yes, but that's not the purpose of this place. This place is consecrated to be a household of prayer to God the Father. You conduct your commerce elsewhere."

Do we understand the exclusivity of anything in life? We're a multitasking people. We like things that are diverse. We like our phones to have everything from e-mail, telephone numbers, and games on it. The more we can pack into one thing, the more we like it. We like multi-use facilities. The idea that a place would be consecrated just for one purpose seems to us to be a waste of space.

We can improve the definition by pointing out that sanctifying an object or person commits them to that single purpose and removes them from the defilement of the world. They are committed to one purpose, and they are taken out of any other. So it means separation and devotion. This is what it means in verse 19 when Jesus says that He has consecrated Himself. He has sanctified Himself. Since He has no inner defilement, He can't be speaking of an inner improvement. He's talking about His being separated from defilement and the commitment of His life to being God's purpose.

It's also used of you and me in 1 Corinthians 6:11. "And such were some of you. But you were washed, you were sanctified, you were justified in the name of the Lord Jesus Christ and by the Spirit of our God." Notice the word *sanctified* actually appears before the word *justified* in the passage. Placing *sanctified* before *justified* means that we've actually been set apart by God and taken out of the world by God, before all else. We are then cleansed and made fit for service by Christ. *Sanctified* describes our position. We are out of this world. Jesus has already affirmed this in verse 16 when He said, "They are not of the world, just as I am not of the world." People, we are not of this world, and this world and its ways will never embrace those who embrace Christ. We must forfeit Christ if we are to be received and embraced by the world.

One of our greatest handicaps today as Bible readers is that we take absolute statements like I just made, and we make them mere religious platitudes. We say things before it like, "All things being equal," or "You don't know my circumstances," or "This is not the right season of life for me." And we do everything we can to set aside any absolutes upon our lives which Scripture puts before us. But Jesus points out that we will remain in the world, but the world will not remain in us.

This takes us to the second meaning of the word *sanctification*. It not only brings us to the Lord, but it signifies that God is in us. In Ezekiel 36:23–27, we read these passages:

> "And I will vindicate the holiness of my great name, which has been profaned among the nations, and which you have profaned among them. And the nations will know that I am the Lord, declares the Lord God, when through you I vindicate my holiness before their eyes. I will take you from the nations and gather you from all the countries and bring you into your own land. I will sprinkle clean water on you, and you shall be clean from all your uncleannesses, and from all your idols I will cleanse you. And I will give you a new heart, and a new spirit I will put within you. And I will remove the heart of stone from your flesh and give you

a heart of flesh. And I will put my Spirit within you, and cause you
to walk in my statutes and be careful to obey my rules."

This shows us the blessing for which we are sanctified. First, God
will take us out from a heathen world. He will gather us to our own land
and our own people. The Church is the visible kingdom of God. It is
imperfect still, as it is mixed with wheat and tares, and we know that, but
it is what we have as we await the kingdom which is to come. Second,
God says He will sprinkle us, and He will cleanse us from our sins and
defilement. He is going to give us a new heart. He's going to take from us
a hard heart, full of vindictive hatred, vice, and avarice, and He will put
His own Spirit, the Holy Spirit, in us. He will cause us to walk according
to His law, to be an obedient people. He will pull all of this together, and
we will have a full definition of our own sanctification.

Essentially it is this: God sets His people apart. He manifests Himself
in them as a testimony to the nations. He changes them and makes them
clean in His sight, and He makes them to order their lives to be in compliance and obedience to His will. Jude 1 is a great New Testament summary.
"To those who are called, beloved in God the Father and kept for Jesus
Christ." We are called, and we are kept.

Jesus goes another step in His prayer to show us the instrument
which God uses to sanctify His people, that is truth.

Marcus Rainsford said, "As Satan corrupts through falsehoods, our
God sanctifies us through the truth" (307). It is through truth that God
is revealed. It is through truth that God's love is proclaimed and demonstrated in Christ. It is the Spirit that acts as the sledge which shapes God's
people against the anvil of God's truth in the heat of conflict with the
world. We are like iron that has been heated to become pliable, almost
to the melting point. As we go through the trials and tribulations of this
world, we are placed against the anvil of God's truth, which is unchanging
and immovable, and then the Holy Spirit does its work upon us to shape
us to be Christlike.

"So faith comes from hearing, and hearing through the Word of
Christ" (Romans 10:17). It is by truth that God is revealed. It is by truth
which takes up residence in us that we are to be changed and made testi-
fiers of the truth ourselves. It is the effect of truth that we see described as
sanctification, a progressive march toward Christlikeness. In Romans 8:29
we read we are "predestined to be conformed to the image of His Son."

Ephesians 4:21–24 opens that subject up plainly for us.

> Assuming that you have heard about Him and were taught in Him, as the truth is in Jesus, to put off your old self, which belongs to your former manner of life and is corrupt through deceitful desires, and to be renewed in the spirit of your minds, and to put on the new self, created after the likeness of God in true righteousness and holiness.

There is a fundamental change from the person we were to the person we are becoming, but it is not we who determine what that new man is to look like. God has determined what that new man is to look like. By the Holy Spirit, through the instrumentality of the Word, we are predestined to be conformed into the image of Christ. The end of this progressive work which God is accomplishing is that we would be like Christ, and by the Holy Spirit and through His Word, that we would be holy as He is holy. All the way back into Leviticus 19:2, we are commanded to be holy for our Lord God is holy.

Sanctification then is accomplished by the Holy Spirit, but it is also the work of man. That is, the work that men are engaged in. We are active. We are not passive in the process of being sanctified. That's why Paul was able to say to the Philippians, "work out your own salvation with fear and trembling," and at the same time he acknowledged that it is God who is at work in them. As for himself, Paul said, "I press on toward the goal for the prize of the upward call of God in Christ Jesus" (Philippians 3:14).

In Colossians 3, Paul makes it the believer's responsibility to "put to death therefore what is earthly in you." In Joel 2:13 we are commanded to rend our hearts. In Romans 6:11 we are told to die to sin. In 1 Timothy 6:11 we are told to flee carnality and pursue righteousness, and Jesus gives us the method by which we do all of these things, and that is truth.

How do we become holy? How do we become sanctified? By truth. J. C. Ryle said, "When I speak of means, I have in view Bible reading, private prayer, regular attendance on public worship, regular hearing of God's Word, and regular reception of the Lord's Supper. I lay it down as a simple matter of fact that no one who is careless about such things must ever expect to make much progress in sanctification" (13).

God has provided the means for our growth in truth. To be careless in our attendance upon these things, to be negligent in the listening of God's Word and the preaching of it, to be negligent in attendance to the

Lord's Supper, to be negligent in our prayers, to be negligent in our Bible reading and study would be to avoid the very means necessary for God to sanctify us and make us Christlike. It's our abiding in the Word and in the ministry of the Word that puts us in a place for the truth of God to have its work in us to produce sanctification.

So how does it work? Not magically, nor is it easy. Staying in the Word of God, which is truth, will reveal God to us and expand our love for Him. Our convictions will grow when we lose our love for the besetting sins in our lives. Martyn Lloyd-Jones put this eloquently and well. He said, "Some teach that all we have to do, having told God we want to be delivered, is to believe He has done it, and then we shall find that is has happened" (400).

What does the scripture say in Ephesians 4:28 to a man who finds himself constantly guilty of stealing? Am I to say to that man, "Take that sin to Christ, and ask Him to deliver you"? No. What the Apostle Paul tells him is this, "Let him that stole steal no more."

The key to progress in sanctification is not to appeal to some mystical change, but to simply stop the sin. We're not able to stop unless we are in possession of the Holy Spirit, but Paul does not instruct us to say, "Yes, just deliver it up." that God would take the sin away as if it was something foreign and alien to us. It is of the flesh, but because of the Holy Spirit we are empowered to stop sinning.

In First John we are told the children of God will not sin. Paul says, "What do you say to a man who steals and steals and steals"? Do you say to him, "Go and lay down your sins at the Cross of Jesus that God would take them away"? We do that in confession, but the answer is stop. Stop stealing. In the power of your own flesh? No. In the power of the Holy Spirit, stop the sin. God is already equipped for us to stop the sin.

Let us not appeal to a lack of passion to stop sinning. Let us not appeal to a lack of our own activity and exertion. Paul said, "I press on toward the goal for the prize of the upward call of God in Christ Jesus" (Philippians 3:14). "As obedient children, do not be conformed to the passions of your former ignorance, but as He who called you is holy, you also be holy in all your conduct" (I Peter 1:14). There is nothing passive in that command. Sanctification isn't passive and directionless; it's an action based on light and based on knowledge, an instrument received by those who have had the eyes of their hearts enlightened in order that the Spirit can apply the truth to their soul to this end.

In Romans 8:29, we are "predestined to be conformed to the image of His Son." Think for a moment about your own life. What are you consecrated to? What do you give your time to? What do you give your money to? When you argue, what are you defending? How often do you have to use phrases like, "I'm just going to go where the sinners are," or "Nobody's perfect," or "Don't be judgmental," or "I don't want to be a hypocrite and not advertise my sin" or "I've always done that," or "It's just something I enjoy"? "I hate the double-minded, but I love Your law" (Psalm 119:113). James 4:4–9 teaches the same thing.

God has called us out of the world. He requires us not to be double-minded, but to use the means of grace to grow in Christ by the power, not of the flesh, but of the Spirit. He knew us before the foundations of the world. Before we were knitted together in our mothers' wombs, God has known us. He justified us in Christ, and now, He has made us His own, and we are on a journey with one purpose: to glorify God by being consecrated and transformed into Christ's likeness.

So ask yourself, *How's it going?* How are you doing? Those sins that you know; have you pushed them aside, or are you seeking to justify them? Do you want to cling to them more than to Christ?

13

Resident Aliens: Going Into the World

(John 17:18)

"As you sent me into the world, so I have sent them into the world."

VERSE 18 IS A stopping point or a summary place. For it seems in this verse, there is a gathering together of all of these virtues of the Church, which we have already been speaking of. Verses 18 and 19, together close out this second phase or second epic of Jesus' prayer.

You remember there were three major sections of that prayer. Jesus opened the prayer with the petition for Himself that God would glorify Him with the glory which He had before the world was made. The second petition is most particularly for the apostles, though we are finding so many parallels to our own life because we are the Church, also indwelled by the Holy Spirit.

The third petition of Christ, which begins at verse 20, will be for those who believe the testimony of the apostles and then follow Christ. So we see that as most directly applicable, or most directly pointed, towards us. Jesus has been praying that the disciples would be known by their joy, by their holiness, by their truth and love of truth, and, here, by their mission, and then finally by their unity. These were the characteristics and the traits of the apostles which became the characteristics and traits of the Church and, consequently, of all God's people.

We have learned that we are called out of the world, hence the theme which we have kept of being *resident aliens*. We are alien to this world. We are pilgrims, sojourners, yet we're residents here, so we are resident aliens. But we are to be a people who are known by being filled with joy. We are a people who are to be known by our holiness, our being consecrated to the Lord, and becoming more and more Christ-like each and every day by our commitment to and adherence to truth.

In fact, it's not too much to say we are absolutely dependent upon God's Word. We are to be a people who don't just simply carry God's word and speak of God's Word as we would a math book or a science book, but to be dependent upon God's Word as if it were the very air that we breathe. And now we are to learn that all of these taken together, brought into a single and unified body, become testimony.

They become our mission. Jesus is speaking principally of these disciples—11 at this point, Judas having been gone—who are around Him. Verse 20 is where we introduce the broader group, but these same principles that were given to the apostles were communicated to the Church, and the Church, like the apostles, is on a mission. The apostles were given a mission by Christ to go and to speak and to tell authoritatively everything they had heard.

The Church has taken the apostles' teaching, along with the teaching of the prophets of the Old Testament, and the books of history of the Old Testament and the Gospels themselves—the Church has taken these, authoritative teachings of the apostles, and speaks authoritatively of them. And so we find the Church continuing that same mission which is put forth to the apostles here.

When we think of mission, we usually think of going on from here to somewhere else, to carry the gospel from where we are to somewhere that the gospel isn't. The Church has long understood that missions are to be the focus of the Christian life. Emil Brunner said, "One who receives this Word, and by it salvation, receives along with it the duty of passing this Word on. Where there is no mission, there is no Church, and where there is neither Church nor mission, there is no faith" (108).

G. Campbell Morgan said very simply, "To call a man evangelical who is not evangelistic is an utter contradiction" (2). Jesus had promised them a place with Him in eternity. Do you remember? He said, "I'm leaving." And they said, "But where are you going?" He said, "I'm going to the Father." They said, "Well, can we go with you?" He said, "I'm going to build a place, to prepare a place for you. There will be a mansion, a home, for you there with my Father, but you cannot go now." And then He turns in prayer, and He says, "Father, I'm not praying that you would take them. I want them to stay here. I'm going to leave them here in this place."

We can all admit to a little impatience from time to time. As one grows long in the tooth, so to speak, can't we recall hearing many of our elders complain that God is delaying calling them home? Why doesn't God just take us the moment we believe? If the objective is simply the salvation of our soul, then as soon as we believe and confess, then it's all done. It's all finished. Why doesn't God just take us then? Why are we made to stay? With our soul secured, with our citizenship confirmed, why aren't we deported as it were from this life and received into the next?

Our answer can be found in the first question of the Westminster Shorter Catechism. That question asks what our chief end, or our highest purpose in life is. The answer is simply to glorify God and to enjoy Him forever. We glorify God by magnifying His name and by being a living testimony that we might serve Him by seeing others come to faith. That's the only reason we're here. Let me repeat that because we often think we are here for a lot of different reasons. To glorify God and to be a living testimony is the *only* reason we are here.

The only reason that we are here, if we have received by God's grace the gospel of Jesus Christ, is that we might speak the gospel as testimony and establish the gospel in this world that others might receive salvation. Billy Graham said, "We are the Bibles the world is reading. We are the creeds the world is needing. We are the sermons the world is heeding" (400). This is the fourth mark of the Church, the mark that distinguishes God's people who know joy, who are sanctified, who were made holy and who are distinguished by being marked by truth. They are also missional, a people who are on a mission in a world of instant coffee, instant messaging, 24-hour news cycles, drive-thru restaurants, direct deposit, 10-minute oil changes, TurboTax, and Wikipedia. The inclination towards impatience has become a crippling defect of the modern mind, a crippling handicap to the Church. Even worship is not immune from the impatience of modern man. Thus, we realize the truth of the words, "Patience is a virtue."

In the past, men were more accustomed to waiting. It's not that they weren't impatient, but they were more accustomed to waiting. They didn't seem to feel that they, themselves, were so sovereign over every aspect of life to where their own sense of sovereignty drove them nearly to insanity. They were accustomed to waiting long periods of time on harvest. They were accustomed to waiting long periods of time on many aspects of life to mature. The Greek historian, Herodotus', writing in 500 BC recorded a workforce of 100,000 that worked on a pyramid, saying that it would take an entire lifetime to complete it. At best, some estimate that to build a pyramid would take, at best, about 30 years. The Norwich Cathedral was begun in 1096 AD. It was completed in 1145. Generally speaking, however, cathedrals in Europe took about 38 years to build—38 years before, after the first stone was laid, the first service would be held.

After World War II, American forces were garrisoned in Germany. They were garrisoned in Japan to provide security and stability. When did that end? We're still there. Now, we want to know, before we go on a mission, when do we get to come home? This present generation, of which I would include myself, knows nothing of things like *Hundred Years' War*, which we learned about in history. Everything is now. We're addicted to adrenaline. Boredom comes in an instant And missions have become an unfulfilling, time-consuming work that fewer and fewer take any real interest in.

Jesus opens this issue up in a very interesting and captivating way. However, He begins our passage by saying, "As you sent me into the world. . . ." "As you sent me. . . ," how deep the subject of that short, little phrase. *Sent* is from the Greek word *apostolos*, from which we draw the word *apostle*. Apostle, then, we could simply abbreviate by saying, "They are *the sent*." This is the work to which they are sanctified. It's the work to which they're set apart, but uniquely—and particularly—to be *the sent*. We can observe that Jesus, Himself, was *the sent*.

This means that Jesus existed prior to the incarnation because He had to be *sent* from where He was. It also means that the incarnation was of the Father's will because it doesn't say that Jesus *came*. It says that He was *sent*. Jesus is professing His subjection to the Father's will.

In John 8:42, the second part of the verse, Jesus said, "I came not of my own accord, but He sent Me." Jesus delighted to show that His mission was based on and motivated by the Father's love for His people. Jesus came and He said, "I am here not because I come unwillingly, but I'm coming because it was the Father's will to show His love for His people."

"For God so loved the world, that He gave His only begotten son. . . ." He came as demonstration of God's love.

"But now I am going to Him who sent Me. . . ." (John 16:5). Jesus emphasized this even at the end. Before ascending to the Father, He simply reflected upon the fact that it was the Father who sent Him. So first of all, Jesus was the one that was sent, and Jesus was also sent officially. This means it was His responsibility to discharge all the duties of His office.

In John 9:4, "We must work the works of Him who sent me while it is day. . . ." Notice the imperative. "We must work the works of Him who sent me. . . ." He doesn't say we *ought* to work the works, or we *should* work the works. He doesn't say all things being equal, you *should* work these works into your life. He doesn't say you should *gradually* accomplish the works. He says, "We must work the works of Him who sent me while it is day."

When our Lord was sent into the world, there was no part of His mission that He imagined He must not do. Was there any part of Jesus' work that He said at any point, "I have done nearly all that the Father sent me to do. I accomplished all that was practicable that the Lord has sent me to accomplish. I have done all things that were within my finite ability, given that I have been burdened with this flesh, that God would have desired for me to do." Jesus said none of those things. He said, "I have accomplished all that my Father has sent me to do."

Jesus was sent officially to accomplish God's mission, and Jesus was sent from God. We ought not overlook that. It seems so obvious but so important. Philippians 2:6, ". . . though He was in the form of God, did not count equality with God a thing to be grasped. . . ." He was at home with God, and it was from God that He was sent. He was sent from God with God's authority. To accomplish the mission, which God had given Him to do, He was the one sent *by* God to *do* God's work *in* the world.

Jesus was sent into the world. He wasn't sent to those who received Him or gathered to hear. He was sent to save the lost. He was sent to restore sight to the blind. He was sent to free the captives. He was sent into the wilderness of a fallen world, into the chaos of this world, a chaos which, even now, is on the ascendancy, especially in man's thought. But as in man's thought, chaos continues to gain ascendancy. We see that thought breaking down culture and breaking down our communities as we know them—families disintegrating before our very eyes, morality disappearing and evaporating before us. This is where He was sent. And as the gospel has become quieter, we have seen in its place not nothing, but the thought of man. And what has the thought of man brought except discord and disunity and destruction. ". . . The reason the Son of God appeared was to destroy the works of the devil" (1 John 3:8). He was sent to seek and to save the lost and destroy the dominion of sin.

Marcus Rainsford summarizes this so well. "It was for the greatest cause He was sent—even the glory of God; the greatest object—the salvation of sinners; and for the greatest results—even that He might subdue all things to Himself. He only could do it, therefore He was sent; He could do it only in our nature, therefore He assumed it; He could do it in the world only, therefore He dwelt amongst us" (322–323).

This brings us to the second half of the verse. Jesus said, "As you sent me into the world, so I have sent them into the world." The fact that this statement is yoked to the first should stagger us. While the apostles were unique in their inspired teaching, to continue the mission and work of Jesus, like the apostles, we are sent. We are not our own. We are sent. We aren't here for our own business except as it is our business to glorify God. That's why we have remained here. That's why we were not evacuated immediately. We are sent. We are here by compulsion, not choice. What do I mean by that?

Not one of us here willed ourselves into existence. We did not decide to be born. Not one of us here pressed our way into heaven by our own strength. We have not put our shoulder to the gates of heaven and pried them open to work our way inside. Here, we remember Jesus' prayer that He deliberately asked the Father not to remove us from the world. If anyone here, who knows Christ, were asked at this very moment if you could remain in this world or enter into eternity with all of its blessedness now, where would you rather be? Those who know Christ know, in their answer right now, that they would prefer to be with Christ now.

But we are compelled to be here, so it's not by our own will that we remain. Jesus prayed, "Father, don't remove them from the world. Leave them here in the world." Is that an act of cruelty by our Savior? Certainly not. The apostles in the Church remain because they continue planting, for that is a continuing of the loci of John 3:16, "God so loved the world that He . . ." *sent* . . . his son. He sent the apostles. He sends us.

The word *mission* comes from the Latin *mitto* or *misi,* and it means *to send or to dispatch.* Where are we sent? We are sent here to the world, in some cases simply into our own communities. In other cases, we are sent around the world. Wherever there is one soul dwelling in darkness, that's where we're sent. Maybe you were sent to your own den. Maybe you were sent to your own dining room table. Maybe you were sent to a family member's table. Maybe you were sent across the street. Maybe you were sent across the world.

Wherever it is that you were sent, if there is one that doesn't know Christ, then that is your mission. Why are we here? Is it so that we can survive the course of our days and "eek" out a little bit of joy even as our bodies age to death? No, we are left here—not abandoned—but with a mission. We aren't left. We are sent. We're called out of the world, and then we are sanctified in Christ and sent back into the world to accomplish a mission. We are sent.

Jesus entered the world by incarnation, and we learn even from that. He took on flesh yet remained consecrated and holy. We must enter the world in people's lives as well so that we might show them Christ who lives in us. Jesus was incarnated. That means He took on the flesh of the people He was sent to. We go into the world, but we are not to become a part of the world. Jesus didn't become unholy and a sinner when He came into the world even though He became incarnated in the world. We must enter into the world and become not a part of the world, but in the world that we might impact it rather than be infected by it.

Let me remind you again of the words of Billy Graham, "We are the Bibles the world is reading. We are the creeds the world is needing. We are the sermons the world is heeding."

"But if the salt loses its flavor, of what use is it? It is of none. The salt goes in to preserve the world" (Mathew 5:13).

I would submit to you with absolute confidence that because Christians no longer sense that they're being sent, the salt is losing its flavor, and we are seeing the decay of society as a result. Those who would seek to have a voice in society to preserve it through some sort of utopian vision of socialism or communism or any other *ism* that has proven historically to be a failure throughout man's history, are once again showing that they cannot learn from those lessons. And so they're trying to do it again, and once again we're seeing disunity and an erosion of everything from morality to culture to society itself—everything from education to family. And why is this occurring? Because the salt is not present in the world, no longer a society being preserved, and so it is in decay.

Jesus was sent to be the light of the world. We are sent to carry His light in the world. "In the same way, let your light shine before others, so that they may see your good works and give glory to your Father who is in heaven" (Matthew 5:16). As Jesus was qualified for His mission, He has qualified us by giving us His spirit. "The spirit of the Lord is upon me... to preach the gospel . . ." (In Luke 4:18). "'. . . as My Father has sent me, even so send I you.' And when He had said this, He breathed on them and said to them, 'Receive the Holy Spirit'" (John 20:22).

What does this mean? This means that we can draw a strong connection, not to us being the power of Christ, not for us being Christ, but being indwelled with the Spirit so that the words of Scripture are true. Wherever the Word goes out, the Spirit goes with it, and it does not return void. So our mission is to preach the Word. The Word of Christ, the word of God, and the Spirit going with that word, changes men's hearts, souls, and minds. ". . . As He is, so also are we in this world" (John 4:17). Is that true of you, and is it true of me?

Jesus sent His apostles into the world with the very same mission that the Father sent Him on . . . the very same mission; "As you sent me, so send I them." In Luke 4:18, Jesus said, ". . . 'He has anointed Me to preach. . . .'" In Mark 16:15, "And He said to them, 'Go into all the world and proclaim the gospel to the whole creation.'"

Brothers and Sisters, ask yourself this: If we are sent as Christ was sent, what would be our state if Christ had done as we do? We are the benefactors of a great work of grace. Its greatness becomes all the more apparent when we see how poorly we carry on the work of Christ. We aren't called to observe the work of Christ, but to participate in the work of Christ.

We're even told that it is not our own power that will make it effective, but Christ who works through us will make it effective. And even with that, with the simple task of *preach the gospel* and not by your power will the effect be drawn, but from God's own power, even with that simple task and promise, we still falter, and we still fail. As long as there remains one of Christ's own not yet confessing the Lord, then there remains a work for us as aliens in this world. As a people in the wilderness, we are still called to labor for the kingdom.

In his book *The Four Loves,* C.S. Lewis talks about this working and observing a greater power than ours that brings a result:

> A garden teams with life. It glows with color and smells like heaven and puts forward at every hour of a summer day beauties which man could never have created and could not, even on his own resources, have imagined. When the garden is in its full glory, the gardener's contributions to that glory will still have been, in a sense, paltry, compared with those in nature. Without life spring-

ing from the earth, without rain, light, and heat descending from
the sky, he could do nothing. (17)

When he has done all, he has merely encouraged here and discour-
aged there powers and beauties that have a different source, but his share,
though small, is indispensable and laborious. When God planted a garden, he set a man over it and set the man under Himself. When he planted
the garden of our nature and caused the flower and fruit he loves to grow
there, he said, It is "our will to dress them." Unless His grace comes down
like rain and sunshine, we shall use the tool given to us to little purpose.
But its laborious and largely negative services are indispensable."

We recognize that the power of God over history, the power of God
over the hearts and the minds of men, is something that we can hardly
even fathom. And so we sometimes, feeling so small and insignificant in
the work of God, fail to apply ourselves, believing that what we do is so
small and inconsequential that God's work will go on without us. But
we are like a gardener, whose work compared to the sunshine and the
rain, is so small. Pull a weed here; till the soil there; plant a seed here. But
yet without the work of the gardener, the sunshine simply works to dry,
and the rain simply brings flood because it has been ordained that for a
beautiful garden to exist there will be a gardener doing the small work of
gardening.

As Christ was sent, so we are sent to do that small work of preaching
the gospel. Through the foolishness of preaching, comparatively a small
word spoken, God causes the dead to come to life. Compared to Christ,
our best labor seems like nothing. But love compels us not to measure our
own results, not to measure our own strength and ability, but instead to
measure our heart's desire simply to obey because that is our calling.

14

Resident Aliens Sanctified through the Truth

(John 17:19)

"And for their sake I consecrate Myself, that they also may be sanctified in truth."

IN FIRST CORINTHIANS, CHAPTER 1, the second verse, Paul, in addressing the church says, "To the church of God that is in Corinth, to those sanctified in Christ Jesus, called to be saints together. . . ." Here he addresses the church, calling them those that are *"sanctified in Christ."* We read in verse 7, "So that you are not lacking in any spiritual gift. . . ." That is, Paul addressed the church as those who are in fact sanctified, already accomplished, and says to them, "You do not lack any spiritual gift," thus pointing to God's pouring out to the Church all of His blessings. In verse 8, we see that we receive our confidence in this because it is Jesus Christ "who will sustain you to the end, guiltless in the day of our Lord Jesus Christ."

The Church of Jesus Christ can be properly called *those who are sanctified, those who are saints of God,* and there is no blessing of God that is not available and given to them. They are not lacking in any spiritual gift. So, the Church has a confidence that there is a sanctification already accomplished in Christ, and as a result of that, there is no blessing that is lacking which we need. Now, that does not imply that everything that *can* be given is given as far as spiritual giftedness, but it is saying that anything that the Church *needs* is given. We are not lacking in any spiritual gift.

What is the foundation of this? Jesus Christ, who sustains us and presents us guiltless in the day of our Lord Jesus Christ. That is the definition of our sanctification. Our Lord Jesus Christ has preserved us to the end and presents us guiltless before God. We are called out, made holy, separated from the world. We are justified by the atoning work of Christ on the Cross. That is, we're declared not guilty in a judicial action of God. And we who are those people called out, made holy, separated from the world, who are sanctified in that action, are then preserved by Christ.

I would submit that much of the Church's lack of enthusiasm, or lack of activity, comes from a lack of this confidence that we are in fact sanctified as saints, preserved by Christ, given all that is necessary for whatever God calls us to. And so, we can step out on the mission that God has called us to with all confidence that we lack nothing, that we ought not look to ourselves to provide a resource that God has not provided. If He calls us to a work, He has provided for that work. To say anything less would be to say less of God. Paul's words are true, and it is left to us to appropriate that truth and act accordingly, not to doubt. It is a true statement. How do we respond to that? How do we act according to that?

The idea of sanctification is not limited just to this aspect in the Scriptures. No, we read throughout the first testament that word *sanctification*. In Genesis 2:3, "So God blessed the seventh day and made it holy. . . ." He sanctified that day to Himself. He said, "This day is My day. The seventh day, the Sabbath, will be My day." And He determines how that day is to be used and regulated because it is not a day of man. It is a day that God says, "I will take that day. I sanctify that day to Myself."

The Tabernacle, the Temple, are both sanctified to God's service, and all the instruments in it, be they silver, gold or anything else. Everything that is in the Tabernacle is also sanctified to the service of God. What does that mean? It means that those, the Tabernacle, the Temple, and all of those utensils can be used for nothing else except in the service of God. Now, if we take that as our understanding of the word *sanctified*, what does that mean of our own persons, our own lives, of this place, of our church, of our body? It means that if we are sanctified to the Lord, then we have one purpose—to glorify God and enjoy Him forever, which we say over and over again, and yet each one of us fails to fully realize its practical application in our lives.

In John, chapter 10, verse 36, Jesus said, "Do you say of Him whom the Father consecrated and sent into the world, 'You are blaspheming,'. . . ?" Jesus is sanctified by God, consecrated by God, to a particular purpose, to a particular function. In First Corinthians 1:30, Jesus is consecrated, that is, sanctified, as the "wisdom from God, righteousness and sanctification and redemption. . . ." In a sense, Jesus Himself is our sanctification. Here is where we begin if we're going to understand sanctification.

I agree with Martyn Lloyd-Jones when he says, "If anyone can present a doctrine of sanctification in one study, there is something wrong with that doctrine." Sanctification is too large a topic even for the amount of time that I will spend, which probably will bore some readers. But nevertheless, whatever time I spend would still not be sufficient to really understand sanctification. And so, we will try to provide not an overview, but to touch on the broadest strokes, or the keys to understanding this, trusting the Spirit of God to continue His instruction to us.

Consider the verse quoted at the beginning of this chapter. "And for their sake I consecrate Myself, that they also may be sanctified in truth." Look at the words. "that they. . . ." *That they* points to our sanctification, which is grounded in His own sanctification, His own consecration. Jesus is here saying, "And for their sake I consecrate myself. . . . For their sake, I separate myself to a singular service of ministry which the Father has sent me on, and that is for their salvation. I have consecrated myself." But for what purpose? "That they also may be sanctified in truth." All of God's dealing with His people are through Christ.

I want to emphasize a couple of words because I hope that you will grab hold of these words. God does *to* Christ and *with* Christ what He has purposed to do *to* and *with* His people. He has done to Christ—what did He do to Christ? He separated Christ out and He punished sin on the Cross. What did God intend to do to His people? Because we were condemned and under the curse of sin and the wrath of God, He intended to do to us what He did to Christ. And He does with Christ what He purposes to do to His people in the resurrection and glorification of Christ.

To get a sense of this, visit Isaiah 53, verses 4 and 5 and verse 8. "Surely He has borne our griefs and carried our sorrows; yet we esteemed him stricken, smitten by God, and afflicted." Look carefully at what He says. *"Surely He . . ."* that is, Christ as the fulfillment of this, ". . . has borne our griefs." What was done to Christ is what was intended to be done to us. Verse 5: "But He was wounded for our transgressions." His wounds, the wounds inflicted upon Christ were intended for us. "He was crushed for our iniquities; upon Him was the chastisement that brought us peace, and with His stripes we are healed." The stripes on Christ's back were the stripes that were intended for us.

Verse 8: "By oppression and judgment He was taken away; and as for His generation, who considered that He was cut off out of the land of the living, stricken for the transgression of My people?" I repeat again because it is worthy of repetition. What God did to Christ was intended to be done to us, and what He has done with Christ, He has purposed to do with His people. Why emphasize that so much? Because we find that to truly understand the width and the depth and the breadth of the gospel, we have to understand our unity with Christ. We have to understand our union with Christ. If we're to understand the Lord's Table rightly, we must understand our union with Christ.

It's a topic that is not necessarily preached on so directly in our modern day because union with Christ is a difficult topic, and given the time allotted for preaching, it is hard to arrive at something that is a bit more in depth than a gospel presentation or a call to moral and ethical living. To arrive at something of that depth takes time to develop in an idea. And so, most of us perhaps have gone through our days without hearing much about union with Christ. And yet, union with Christ is fundamental to understanding our being in Christ and His being in us.

Certainly, Jesus Himself referred to union in Christ a great deal. The whole allegory or metaphor of the branch and the vine is an instruction of union in Christ. When Jesus said to the Father, "I am in you, and they are in me," was He not talking about union in Christ, and He in us? How can we understand the indwelling of the Holy Spirit unless it is that we are in union with Christ? Otherwise, we're left with a superstitious notion of being somehow possessed by a spirit that is separate from us, and we wonder what the Spirit will do inside of us. Does it take over? I would submit to you that many of the Pentecostal expressions that we fail to understand result from the superstitious notion of possession rather than unity, that somehow something takes over us as if we are possessed by an external spirit instead of in union with Christ by the Holy Spirit.

But, if we don't take time to examine it, if we don't take time to understand it, perhaps we shouldn't be so critical. At least in that case, they are trying to find some way to express the occupation of the Spirit inside the believer. God first unites Christ with Himself and then He unites Himself to His people through Christ. "For we have come to share in Christ, if indeed we hold our original confidence firm to the end" (Hebrews 3:14). Christ is the firstborn of many brethren; then we are begotten in Him.

Christ is the most blessed forevermore, and we are blessed in Him with all spiritual blessings.

First, the Father gave to Christ to have life in Himself, then He gave us life in Him. Christ was manifested and declared to be the Son of God, then we are sons in Him. Christ was crucified for our sin, and we are crucified with Him. Christ is risen, and we are raised together with Him. Christ is more than a conqueror, and we are more than conquerors through Him. Christ sat down at the right hand of the Father, and we are sitting at God's right hand in the heavenly places. And so, there is an inseparable connection between His life and our life. As He is sanctified, so are we. Hebrews 3:1 begins with "Therefore, holy brothers, you who share in a heavenly calling, consider Jesus. . . ." And then, it goes on to contrast believers with the disobedient.

In Jesus, there is an analogy of faith. In Galatians 2:20, we read, "I have been crucified with Christ. It is no longer I who live, but Christ who lives in me." Paul is saying, "As Christ went to the Cross and died, what Jesus experienced from God as God did to Him what He meant for me and to me, it was I who also was crucified with Christ on the Cross." "And the life I now live. . ." Paul goes on to say, ". . .in the flesh I live by faith in the Son of God, . . ." Having died in Christ, we are in Christ, are found complete only in Him—only in Him.

We discover here in First Corinthians our union with Christ which is described as a washing and a purification.

> Or do you not know that the unrighteous will not inherit the kingdom of God? Do not be deceived: neither the sexually immoral, nor idolaters, nor adulterers, nor men who practice homosexuality, nor thieves, nor the greedy, nor drunkards, nor revilers, nor swindlers will inherit the kingdom of God. And such were some of you. But you were washed, you were sanctified, you were justified in the name of the Lord Jesus Christ and by the Spirit of our God. (Corinthians 6:9–11)

Our union with Christ is categorized as a washing and a purification of sins that makes us complete in Christ. Our sanctification in Christ is complete without any reference to any degree of response in us. Did you note that? It doesn't talk about our faithful response, or our appreciation, or our reaching and grasping, or our obedience at that point, all of which are biblical terms and biblical themes; but when it talks about this sanctification, this justification, it is without any reference to any degree of worthiness in ourselves. It is complete in Christ.

First Corinthians 1:30: It's through the offering and sacrifice of our Lord that we are found complete. Our sanctification consists in fellowship with Him and participation with Him in all that He is. Paul makes it clear in Romans, chapter 6, verses 3 and 4; he talks about the baptism, which is a baptism of the Holy Spirit, and that we are united to Him by baptism, represented by water. That is the Spirit's representation coming into us. We are baptized into His death and His resurrection. With this picture in mind, we can perhaps grasp the words in Hebrews 13, "So Jesus also suffered outside the gate in order to sanctify the people through His own blood." Jesus suffered in order that we would be sanctified through Him.

In John 17:9, Jesus said, "And for their sake I consecrate myself, that they also may be sanctified in truth." *I consecrate myself to the Father for their sake.* He gave His whole person as an atonement on the Cross. His blood sanctified us and justified us. Our sanctification is the fruit and result of that sacrifice. "Now, we know the Spirit is at work in us to complete His work. And we all, with unveiled face, beholding the glory of the Lord, are being transformed into the same image from one degree of glory to another" (2 Corinthians 3:18).

It's here that we have to make a distinction in that word *sanctification.* There is the sanctification we've been addressing, which is a calling out, a declaring holy, a setting aside, a making of one purpose, and that is to serve God. Then there is a sanctification we understand Scripture to teach, which is progressive. That is, for the rest of our lives, we will be doing what? Becoming more like Christ, as we just read in 2 Corinthians. We "are being transformed into the same image from one degree of glory to another." This is a daily, hourly, moment-by-moment, progressive sanctification, becoming more like Christ, mortifying the sin which is in our own body.

Leviticus 8 and Leviticus 14 are interesting contrasts that show us how a sinner is unified in the sanctifying and the washing and cleansing power of our Lord. In Leviticus 8, verses 22 through 24, we have the consecration of a priest to his work. "Then he presented the other ram, the ram of ordination, and Aaron and his sons laid their hands on the head of the ram." Why would they lay their hands on the head of the ram? They're identifying with that ram. By laying their hands upon it, their sins are transferred, thus giving us the concept of *scapegoating*. They lay their hands on the head of the ram.

"And he killed it, and Moses took some of its blood and put it on the lobe of Aaron's right ear and on the thumb of his right hand and on the big toe of his right foot" (Leviticus 8:23). They lay their hands on the ram, and the ram which then embodies their sin representatively is killed. Christ represented us because He took on flesh, and in taking on flesh, He went to the Cross and was killed for an atonement of sin.

And then, the blood of this ram was placed on the priest's ear and his thumb of his right hand and his big toe. Why would the blood be placed on these? Because it is with the ear that the priest hears the pleas of his people. It is with the hand that the priest serves in the ministry of God. It is with the feet that a priest then travels doing the business of the people before God as he travels back and forth doing his ministry before the Lord.

"Then Moses took some of the anointing oil and of the blood that was on the altar and sprinkled it on Aaron and his garments . . ." (Leviticus 8:30). Interesting to note here, the oil and blood are mingled—are mingled! The oil and the blood. Oil most often represents the anointing of the Holy Spirit, and blood represents atonement. These are mingled together and are put upon the priest Aaron and his garments ". . . and also on his sons and his sons' garments. So he consecrated Aaron and his garments. . . ." This anointing of oil and blood separates these men out as priests. It consecrates them. It sanctifies them to a unique purpose in their lives. They are to serve no other purpose except to be priests before the people and before God.

In Leviticus 14, it's awfully curious that we read in verse 2 and then 13 through 18 some similar language. "This shall be the law of the leprous person for the day of his cleansing. He shall be brought to the priest. . . ." So, now we're talking about an action not on the priest but upon the leper.

> And he shall kill the lamb in the place where they kill the sin of-
> fering and the burnt offering, in the place of the sanctuary. For the
> guilt offering, like the sin offering, belongs to the priest; it is most
> holy. The priest shall take some of the blood of the guilt offering,
> and the priest shall put it on the lobe of the right ear of him who is
> to be cleansed and on the thumb of his right hand and on the big
> toe of his right foot. Then the priest shall take some of the log of

oil and pour it into the palm of his own left hand and dip his right finger in the oil that is in his left hand and sprinkle some oil with his finger seven times before the LORD. (Leviticus 14:13–18)

The same ritual that is used for the consecration of a priest is used for the cleansing of a sinner. What is done to the priest is done to cleanse the sinner.

And so we find here in these two rituals an identification of the leper who needs to be clean with the priest who is consecrated and made clean. We find here symbolically blood that is applied in the same way. You would imagine a leper would be so far from the ceremonies of a priest that you wouldn't even be able to make a comparison, but yet we find an identical description of a ceremony that is used for the priest and the leper, and we find our Christ who is crucified to be in union with His people, for as Paul said, "I am crucified with Christ. I have died with Christ, and it is He who lives in me." Hebrews 10:10: "And by that will we have been sanctified through the offering of the body of Jesus Christ once for all." Isn't this a glorious picture of our sanctification, of our being sealed in Christ?

But it doesn't end there. Our sanctification, be it the initial sanctification or progressive sanctification, we first acknowledge is solely the work of God. Paul says that what God has begun in us, He'll be faithful to complete. It is God in us, coming to us to work and to will for His good pleasure. In Hebrews 12, however, it teaches that God isn't calling us just to wait and see, because He says, "If there is any child of God who is not in conformity with God's will, God will discipline him." God will discipline him to bring him back into the path of righteousness. He doesn't simply allow His children to walk and to stray.

And so, we recognize there is something about the activity of man that we are to be held in account for, that though it is the Spirit of God at work in us to produce sanctification, there is something in the activity of man that is a part of our sanctifying process. We seem to be either like clay in the Master's hand as He forms and shapes it to be Christ like, or we can be like granite. But granite still will be shaped and formed. It will just be formed with a chisel and a hammer. And so, we choose to progress in life, either in obedience to the Father, where we are shaped and changed day by day, or in resistance to the work of the Father, but still being shaped and changed day by day—except now under the stern hand of a disciplining and loving Father. Either way, we will be changed if we belong to Christ.

"Since you have been born again, not of perishable seed but of imperishable, through the living and abiding word of God" (1 Peter 1:23). Here we find the source of our change. We are born not of a seed of man, not of anything that is perishable, but of a seed which is imperishable in the Word of God. Why mention the Word of God? Because that is where Christ has taken us. They are sanctified through the truth. What is the truth? The Word of God.

George Whitefield, a great Baptist minister of many years ago, said, "The renewal of our natures is a work of great importance. It's not done in a day. We have not only a new house to build up, but an old one to tear down" (906). The work of sanctification involves the mortification of sin in our flesh. F. F. Bruce, a great Bible scholar, said, "Sanctification is glory begun, and glory is sanctification completed" (81). I think those are wonderful summations, but yet do they give us a full understanding of the progress of Christian life, the progress of Christian holiness, and how that is accomplished?

We have to take great care here because our own categories of thinking would lend us to a theology of works that cause sanctification, and that is error. We are *not* here advocating that our work, our actions of righteousness, cause us to be sanctified. That is not it at all. Sanctification still remains only the work of the Holy Spirit. "And we all, with unveiled face, beholding the glory of the Lord, are being transformed into the same image from one degree of glory to another" (2 Corinthians 3:18). We know transformation only happens by the Spirit of Christ.

When the eyes are enlightened, faith is present, and then truth is lived. Our present living is to be in constant union and communion with Christ. That is how it will be effected. We are sanctified by truth. And how is it we are sanctified by truth? By remaining in truth, which keeps Christ before us each and every day. That is what is meant by John 17:17, when He says, "Sanctify them in the truth; Your word is truth." Feeding on truth in faith transforms our lives by changing our lives, by burdening our conscience, by transforming our will. This is the means of transformation, and there is no other.

You will not take another path no matter how virtuous it may seem, no matter how high the ethic that you adhere to. There is no conduct good enough to sanctify you. In the eyes of men, you may be a very moral person, you may be a very gentle person, but you have not become in the image of Christ unless it is through the Word of truth God has acted upon you.

The Westminster Confession 13:1 says we are sanctified by "virtue of Christ's death and resurrection, by His Word and Spirit dwelling in them." ". . .God chose you as the firstfruits to be saved, through sanctification by the Spirit and belief in the truth" (2 Thessalonians 2:13). What are we referring to whenever we say "belief in the truth"? The Word of God. Where else would we find truth to believe? By the Spirit and belief in the truth.

"He will present us holy and blameless through the washing of water unto the Word" (Ephesians 5:26). Contrary to those who say we have nothing to do with our sanctification, there are those who would say that we are somehow idle, that we are simply responsible to be aware and to give glory to God. We certainly commend giving glory to God, but nowhere does the Scripture call us to do nothing regarding our sanctification. For those who would say we have nothing to do with our sanctification except just simply to wait on God to make us holy in our living, we find that God's ordained means to make men's lives holy are the Scriptures themselves. That is what frees us from persistent sin and willfulness and makes us into the image of His Son.

Bernard of Clairvaux said, "He is not a Christian that thinks he is a finished Christian and is insensible how far he falls short. That man without doubt has never so much as begun to be renewed, nor did he ever taste what it is like to be a Christian" (905). Bernard of Clairvaux is simply saying, "Anyone who says he is complete in Christ and cares not a whit about his progress in the Christian faith has not even begun a journey in Christ, and probably doesn't even know what it means to be a Christian."

Therefore, against the argument of God's direct work of progressive sanctification, we would argue that God works indirectly through His Word. The means that God has appointed for our sanctification is His Word. There is no other way. Not hymns, not good works, not ministries, not attendance, not holding or hosting or teaching or providing money for any sort of ministry or study anywhere, not the support of missionaries, not even new seat covers. None of that will sanctify us. Only the Word sanctifies us. Only the Word because God has appointed that as the means for sanctification, and nothing else.

The means that is still not and never shall be any reward for the works of righteousness, but is the vehicle for the transformation of the will from which flows the works of righteousness and unrighteousness, is the Word. Scripture speaks of babes, young men, and old men in terms of faith, indicating progress and motion. Peter exhorts his people, "But grow in the grace and knowledge of our Lord and Savior Jesus Christ" (2 Peter 3:18).

The exhortation of Peter is growth. How do you grow? Do you grow by imagination? Do you grow by good intention? Do you grow by hanging out with Christians who don't curse and smoke and drink and commit all those vices? No! You grow through the Word. Pay no attention to the Word, and you have no growth. You have good moral and ethical behavior in the eyes of men. Perhaps you can speak a good religious talk, but there is no true growth of the soul nor a changing of the mind and the will to be like that of Christ unless you are in the Word.

My daughters have tick marks on their doorframe that mark their growth over the years. Each one marks continued progress and height, which young people strive after. There is, however, a time that comes when they back up to the door, and this year's tick mark is the same as last year's tick mark. What does that mean? That means that they have stopped growing. The progress that was seen has ceased.

As you observe the tick marks of your own spiritual growth, would you say you are seeing a progressive change in your becoming like Christ year after year? Are you growing in holiness? Are you being more and more sanctified because of the truth which is changing your life? Or as you look back over the past five or ten years, have you been more interested in holding on to those habits, those ideas, those activities that you somehow captured and learned to enjoy years ago and have preserved rather than changing to become like Christ? Are you experiencing a stunted growth or a progressive growth? You won't grow by wishing it. You're not going to grow through your works, but you will grow through faith that feeds on God's Word and acts by the Spirit's power on your mind and on your heart.

Is that hard to understand? Is it hard to grasp these two uses of the word *sanctification*? Think of it this way: God calls us His people by sanctifying us and separating us out from the world. In this sanctification, we are known by God before the foundations of the world, and so we do nothing as it is all God's will. He effects this sanctification through the blood atonement of Christ, and so we are sanctified and separated out to Him. Secondly, God calls those people to be changed progressively by faith. Our eyes are illumined to see the truth of the Scripture. We're able to see our Savior, we're able to hear our Father speak to us, but again, it is God who is at work to transform us. And He effects this sanctification through His Word which is truth.

Augustine said, "Where I found truth there I found my God who is truth itself" (187). Again, 2 Corinthians 3:18: "We are beholding the glory of the Lord with unveiled faces." Where do we behold that glory? In the Scriptures which are truth. There is where we find the standard that God has given us.

Again I'm drawn to the teaching of Marcus Rainsford who preached on sanctification in 1885 in several sermons. He said, "What is the standard of Christian holiness? The same image. Don't let us be led away by what one hears and reads now about holiness. Some talk about being holy according to their conscience. Is a man's conscience the standard of holiness? The same image. Is it walking according to our own light? If the light that is in you be darkness, how great is that darkness. No, His image is the standard. Here is a standard, and it does not change. It is perfection. The image of God, and we are called to it, and shall attain unto it" (Straight Paths, 155). Is that sanctification anywhere else except to be found in the Word? It is through the Word. It is the Word. Our sanctification doesn't consist in grasping some formal or mystical doctrine, except as we find doctrine in Scripture. By this, we are sanctified by the Spirit of God through our feeding on the Word.

Martyn Lloyd-Jones has these three points of reflection, and I've reversed the order. The first, which was his last, is that we have a trouble with our will when it comes to sanctification. We struggle with self-delusion here. We believe our whole will is in it, and we simply can't progress. If the Spirit of Christ resides in us, that excuse is patently false. We can progress, so reflect on your own life, and then as you decide that you can't move past this, you can't get past this besetting sin, you can't set down this habit, or you can't progress and become better in this way or that way, you need to know the issue is not that you can't, because God is able to do all things in you through Christ. It is a problem with the will. The will simply doesn't will it to be done.

Secondly, our primary need in the progress of sanctification is not more power for sanctification. It is not calling down, "Spirit, give us more power for sanctification." It is light and knowledge and instruction. Do we in asking for more power believe God has not given us enough power in the Spirit already, that He somehow has given us a measure of the Holy Spirit that is inadequate for what He has called us to do, and only when we ask for more of His Spirit are we able to progress? It can't be. So much of what people are asking for from a pastor in his preaching is motivation rather than instruction. They want to be somehow empowered, but what they need is to be illumined. They need to know. They don't need some sort of a pep talk. They don't need more of what God has already supplied. They need to be convicted so that they have a will that is changed in order to live it. They often want people to fan the flame rather than explain the truth, but the flame is only properly fanned by the Holy Spirit who blows on the flames ignited by the truth from God's Word. Scripture warns of our seeking to have our ears tickled, and for good reason. Tickled ears don't shape the will or transform life. They just leave us giddy.

Third and finally, sanctification is not primarily an experience in the Christian life. It's an application of truth to ourselves. We must first hear, then receive, then apply the truth. Giving ourselves to a life of study in God's Word gives us the ability to discern what is true and what is false. Hebrews 5:14: "But solid food is for the mature, for those who have their powers of discernment trained by constant practice to distinguish good from evil." Isn't this the foundation of Paul's prayer for the Ephesians when he says in Ephesians 1:18, "I pray that the eyes of your hearts may be enlightened, that you may know what is the hope to which He has called you, what are the riches of His glorious inheritance in the saints. . . ." The eyes of the heart illumined? These were the prayers of the apostles for the believers, that they would understand, and understanding, be convicted by the Holy Spirit, not themselves, and in understanding and being convicted, have their wills shaped and changed to be more like Christ.

Sanctification is not a practice of getting rid of this sin or that sin. It's being rightly related to God and submitting to His work as we daily spend time in His Word. How are you doing in sanctification? Are you willfully resisting what God is doing in your life, or are you clay? Granite or clay? You actually can be one of three. Either you aren't a child of God, and nothing is going on, or you're a child of God like a piece of granite where He is taking a chisel and a hammer and painfully sculpting the image of His Son in your life, or you're like clay, soft and pliable, being shaped gently over time as God continues to open the Scriptures to your understanding.

Are you becoming more like Christ by setting aside what you were yesterday to become what He has called you to be tomorrow? For tomorrow you will not be the same as you were yesterday if in fact God has His hand upon you for His purposes Are you becoming like Christ? You must. It's not a wish that it could be. It *is* to be because that is what is happening while we remain here. Measure your tick marks. Consider in your own heart whether you're growing in Christ.

15

One With the Lord

(John 17:21)

"I do not ask for these only, but also for those who will believe in Me through their word, that they may all be one, just as You, Father, are in Me, and I in You, that they also may be in Us, so that the world may believe that You have sent Me. The glory that You have given Me I have given to them, that they may be one even as We are one, I in them and You in Me, that they may become perfectly one, so that the world may know that You sent Me and loved them even as You loved Me." (John 17:20–23)

A ARON THE HIGH PRIEST of the Israelites went before God in prayer "So Aaron shall bear the names of the sons of Israel in the breast piece of judgment on his heart, when he goes into the Holy Place, to bring them to regular remembrance before the LORD" (Exodus 28:29). And we imagine that just as Aaron bore the names of the sons of Israel in the breast piece he wore as he came before the Lord God in prayer, just as Aaron provided an early picture for us of that high priestly work, so Jesus, who has all of our names inscribed upon His own breast piece over His heart carries us before God, likewise that God the Father would have us in regular remembrance before Him. Jesus Christ makes continual intercession for us, Hebrews teaches. Continual intercession. We are ever before God by name as our Lord Jesus Christ makes intercession for us, even today—even in this moment. Even if our minds wander from our gathering for worship, our Lord continually prays for us, perhaps even praying that we would have a disciplined mind when it comes to worship and be able to remain engaged in the worship of God our Father.

That prayer for us which is given by Jesus is heard by the Father and answered. That is the point worth making. Our Lord does not pray in vain. Our Lord's prayers are answered. In verse 20, Jesus testifies of His own unity with the Father and the Father's unity with Him. And then, He prays that that unity would also be displayed among His people. We can be assured that His prayers are not only heard, but they are accomplished, and He is praying for our unity, unity with one another, unity with both Himself, and with the Father.

Union with Christ, by means of the Holy Spirit is not a peripheral matter. It's not an addendum or a footnote to our faith. It's not a peripheral matter in biblical theology, although it is widely neglected. It's a key thought in the Lord's teaching. The Lord just doesn't simply mention it as some sort of a warm correspondence in passing. Instead, the Lord emphasizes this idea of unity, this idea of our unity, the idea of His unity with the Father. In fact, the whole idea of the Trinity is one of unity, and we are drawn into that theology of unity. But I would dare say that in most Christian minds, even though genuinely converted, there is an absence of thought when it comes to the topic of unity.

James Montgomery Boice points out the commentator James Stewart's observation that "Union is the heart of Paul's religion." What a profound statement for an idea that escapes most of us that at the heart of Paul's entire theology is the idea of union. Well then, that necessarily implies that if we haven't grasped this idea of union, if it is indeed at the heart of Paul's theology, then we really haven't grasped the heart of Paul's theology. Instead of union being on the periphery, it seems that most of our knowledge is in fact on the periphery and we've missed the core of Paul's teaching, which is the idea of unity.

Most emphatic of all in biblical scholars would be A. W. Pink, who said, "The subject of spiritual union is the most important, the most profound, and yet the most blessed of any that is set forth in the sacred Scriptures, and yet, sad to say, there is hardly any which is now more generally neglected. The very expression 'spiritual union' is unknown in most Christian circles" (7).

Before I proceed into an explanation of Christian unity, we may pause only long enough for you to ask yourself and answer honestly, *Do you have a fully developed theology in your own mind of Christian unity with one another and also with the Lord?*

When we say we believe in the communion of the saints, what would be your explanation of that which you profess at nearly every church gathering, this communion of the saints, this unity of the saints? If all churches truly held to that as the Scripture teaches, we would never hear of a church split, ever. Never. How can there be a church split when we are living according to the Scripture's teaching of communion of the saints? How can we read in 1 John of that communion of the saints which is characterized by genuine selfless, and self-abasing love and yet there be a wedge between people in Christ's church? The wedge is not of God because love is what characterizes the people of God.

Nearly every commentary begins a discussion on our spiritual union with Christ by bringing forward the passage in John 15, the word picture of the vine and the branches. In John 15, just the first two verses we read, "I am the true vine, and My Father is the vinedresser. Every branch in Me that does not bear fruit He takes away, and every branch that does bear fruit He prunes, that it may bear more fruit."

The pastor Maurice Roberts, a pastor of the Free Church of Scotland who still ministers in Scotland remarks that, "All our spiritual life, if we have any, must come from the Lord Jesus Christ. It flows from Him to us as believers by the gracious activity of His Holy Spirit. The *only* evidence of real Christian faith is to be seen in the character we possess. Where Christ is in a man's soul, the fruits of love, peace, and holiness will be visible" (8, emphasis mine).

Herein lies the great danger of not listening carefully to Jesus in John, chapter 15. When Jesus speaks of the branch that doesn't bear fruit, He is speaking of someone who will profess to be a Christian, and who is in all likelihood believes that they are a Christian but who is not actually in union with Christ, as evidenced by the lack of fruit of the Spirit. That is a sobering thought, I believe, because the teaching of the vine and the branches is that the branches which are grafted into the vine receive life as it flows up from the vine, or the trunk, into the branches, and though there be many branches, they all receive life from that same trunk.

And so, that same trunk or that same vine that pushes life out into the branches produces various fruits, but those fruits must be of a particular kind—we call them the fruits of the Spirit—if in fact they can find their source in the Lord Jesus Christ. We all produce fruits. Believer and unbeliever alike produce fruits. So, fruit production is not in itself evidence of salvation for there are fruits that are unrighteous. But there are some particular fruits, and the Scripture doesn't leave us to guess. God gives us particular information that we can be a discerning people.

It's not necessarily what is spoken by the lips, for there are many we read in Scripture who will profess with their lips that Jesus is Lord, but even among them, some will not have those fruits that bear testimony of the truth of their confession. Particularly heartbreaking is that many believe that in simply saying they are believers, and by hanging around long enough, and be doing enough Christian work, that they are believers. Such were the Pharisees, such were the Sadducees, and such have been many religious people in many religious vocations. Some of the finest preachers and theologians I imagine we are going to find not in heaven but in hell because they simply are not in possession of the Spirit of Christ. "On that day many will say to Me," (I'm forced to emphasize the word many) ". . . many will say to Me, 'Lord, Lord, did we not prophesy in Your name, and cast out demons in Your name, and do many mighty works in Your name?' And then will I declare to them, 'I never knew you; depart from Me, you workers of lawlessness'" (Matthew 7:22, 23). In Matthew 7, Jesus warns every one of us to look to our own lives, to conduct an inventory, a spiritual inventory of our own character to see if our assurance is in fact real.

Jesus tells us to take heed of those whom we are in fellowship with—not to their resume, as many a pastor and theologian as I've already mentioned along with philanthropists will actually be in hell, but to their character. Is their character like Christ? Are they manifesting Christlike virtue in their lives? Are the fruits of the Spirit present? When they open their mouths to speak, do you hear peace, and love, and contentment, and building up in Christ, or instead do you hear cynicism, and plots, and disgruntlement, and disenchantment, and gossip against the very Body of Christ?

Roberts comments, "Where Christ is in a man's soul, the fruits of love, peace, and holiness will be visible. The Holy Spirit is not so much given to impart gifts to men as to create in them a likeness to Christ" (9). Oh, there are spiritual gifts. We wouldn't deny that, but that primary vocation of the Spirit is to transform us into the likeness of Christ, to make us like Christ. So, consequently, there must be—there *must* be evidences of transformation. And what are the evidences of transformation? The fruits of the Spirit are the evidences. Those are the fruits of God's vine.

But what of, we might ask, what of this work? What of this duty? What of this office? What of this tenure of teaching? What of this vocational calling to ministry? What of this time or this family legacy? What of this and what of that? None of it answers the question. The fruits of the Spirit in the life of the individual are the evidences of the activity of the Spirit of Christ in the soul of an individual person. There are no other. We cannot neglect the manifestation of these fruits. We cannot neglect them because they do distinguish us from the world.

All these other traits, the cynicism, the plots, the disgruntlement, the disenchantment, the gossip, what is different from that in the place that you work which is completely secular? Nothing. Nothing at all. These fruits will be present in some degree in every believer. Now, we need to acknowledge that for those who are young in faith, for the immature believer or the weak believer, the fruits will be imperfectly present. The fruits may in fact be weak, and they may in fact be infrequently seen, as the war that wages within between the flesh and the spirit has just begun in a young or an immature believer. And so, their flesh, and their desire, and their habits of the flesh still have ascendancy over the spirit. But the flesh has already been cut off from its root, and so it begins to bleed out and die as the spirit overcomes and overwhelms with the result of the mortification of sin in the flesh.

And so, even in the immature believer, we can begin to see those early evidences of the work of the Spirit of Christ which will grow and which will gain. So, what of the one who appears so godly in youth, but seems to have lost something in older years? As life begins to close in upon an individual, they find themselves leaning not upon the resources of God, but turning again to the world from whence they came because it is there that they draw their comfort.

Always remember the fruits are expressions of the character of Christ into whose image we are being shaped. How can we negotiate that? How can we cut a corner on that? How can we somehow soften those words? We are either being shaped into the character of Christ or we are not. And if we are, there are certain characteristics and traits that are indicative to that And if they are not present, it is not occurring.

Now, we want to find a middle road, and the Church has sought one by having backsliding Christians as some middle ground or third place for man to be. But there is no description of such a place in Scripture. Now, we do know that there are seasons of life where people may struggle mightily, but will not Christ gain victory even then?

The first petition in verse 21 in Jesus' prayer: ". . . that they may be one. . . ." That we may all be one. That is, that there will be a unity among believers. Any hope for unity must have something tangible that serves the whole people together. In our creeds, we profess that we believe in the communion of the saints, but without actual union with Christ there is no communion of the saints. There is no unity among us if there is no unity with me and with you in Christ. We can't build a community that is Christian if we don't first have a unity with Christ.

In Philip Ryken's book titled, *The Communion of the Saints*, he comments, "The word *communion* can't even be spelled without *union*. In order for people to have communion with one another, they must be connected by some common bond. For example, motorcycle enthusiasts are united by their love for a Harley-Davidson or some other motorcycle brand. Basketball players are united because of the uniforms which they wear. The teamsters by the labors that they perform. Family members are united by flesh and blood. The United States are united by a common Constitution. And the same is true for Christians. There is no communion of the saints apart from a union in Christ" (15).

The Westminster Confession teaches us in chapter 26 that "All saints, that are united to Jesus Christ their Head, by His Spirit, and by faith, have fellowship with Him in His graces, sufferings, death, resurrection, and glory. . . ." Here we find represented the Scriptural teaching of the nature of our union with Christ. It's not a sentimental attachment. It's not simply saying, "Oh, I just love Jesus so much," and then singing a song about it. Our union with Christ is built upon very tangible and very real historic events in the life of Christ in which we enter spiritually with Him.

Paul teaches that in Romans 6, verses 3 to 5.

> Do you not know that all of us who have been baptized into Christ Jesus were baptized into His death? We were buried therefore with Him by baptism into death, in order that, just as Christ was raised from the dead by the glory of the Father, we too might walk in newness of life. For if we have been united with Him in a death like His, we shall certainly be united with Him in a resurrection like His.

We who were once of the world and the flesh are united with Christ in His death, and we will be united with Him in His resurrection. Spiritually, that is already fact. We're united with Him in His death and united with Him in His resurrection. This is our bond and the formation of our fellowship—unity in Christ, in His death and in His resurrection.

We may have come to Christ as many people, but we converge in Christ as one. You may have come to Christ as an individual from a certain place in life, but as you come to Christ, and as I come to Christ, and as another comes to Christ, when we find ourselves in Christ, we converge there as one people—one people in Christ.

There is a death of the old, there is a rebirth of the new. Our fellowship with one another is dependent on and flows directly from our fellowship, that is, our union with Christ. And this union is so often referred to in Scripture as being in Christ. It's simply put that way. When you read *in Christ*, here we're talking about our union with Him. It's assumed by the writer that already we're beginning to come to an understanding of our union with Christ. And so, the shorthand is simply to say *in Christ*. Such as, in 2 Corinthians 5:17, "Therefore, if anyone is in Christ, he is a new creation. . . ."

Philippians 1:1 is addressed to ". . .all the saints in Christ Jesus who are at Philippi,. . . ." Galatians 3:28 describes that union this way: "There is neither Jew nor Greek, there is neither slave nor free, there is no male and female, for you are all one in Christ Jesus." A unity of the people in Christ Jesus—again and again Scripture frames the teaching with our union in Christ. It's common, and it's foundational to the gospel.

Some might even say, and it wouldn't be an exaggeration, that the idea of our unity with Christ might even be said to *be* the gospel expression, for we are united with Him, remember, in His death and in His resurrection. The proclamation of atonement—the proclamation of resurrection. Unity is the frame in which the gospel is set. When we hang a beautiful portrait of the gospel upon our soul's walls, isn't it framed with the idea of unity? Unity with Christ and unity with one another.

John Murray observed that our union with Christ "is not simply *a* step in the application of redemption. It underlies every step of the application of redemption. Union with Christ is really the central truth of the whole doctrine of salvation." Appealing to none other than the venerable John Calvin himself where he explained, "We must understand that as long as Christ remains outside of us and we are separated from Him, all that He has suffered and done for the salvation of the human race remains useless and of no value for us. All that He possesses is nothing to us until we grow into one Body with Him."

In the Lord's prayer, John, chapter 17, we find an assurance however in verse 21. Remember, when Jesus prays, His prayer is answered. He does not pray in vain. What He asked of the Father is accomplished, and He asked of the Father that we would be one. And so, we can be assured that those who are in Christ are in fact one. This is not an ideal that we simply are shooting for or hoping for perhaps after the resurrection. This is Christ's prayer which is accomplished now. It is accomplished. I'm not saying to you that it ought to be. I'm saying to you that it *is* accomplished now, which is all the more reason for our discernment of those who are in possession of the gifts of the Spirit.

Although we are one, we can observe this prayer doesn't mean we are all alike without distinction. We look around, and we say, "Well, if I'm being shaped into the character of Christ, why do all of us seem to be so different?" We observe that we are different. We observe that Christ's prayer is accomplished. We observe that there is a spiritual unity between us in Christ, and that we are in fact becoming like Christ by virtue of the manifestation of the gifts of the Spirit, and so we acknowledge that unity is true even while there is diversity among the people.

But isn't that the doctrine of the Trinity itself? There is unity in the Godhead between the Father, and the Son, and the Holy Spirit, and yet there is a diversity among the persons, the Father, and the Son, and the Holy Spirit. Can't we see that as an observable truth within the Body? Perhaps our lack of ability to grasp the Trinity is because we haven't even grasped ourselves as being united and yet diverse in Christ.

So, though we have distinctions among us, and though we would recognize that there may be many denominations, none of that will destroy the truth of the communion of the saints because it isn't our present circumstances that make us one; it's our union with Christ, and it's His union with His Church. The unity of the Church extends into the past. It's connected with the election of God by men to the salvation of Christ.

In Ephesians 1:3 to 5 we read, "Blessed be the God and Father of our Lord Jesus Christ, who has blessed us in Christ with every spiritual blessing in the heavenly places, even as He chose us in Him. . . ." Here we go again—*in Him*. We are in Christ. ". . . even as He chose us in Him before the foundation of the world, that we should be holy and blameless before Him. In love He predestined us for adoption as sons through Jesus Christ, according to the purpose of His will. . . ." So, as far back as we can go, the purpose of God has been our salvation in Christ.

The great pastor, preacher, Donald Grey Barnhouse explains this. "The first work performed by the Holy Spirit in our behalf was to elect us members of Christ's Body. In His eternal decrees, God determined that He should not be solitary forever, that out of the multitude of sons of Adam, a vast host would become sons of God, partakers of the divine nature, and conformed to the image of the Lord Jesus Christ. This company, the fullness of Him who fills all in all would become sons of the new birth but members of the Body by baptism of the Holy Spirit" (391).

Our new birth is pictured somewhat even in the incarnation, as God, who is Spirit, in the second Person of the Trinity became man, took on flesh and became man. And yet, there was no violence done to the second Person of the Trinity. Christ remains fully God and a full participating Member of the Trinity, and yet also fully man. Fully man, not handicapped in His manhood. He was fully man, and yet in becoming fully man, He never became any less God. When we are in Christ, we are a new creature in Christ. We don't become divine, but the life of God is made to dwell in us and bring us into union with Him through His own life. It is His own life that dwells in us.

God shows us what this means in Scripture in several pictures, and I'll just touch on them to help us understand. In Ephesians 5, we have the picture of marriage. It's one of the most powerful examples of unity when we approach marriage. Even if we never marry ourselves, we certainly know of marriage and observe marriage. We've seen good marriages, we've seen bad marriages, and we have seen everything in between. But it remains a powerful example of unity—the union of a man and a woman to become one as husband and wife, a union founded on love with harmony of heart and mind and sharing of life's goals and ambitions, a reflection of the Christian's attitude toward God, that we should love Him with all of our heart, soul, mind, and strength.

There is an economy of function in the relationship even as the two are equals in Christ. In marriage, a man and a woman enter the church as two people with two names. They leave as a couple with one name. In the morning before the marriage, they may both buy and sell their property as they wish, but after the marriage, what's mine is yours, and what's yours is mine. Before marriage, they floated through social circles that may never have intersected one another, but after marriage, the couple now as one is supposed to be established in a community together, to share a life, to share work, to share friendships, to be one in unit, a perfect unit in perfect harmony one with another. And yet, there remains two distinct individuals.

Ephesians 1:22 and 23 gives us the example of the human body itself. God has put all things under Jesus' feet and made Him the Head of the Body, we are told. Colossians 1:18, He is the Head of the Body, which is described as the Church. In 1 Corinthians 12:12 through 27 we find the fullest development of the image of a body. "For just as the body is one and has many members, and all the members of the body, though many, are one body, so it is with Christ. For in one Spirit we were all baptized into one body. . . . Now you are the body of Christ and individually members of it."

The head of a body thinks for the body, provides for it, rules it, receives nourishment for it. The head leads the body by seeing for the body by looking in a true direction. It is a sad state of paralysis when a body will not respond or listen or obey the head.

The vine and the branches are meant to show that our union with Christ isn't static but fruitful, and that there is one vine though there are many branches. And then, finally, Scripture describes our union in terms of a building, a building in which we are the building blocks, or the bricks, and Christ is the Cornerstone where the whole structure is joined together.

When we take the Lord's Supper together, don't we see there a figure of our unity together—one cup and one loaf of bread together at this one table? Can it have any fuller meaning than one that is tied to the realities of union? Christ feeds us with His body. And as the bread would be incorporated into our flesh which we consume with our mouth so Christ is also united by faith with our spirit. His blood sealed the covenant of salvation for us, the covenant of grace, and as we take the cup of His blessing, aren't we acknowledging that we have also died with Him and His blood is associated and mingled with our own?

In the Church in the wilderness, the worshipers brought an animal. It was slaughtered to atone for their sin. It was cut up and made fit for burning, and it became smoke that was smelled by God, we're told, as a fragrant aroma. Smoke, as it ascends, mingles with the glory cloud of God, and in that we find unity as it hovers there above the Tabernacle in the wilderness. By faith, we eat the bread and drink the cup and understand our unity at this table through our union with Christ, who is Himself the meal which we consume.

16

In Us, United by Christ with God

(John 17:21)

"I do not ask for these only, but also for those who will believe in me through their word, that they may all be one, just as you, Father, are in me, and I in you, that they also may be in us, so that the world may believe that you have sent me. The glory that you have given me I have given to them, that they may be one even as we are one, I in them and you in me, that they may become perfectly one, so that the world may know that you sent me and loved them even as you loved me." (John 17:20–21)

Has there ever been so great and so magnificent a theological truth as our unity with God? Union with God! Let those words hang in the air for just a moment. Our unity with God. Not a philosophical unity where we just agree on some things together. Union, spiritual union with God the Father. We in union with God.

And yet, as great and magnificent and wonderful as that is, it probably is also one of the most neglected areas in Christian understanding. It shouldn't seem like a small matter that the transcendent God of eternity would take us into union with Himself. We can't become confused in thinking that our being united with God somehow makes us God. That would be blasphemy. So, it's not as simple as saying, "A plus B equals C, therefore we are God because if we're in union with God and He is God, we must be God." That is blasphemy.

As we continue the subject of unity, I have to tell you that this is probably one of the, if not most misunderstood, and neglected subjects of the Scriptures and of the Gospels. That is tragic, because as we study the Bible together, we come across the many different ideas or themes or theologies, whether it's God's providence, whether it's concerning evangelism. And all of these, if you picture a great oak, are like leaves hanging there, and we sometimes find it so easy to describe every detail of a leaf. But how much harder is it to describe what it is that gives life to the oak itself?

We can describe the bark, we can describe the meat of the tree, we can describe the fruit or the leaf of the tree, but what of that which gives the tree life? How do we describe that? And we find ourselves dealing in this area of unity and particularly of the Spirit's function in unity with something like that before us.

In the environment in which I work at Fort Jackson, there are a number of people of many different faiths. And there are Methodists, and there are Catholics, and there are Seventh Day Adventists, and there are some that I dare not mention. There are Presbyterians and Baptists of many different associations and flavors and colors.

During the Christmas season, it's interesting to hear the conversations and to realize the sources of many of our traditions. I've had a number of people come to me and mention this tradition or that tradition, and there are several, there are many.

We could do all of those things that every tradition under the sun has developed in the history of the Church, but I have to confess to you that I've come to the startling realization that for us to really understand them, I probably would need to bring a Catholic priest in here to describe them for us and explain why it is they do the different things they do. And then, we need to decide whether we are Protestants or not, whether we want to adopt those traditions.

Now, lest we think they're innocuous, I need to let you know that Catholic priests are celebrating to the high heavens the adoption of Catholic tradition by the Protestant Church, and they talk about it a lot. They see it as part and parcel to the re-assimilation of a people who they see as simply venturing away from the Church. And the more we fall in love with Catholic tradition, the more excited they become.

And now, there is this Manhattan document that is floating around about how we need to join forces on issues such as abortion and social justice. So, if we work together in social areas, if we celebrate on the Lord's day essentially the same, that only leaves one or two issues before us. What do we do with the Pope and a couple of other ideas? But if our worship looks the same, and if our outside ministry is the same, then where are the distinctions because we are a people who apparently have lost our Protestant theology? Somewhere along the way we laid it down. We began to observe a lot of things, but we laid our belief down. We just believe some things, but as they are associated with what we do, we divorced ourselves from solid theology and relegated it to the halls of seminaries where people who actually have an interest in the Word are supposed to go.

Let me encourage you to feel some conviction about this. It's not just a thing, and it's not the pastors' issue. It's an issue with the Church, all churches. There are churches who consider accurate theology a vice, something that is divisive. Imagine that the truth about God is divisive! The only thing divisive about it is dividing the people of God from those who are not the people of God because the people of God cherish God's Word. Are these hard words? Yes, they are.

So how are we to understand union? George Newton warned, "Let us tremble to consider what a weight of duty and obedience lies upon us to walk answerably to it, and how exactly pure and holy they should be who are in any sense in God, in the Father, and in the Son" (317). Our union with God is not simply a footnote. Our union with God is not simply words which we use like platitudes to say, "Oh yes, we're very important to God." Union with God, a spiritual indwelling by God, calls us to the highest accountability, the highest degree of accountability because what we are doing affects our heavenly Father. We are in union with God. Is there any higher calling to duty and obedience?

In the first part of verse 21, Jesus prays that His followers would be one just as He had already prayed in verse 11 the words, "Holy Father, keep them in your name, which you have given me, that they may be one, even as we are one." Jesus' emphasis on unity in the fellowship of believing saints, such unity as He was emphasizing has a practical effect, of course. It's not without some application. A call for unity has consequences.

We can't simply say, "Yes, we are one in the Spirit, we are one in the Lord," and then walk about in disunity. A people in union are able to direct all of their efforts and resources to the mission Christ has given them, the Church's mission of making disciples. A people who are not in unity have to expend energy and time and resources on peripheral matters, on solving issues, of answering complaints, of reconciling quarrels and disputes, of disciplining schismatics who would seek to come in and separate the people of God by bringing in some transient issue or matter.

If the people are dwelling in unity, then they can work with single minded purpose for what God has called the Church to do, but if there is disunity, then all of that energy is diffused out into other areas.

It's not just pragmatic though. It's not just a matter of us doing those things that God calls us to do. Unity among believers is also the testimony of believers. Unbelievers certainly understand this as they so often criticize the Church with the charge of hypocrisy because of the divisions and the infighting and the strife that is so apparent in so many Christian congregations. We'd call a man biting his own arm mad, but when we see the Body of Christ doing what they routinely do in biting themselves, we accept it as just part of church life.

When Jesus cast out demons and was accused of being one Himself because He seemed to have power over demons, He refuted the charge by pointing out how absurd it would be for Satan to work against his own cause by casting out his own demons, showing that even in the dominion of darkness, the dominion of the devil, a house divided against itself will not stand.

Even as we consider unity in the Church, we fall short of grasping the scope of Jesus' teaching. Marcus Rainsford says, "[Jesus] evidently means, as indeed the most full expressions, not only that all His believing people shall be united to one another, whether believers in old times or New Testament days, whether Jew or Gentile, whether believers in the past, present, or future, but that all should be united as children of the same heavenly family of which He Himself is the firstborn" (385).

All true believers are united to one heavenly family, a people who across the ages are being built into a single, unified, spiritual temple. The Church of Jesus Christ is formed of many different sizes, shapes, nationalities, circumstances, and yet formed together into a unified whole. It reaches back to the past and extends into the future as one Church.

As if this weren't enough for our own finite minds to struggle to understand, Jesus now prays further in that verse. He says, "that they may all be one, just as you, Father, are in me, and I in you. . . ." These two words "just as" connect our unity as being like the very nature of the unity of the Son with the Father.

Now, we have these two side by side—the unity of the people of God and the unity of the Son with the Father. And there they sit before us side by side—the unity of the Trinity, Christ as the second Person in the Trinity, and the unity of God's people. Jesus is saying that there is a sameness quality about those two. He said, "May they be one, may they be in unity, just as I am in you and you are in me," speaking here of Christ and the Father. There is a two-fold union between God and Christ. God is in Him and one with Him. Jesus shares a unity with the Father in the relationship of the Trinity.

Here we're open for error. In the third century, Sabellius wrestled with the idea of Trinity and went so far as to lose the distinction of the Persons in the Godhead. The result is called Sabellianism, or sometimes it's called Modalism. He taught that the appearance of Christ after the resurrection and the Holy Spirit were but modes of one God rather than three distinct Persons of the Trinity. It's like saying that God would have three faces on one Person.

The error in the opposite direction was Arianism, which came around 320 AD in Egypt. The Council of Nicea declared Arius of Alexandria a heretic and they exiled him. But Arianism became one of the greatest heresies of the Church and remains with us today in the teaching of the Mormon Church and the teaching of the Jehovah's Witness Church. Arius taught that God was too holy and too pure to appear on earth, and so Christ was created from nothing as the first and greatest creation. That makes Jesus' relation to the Father one that doesn't share in God's nature because He Himself was created.

These two errors, these two heresies take us to the extreme, and now we find ourselves, as I have often repeated, in the awkward position of having to remain in the center of biblical tension without going to either of the logical extremes. But Jesus is clearly saying that the Father is in Him and He is in the Father. So, there is what is called formally a *consubstantial unity*, meaning that the two, that is, the Father and the Son, are distinct Persons, but are of the same essence. So, there is a unity even though there are two distinct Persons.

The Scriptures try to help us to understand this by teaching us about marriage where it says that two people of two flesh become one flesh spiritually. If you're in a marriage, particularly one that is sanctified unto the Lord, then you know that as two people grow and they mature through the years, there is a sameness of the spirit that should develop so that their minds become as one, and their purposes become as one, and their lives become as one. That spiritual unity and spiritual purpose is symbolized in the physical acts of intimacy, but yet that is only symbolic of the spiritual unity that is to exist between two who are married. No longer two people living two lives, but one. And so it is with Christ.

There are two Persons of one essence—one essence in the Godhead though two distinct Persons. A husband and a wife remain two, and yet there seems to be in a married life the joining together in one essence of living. Therefore, Jesus is the same as the Father in His power, and in His will, and in His purpose. In that there is no division between them. What God the Father does, so God the Son does, as Jesus would say in John 5:19, "For whatever the Father does, that the Son does likewise."

As one, they are worshiped together and glorified. In John 5:23, Jesus says, "Whoever does not honor the Son does not honor the Father who sent Him." We can see throughout the Scriptures Jesus is teaching the personal union between God and Himself. He is called Emmanuel, which means God with us. In this Person, there are two natures, but one body in His Person.

Thomas Manton describes it, "It is so united that the human nature is the instrument. The hand is man's instrument not separated from the communion of the body or as a pen or a knife would be. It is man's instrument, but yet it is a part of himself. So is Christ's human nature joined to His divine nature and made use of as the great instrument in the work of redemption" (34). Here is the incarnation. When God came in that manger so many years ago, in the incarnation we had the joining to the nature of God the nature of man in perfect unity, and yet, in these two, there was still one Christ.

The example that is used by Manton is the example of a man's hand. This hand is an instrument. It's a tool for me to use; I would be a fool to think that it is somehow separate from me, and yet I can describe it as an instrument and a tool. It does seem to have function that the rest of the body may not participate in, and yet it remains a part of me. Not like this cup, which is also a tool. It holds water, and I would drink from it. And so, in my hand, I can use the cup, but it's not a part of me. Christ is in unity with the Father in much that same way. It's an organic unity that He has with the Father, and yet He remains one hundred percent God and one hundred percent man in the incarnation.

We learn of our union with Christ, the Author of that union being the Father Himself, who in Ephesians 1 reveals it was His purpose to unite all things to Him, things in heaven and things on earth. So, Paul is able to say, "It's not longer I who live, but Christ who lives in me." Our union with Jesus makes our bodies members of Christ as the hand belongs to a man.

I'd like to let you ponder that for just a moment because I don't think that we meditate upon deep spiritual truths. We hear them, we appreciate them, and we move on. Let me say that again. Our union with Christ makes our bodies members of Christ as the hand that belongs to a man. We're described as much as being parts of the Body of Christ in Scripture. We're described as being parts of one organic whole, and yet how many of us like a cancerous cell are off doing something else, our own thing, so that the Body lives with cancerous cells rather than being a unified whole, working and worshiping together?

Our lives and our resources are owed to Him as belonging to Him, and we should walk with our fellow believers as one, just as Christ and the Father are one. That is our model. Remember, He said, "Just as . . . just as." So, whatever harmony exists between the Father and the Son, that same harmony should exist between the people who are the Body of Christ.

As illustration, wouldn't we consider it mad for a person to injure his own body? And yet, how often does the Body of Christ turn on itself and do itself injury, and we accept it as just part of the Body politic, as part of the give and take of Christian life? We call it democracy in the Church as the Church turns and attacks itself in its own Body.

Then, Jesus takes us further in. Having laid our union with Him alongside His union with the Father to compare and understand the wonder of it, Jesus then tells us the goal of it all. "*. . . that they also may be in Us. . . .*" Here is a beautiful picture in Exodus 24 of really the first worship service. There, the people have come to the mountain where Moses is receiving the Ten Commandments, and there at the first service of worship, the Law is read, the people take vows that they will obey the Law, and then we are told that they are sprinkled with blood.

They are sprinkled with blood from the altar, and the altar itself is sprinkled with blood, the same blood. So as the altar is representative of God here at that mountain, and as the blood represents their atonement, we find here in that sameness of the sprinkling of that same blood a unity between the people as it's sprinkled upon them after they vow to be obedient to God and as it is sprinkled on the altar. And so, there is unity symbolized there in the first service of worship by that sprinkling of the blood. "*. . . that they also may be in Us. . . .*"

How are we to understand such high truth from Scripture? I truly believe out of all that we could study together in Scripture, the idea of me and my soul being in union with God through Christ is too lofty for me to be able to focus on it for long periods of time. I struggle to apprehend this truth. I can state it, and I can believe it, but when I choose to meditate upon it, I find that it is so large that it escapes my grasp. Just when I believe I have my hands on it, it's removed from my mind again because of the weakness of my own mind.

Our whole person, body and soul, are united to His body and soul, even as a whole person as the God man is united to the Father. The Father wedded His divinity to man in the incarnation. So, He sent His Spirit to dwell within man so that we will be one in Him by virtue of the indwelling of the Holy Spirit. So, we become temples of the Holy Spirit and united to God by the Holy Spirit. We are filled with all the fullness of God because of the indwelling of the Holy Spirit.

Doesn't this truth encourage us to hold loosely to the things of the earth? Doesn't this truth cause us to not desire dependence upon the things of this earth? Doesn't this truth drive us to desire worship, not just today, not just tonight, not just tomorrow, but every day? To be at the throne of God every day to worship Him?

Our life and our welfare become God's concern as His Spirit, His own Spirit who is God dwells in us just as it is our own. So, He would tell us through Zechariah that he who touches us touches the apple of His eye. So personal is it to God when violence is done against His own people that it's as if violence is done against Him Himself.

Just as the incarnation didn't make a man God, neither does the gift of the Spirit make man God. Just as the incarnation shows us that the man Jesus was also truly God, so the gift of the Holy Spirit shows us that it is really God who takes up His abode in men. And so, Jesus could say in Matthew 25:40, "Truly, I say to you, as you did it to one of the least of these My brothers, you did it to Me." As you did it to them, so you have done it to Me.

Was this a platitude by Christ? Was He simply empathizing emotionally with His people? No. So identified are the people of God with God that violence to a servant of God is violence against God. So we read in Acts where Jesus appears to Paul, and He says, "Saul, Saul, why do you persecute not them, not my people . . . why do you persecute me? Saul, Saul, why do you persecute me?"

Where does this take us? Our interest in one another isn't fraternal. It's not because we're just good Christian folk. We have taken vows. We've taken vows just as they did at the mountain. We have vowed an allegiance to Christ, and because of Christ, to one another. It's natural and it's spiritual. Our fellowship celebrates a common interest but is born in spiritual sameness. We drink from the same fountain and live by the same blood of Christ. Therefore, our commitment to one another is no less than a commitment to Christ. And to abandon a commitment to one another is to abandon a commitment to Christ. "For as you've done to the least of these, so you have done also to me."

As we together form one body, we have a mutual interest in the spiritual growth to Christ likeness of one another. No single member, no single member can become spiritual perfect until the whole Body does. It's true to say that this Body will never be any stronger than its weakest member. There is strength in union and weakness in division. ". . . If we love one another, God abides in us and His love is perfected in us" (1 John 4:12).

Our society today has placed obstacles in front of us as a church. These obstacles can easily become the object of our vision and attention, but when they do, they are displacing something. And that something is a Someone, which is Christ. It is our purpose that we would all grow through and past those issues which have chained and encumbered us, many which have chained and encumbered us to our delight, but nevertheless because they are not of God, they are not blessed by Him.

Our union with Christ means that we have died, we've been buried and raised with Him, and while our bodies still decay, our spirits have been joined with Him in life. Our lives are forevermore expressions of Christ. Our lives are testimonies because it is God who dwells in us. How can they be anything else? We have died, and it is Christ who lives in us. The old man is gone, and the new man is come. We are new creatures in Christ. The old has passed away. As the Father was seen in Jesus, so Christ must be seen in us.

Finally, first was our union together, secondly, our union with Christ for our salvation, and then thirdly, our union with God means that the Holy Spirit is one and dwells in each of us. The same Holy Spirit who indwells any true believer who is gathered here is the same Spirit who dwells with me and the same Spirit who is Christ's Spirit. The same!

That is why the injunctions in Scripture are so severe about joining our bodies to the body of a harlot—the physical union of a man and a woman being one that is unscriptural when it's done outside of God's decree—because to do that is to take God Himself into the temple of harlotry. Is there any greater offense to the Father?

We're consecrated to God as His own Son was consecrated to Him, and not conflicted with other worldly pursuits or glory. God's interests are our own interests, and His concerns are our own concerns. As God is love, so we are to be known for our love. His Law is written on our hearts so it becomes our conviction rather than a taskmaster. Our lives are to be expressions of the order and majesty of God rather than chaos, darkness, and the despair of fallen men. The love we are commended to in sharing God does not become something that we outgrow. When properly understood, there is no more glorious truth than this. And in verse 22, Jesus says that the glory God gave Him He gave to us for this purpose, that we would be one with one another and with God in Christ. Even blessing is but a means to attain unity.

Ask yourself this—out of any argument that your church has ever had, out of any discussion or division, any issue that anyone has with either the people or the pastor, how many of them revolve around an actual scriptural truth, and how many of them involve things that aren't even in the Scriptures at all? How many times has division been brought to the church over something that wasn't even the truth of Scripture, and yet how willing are people to fight to their very spiritual death for something that God has not decreed? They'll rip a church in two over something, but if it's not of God then it is ungodly.

In fact, Christianity itself, why was it ripped in two? Because the Catholic Church took the gospel and distorted it and turned it on its head and said, "It is by man's works and righteousness he will be saved, not by grace alone." And so, the Church was torn in two. And ever since then, we have shown our propensity to the same sin by focusing on everything but these truths which we have already recognized are so neglected. As if we have somehow mastered the Scripture, we now seek to add things so that we can focused on those as being important instead of the actual truth itself. So, we neglect truth, and we major on things that aren't even in the Scripture itself.

That is the condition of Christ's Church. I see it when I am at Fort Jackson with all the chaplains. They all come with all their own stories from every denomination. Across the spectrum of churches, it's the same story. If we lose our focus on the means of grace, and we displace it with anything else, we will destroy one another because then we enter into the realm of opinion. And opinion is not Christian doctrine. As we celebrate the incarnation of Christ, let's celebrate it because it is our salvation and because we are brought into unity with our Lord and Savior and with one another.

17

Living so that the World May Know

(John 17:21, 22)

". . . that they may all be one, just as you, Father, are in me, and I in you, that they also may be in us, so that the world may believe that you have sent me. The glory that you have given me I have given to them, that they may be one even as we are one. . . ."

So MANY OF OUR Christmas hymns that we sing, so many that the radio waves pump out, thankfully, over so many stations, proclaim that Jesus has come. There are some, of course, which have a very romantic view or a very cherished and a very sensitive view of the manger and the gentleness of that scene, of mother and child being born in a stable in very adverse circumstances. There are some that would take that narrative and present to us that story in a form that really draws us into that story, and there is nothing at all wrong with that. But by and large, if we really were to examine or study our Christmas hymns, we would find that the purpose of the hymn writer seemed to be to say that at this, the first Advent, when God was incarnate in flesh—this is about proclaiming to the world that Christ has come. The miracle of the incarnation is the most miraculous when it is proclaimed as the salvation of man.

Wherever you have had an occasion to share in the joy of a newborn baby, you will likely have heard someone say that it just seems miraculous when a child comes into this world.

What do we do to cause a baby to form or to be born? There is, of course, conception, but from that point, what have we to do—except by maintaining good nutrition and good rest—with the formation of a baby?

There is simply in the birth itself, something that is nearly miraculous to us, the formation and the bringing forth of life.

But the bringing forth of life brings to our mind an even greater miracle—not simply that Jesus was born and not even the warm sense that we get when we reflect upon the conditions of His birth, and the sacrifice which was intended, but the fact that from that comes salvation. All the promises of the Old Testament, all of that had pointed to this event, when God would send salvation among men. Born to die that we might live, and this is what is heralded.

There is a saying, "The good news that isn't told really isn't good." I would say that a hymn that is familiar to us but is often neglected is that great hymn, *Go Tell it on the Mountain* that Jesus Christ is born. It lacks some of the characteristics of what we consider traditional hymns, and so it usually is not in the top five Christmas hymns that are sung.

"Go tell it on the mountain. . . ." In fact you could sing it almost at any time of the year. Perhaps we should sing it more frequently throughout the year, but isn't that really the essence of the birth narrative, that we are to go and tell it on the mountain, to go and speak that Christ was born? The incarnation has occurred. God has taken to Himself the nature of man, remaining fully God and yet becoming also fully man, in order that man might be saved. That's the message the Church has been commissioned to preach, and it's perfectly consistent with our celebration of Christmas, our celebration of Easter, our celebration of every Lord's Day. It is consistent with all of that because it is our hope for salvation.

The verses for this chapter are all about the union of Christ to believers, the union of believers to God through their union with Christ. We've confessed that these are mysteries that have eluded most of our understanding as we've just read through the Scriptures in sort of a cursory reading. We have grasped the narrative of the gospel. We have grasped the birth. We have grasped the life of Christ. We have grasped the atonement, the Cross, the grave, the resurrection.

But this idea of spiritual union has evaded most of Christendom. We can see it expressed—the misunderstanding, that is—through various theologies of the Holy Spirit that simply do not grasp that with the coming of the Holy Spirit, there is a union as Christ dwells in us. There is a union with Christ that is spiritual and yet is also very real. It's not spiritual in the sense of an idea. It's not spiritual in the sense of our simply being moved in an emotion. It's spiritual in the sense that we are spirit, and God is Spirit, and Christ's Spirit dwells within us.

The old man has died; a new creature has been born. It's no longer I who live, but Christ who lives in me, and there is a union there which is symbolized in the sacrament of the Lord's Supper as we take and we drink and we eat. And as we eat and drink and that becomes a part of us, so Christ also is dwelling within us and we are a part of Him, as we are a part of the body. So the theology ripples out as we come to understand unity going not only to the individual believer, but through the Church as well, and from the Church to the world.

Jesus has been describing one of the most vital, deep, and profound spiritual truths of Scripture, and nested right in the middle of His teaching on union, we find these words: ". . . so that the world may believe that you have sent me." This idea of union is expressed both before and after this phrase. So, right in the middle, Jesus is saying that the reason for all of this instruction, at least one reason, is that ". . . the world may believe that you have sent me."

When you purchase and present a Christmas gift, you want the package, the wrapping, the bag and the tissue paper, whatever it might be, to somewhat reflect the contents. If it's a very precious gift, a very special gift, that is, if you paid a lot for it, you don't want it to be wrapped up in something that doesn't communicate the value of the gift. You wouldn't wrap it in a paper bag if it was something you had spent hundreds or perhaps a thousand dollars on. You would take care to wrap it and to present it in something that would represent just how special the contents of that package were.

These words, ". . . that the world may believe that you have sent me" are not uttered in isolation. They are wrapped up, contained in Jesus' teaching on unity with God. There is something about our proclamation that is tied in with the idea of union with God. It's not just an activity the Church performs. It's not just something we do because we are told we have to do it. There is something about our being Church family. There is something about our work and our labor as a Church, our union with Christ, our union with each other and our work for the cause of Christ that are all bound together.

We can't splinter them off. We can't compartmentalize them. That's why our intimacy as a family is so important, and our laboring for the gospel. That's what makes the ministry of the Church effective, we're told, because it is in that unity, the fellowship of the Brethren, the communion of the saints with the Father through Christ by the indwelling of the Holy Spirit, the one Bride of Christ—there is something about all that unity that the world sees and comes to believe about Christ.

In Killian McDonnell's book *John Calvin, the Church, and the Eucharist,* he notes concerning this idea of union: "Among scholars there is little doubt that union with Christ constitutes one of the centralities. Both Calvin's fault and his piety are deeply impregnated with union with Christ" (177). As McDonnell explores Calvin's theology, he comes to realize that whether it's the doctrine of the sacrament or evangelism, the idea of union with Christ permeates all of Calvin's theology. And he goes on further to say, "you cannot properly understand Calvin's theology if you don't grasp, at least in part a growing understanding of the idea of union with Christ" (177).

Union with Christ forms a foundation or forms the ground upon which all the other seeds of theological thought are then placed. They grow up individually, and we can observe them individually. We might talk about six-day creationism, or we might talk about predestination and election. We might talk about the sacraments, the signs, and seals of God's covenant of grace. We can talk about all these things individually, but underlying them all, they are all tied together in their root system with this idea of union with Christ, spiritual union with Christ.

If we take it out, then what do we have? If we're not united to Christ, then we are separated from Christ. If we don't understand union with Christ, then we are still the old creature, because if the old one has died, what forms the new? Do we become a new old-style creature, or are we found in Christ?

There is something about our life in Christ that is so precious that very few of us probably can fathom it, because it would change everything we do. It would change how we live, to consider that we are in vital union with Christ. What this means to us is that we have to give these words, ". . . that the world may believe that you have sent me," as much rank as the doctrine of unity because of its association with unity.

So let's consider just two aspects of this passage. First of all, what? What is it that we are saying here? What is the future that Jesus sees in this prayer ". . . that the world may believe . . ."? Does that mean that all people will come to believe? And then, how does Jesus see this future coming to be? *On account of what?* we ask. How is it that they will come to believe?

Jesus, in His prayer to the Father, expresses His own earnest desire that the world would know and believe that God sent Him. This is going a step beyond what we typically would grant the Great Commission to be teaching us. It's going a step beyond simply saying, "Go out and tell someone." Here He is talking about that day when the world will know.

The great Christmas hymn, "Hark! The Herald Angels Sing!" is an announcement to the world. "Hark! The herald angels sing, glory to the newborn King!" This is an announcement not just to the shepherds. It's not just to those who existed at that time. We still proclaim. "Hark! The herald angels sing!" as a proclamation from the heavens to the world that the King was born, and that the King had come to rule and to save the lost, to set the captives free.

We can note that in our day, many non-Christians will concede that Jesus lived in the past. They can concede that point, but not that He came as the only begotten Son of God, born in a manger as the Messiah, the Prince of Peace, the Savior of man. So when we say, "Hark! The herald angels sing" that Christ was born, they may not buy the angel part of it, but they do concede that yes, in history, there was a good moral man named Jesus. Many spoke highly of God in the Scriptures who never knew His salvation, so it shouldn't surprise us that in our day, there are many who would speak highly of Christ who do not know His salvation. Such was Nebuchadnezzar, in Daniel 2:47, when he was forced to confess to Daniel these words, "Truly, your God is God of gods and Lord of kings, and a revealer of mysteries. . . ." But even with these words of high honor which Nebuchadnezzar paid to God, there wasn't in him a faith that saves, which is why the connection here to union with Christ is so helpful.

After praying for that unity, Jesus contemplates the result in the world, ". . . that the world may believe, . . ." we're told. If we understand this, it dramatically changes the way we think about church, doesn't it? Church isn't just a place where we go and do some things. It's not just simply a time on the schedule where we show up for this and for that or where we decide if we want to attend that or don't want to attend this other. Church is a living entity that we have been called to as a vital organ and a vital part. It is not something we do, but something that we are. We *are* the Church. We *are* parts of the body of Christ.

Jesus is head of the Church, and God has promised Him something even more striking than that. If we go all the way back to Psalm 2, we read, "I will tell of the decree: The LORD said to me, 'you are my Son; today I have begotten you. Ask of me, and I will make the nations your heritage, and the ends of the earth your possession. You shall break them with a rod of iron and dash them in pieces like a potter's vessel.'"

You hear how God has promised the very ends of the earth to Messiah. How broad is God's promise? It's as broad as the covenant He has made with Christ, and the covenant He made with Christ is that all the earth would be His inheritance. Jesus is that promised seed of Abraham, the one that was promised in Genesis 12:3, ". . . in you all the families of the earth shall be blessed." Because of this promise, Paul would reflect in Romans 4:13 that ". . . He would be heir of the world."

We could take at look at Psalm 72 if we wanted to prove the extent of the kingdom of God, which is "from sea to sea, and from the River to the ends of the earth!" But we can bring this to some summary and conclusion by recalling Daniel's promise of the Son of Man in chapter 7.

> "I saw in the night visions, and behold, with the clouds of heaven there came one like a Son of Man, and He came to the Ancient of Days and was presented before Him. And to Him was given dominion and glory and a kingdom, that all peoples, nations, and languages should serve Him; His dominion is an everlasting dominion, which shall not pass away, and His kingdom one that shall not be destroyed."

So here we have heard the promises, but what does the fulfillment of this promise look like practically? Practically speaking, what does it mean that all the world will see and believe? We need only to return to Psalm 22, verse 27, 28: "All the ends of the earth shall remember and turn to the LORD, and all the families of the nations shall worship before you. For kingship belongs to the LORD, and he rules over the nations."

That teaching is picked up in the New Testament as well, in Philippians 2: "Therefore God has highly exalted Him and bestowed on Him the name that is above every name, so that at the name of Jesus every knee should bow, in heaven and on earth and under the earth. . . ." And just to emphasize that this is indeed the view of the culmination of all things, let me go to that favorite book of all good Christians, the Book of Revelation, chapter 11: "Then the seventh angel blew his trumpet, and there were loud voices in heaven, saying, 'The kingdom of the world has become the kingdom of our Lord and of His Christ, and He shall reign forever and ever.'" These are the promises of God that Jesus had in mind when He prayed, ". . . that the world may believe that you have sent me."

So then that leaves only this question. *What does it mean when He says "the world"?* Sometimes *world* is used to mean only those who are blessed in Christ. Sometimes *world* is used as a reference to just the opposite of that, that is, the unbelievers who have rejected God's Messiah. Sometimes *world* is used to reference Gentiles as distinct from Jews, but in each case, the context gives us what the use of that word, the *world*.

In this prayer which Jesus is uttering to the Father, which we are privileged to hear, He has already prayed for the disciples. He has prayed already for those who will believe on Him through their testimony, so here Jesus must be referring in a more general sense to both Jew and Gentile. He isn't praying for those who are in union with Himself already, but for those who are impacted by what they see and learn of His glory in the world. As Rainsford says,

> The means by which the world is to be brought to this true sense and conviction of Jehovah having sent His Son to be the Savior of the world, is not the preaching of the gospel, but the manifested union of the Church of God with one another, and with Christ in the Father. Not faith, but vision; not the preached Word but the effects of the preached Word in the children of the Lord God Almighty, united in one. (400)

Now we know that faith comes by hearing, and hearing by the preaching of the Word of God, but that's not the aspect we're talking about. We're talking about the living testimony of God's people who are in union with one another and the impact that unity makes on the world. I only wish I could give you a perfect example today. We don't have one. We have only fragmented pieces of examples. Even the family itself, which has come under assault and is fragmented and is splitting and breaking—even the family itself no longer bears testimony that is impressive to the world.

But as we see resurgence in those ideas, where families are not viewed as free agents going here and there, individuals going this place and the other, but as they are coming together again as a whole, we see also the

Church of Jesus Christ beginning to draw tighter again. They are gathering around those places where the gospel is being rightly preached, no longer viewing Church as a place where you attend this event or that event, or this show or that show, or hear that speaker or this speaker.

Gradually we are finding that once again, there is a return to the idea of *family* not activity center, not resort—but *family*. And that testimony changes the world. That idea of unity which manifests and displays the idea of covenant fidelity within the body tells the world that there is something that unifies the people of God that is spiritual.

We can, unfortunately, see the negative side, the effects of disunity, as the reputation of the Church has continued to fall. We've tried headliners; we've tried books; we've tired big events. None of that has been effective to convince people that the Church is worthy. But you have a strong Church, a people who are united together, knit together by faith, and that is unassailable, and that changes people's minds about Christ.

And if Ephesians 3:8 is to be believed, it's not only the world of flesh that will be impressed and wonder about this unity of the Church, but the spiritual world as well as even the angels peer and marvel as they learn the power of God by the Church because they can see that the very gates of hell will not prevail against the Church. The Church is meek, and the Church is humble. But as it is found in unity—just like Jerusalem, just like Bethlehem was the smallest of the cities, and from that small city came the salvation of man with the birth of Christ—so the Church, small and meek and humble, is found to be like tempered steel in a world that would seek to crush it.

Where does the strength come from? Not from any single individual, not from a powerful speaker, not from any particular elder or deacon or song leader or women's ministry or anyone else, but from the tight-knit group of God's people because it is the Holy Spirit who dwells there with them.

The union Jesus has been speaking of is seen in the Church. The love of God is seen manifested in the Church. We can't conjure it up. We can't get that Spirit. Going to church is not about going to a football game where you simply have one side that gets the other side up for this for or that. We can't present something to the people in order to get them fired up. That's not what the Church is. The Holy Spirit is the fire behind the people.

The gospel is proclaimed in the Church. Missions are sent out from the Church. The means of grace are held out in the Church. In short, the kingdom of God is manifest and displayed as distinct from the world— where? In the Church. Zion is the Church, which is the city which is set on the hill.

So how tragic and offensive is it to God when His Church becomes like the world; when the Church fails to manifest love; when the church fails to show unity; when the church fails to consider missions; when the church fails to have a disposition of reverence; when the church fails to cherish peace and grace; when people are double-minded; when they are disobedient?

In the Scriptures, we have two agents bearing testimony to God: the Spirit and the Church. Neither is independent from the other. Both serve to convert and convict the world. Both stand as a witness and as heralds of the gospel. And so we are reminded that the Bible the world reads is the character of the people of God, that is, the Church. As the light of the Church's testimony grows bright or becomes dim, so goes the conviction of the world. As the Church is strong, we see society also moral and strong; but as the Church becomes weak, so we see our society becoming weak.

The testimony of the Church is the Scripture, and the testimony of the living Church is a product of the communion of saints which can only be possible when each believer is in vital union with Christ. The great commentator John Peter Lange mentions that "this union is a reflection of the union which subsists between the Father and the Son, the Father and the Son who constitute, along with the Spirit, that Trinity. Consequently it's not merely a moral union and sympathy, but a community of spiritual life, all partaking of the life of Christ as branches of the vine" (522).

The honor of Christ, the evidence of our testimony, the moral progress of the world—all depend on our gathering around our Head, which is Christ; on our serving as we are called in the body; not divided, not disloyal, not distracted. We are to be knit together as a fabric without a seam, so that the world may know. There is a heavy responsibility communicated in this passage. We don't come to church because we personally need a little pep to start the week, or just to be reminded of grace. Those things may occur. We come to church because we bear a responsibility as heralds of the gospel and in forsaking the church, we weaken the Church.

And in weakening the Church, we weaken its testimony, and in weakening its testimony, we do a disservice to the whole world.

We might believe we come for selfish means, but we need to rethink and understand that in coming together as a Church, we are coming together in that vital union which is knit together by Christ in the Spirit not to be neglected, because to neglect it is not only our own personal loss, but also a loss to the Church, and to the world, because we are told that in seeing that vital union, the world believes.

This is the message of the manger. This is the message of the Cross. This is the message of Pentecost, and the Church exists so that the world may know.

18

A Church of One

(John 17:22–23)

"The glory that you have given me I have given to them, that they may be one even as we are one, I in them and you in me, that they may become perfectly one, so that the world may know that you sent me and loved them even as you loved me."

W E ARE COMING TO a conclusion of the Lord's intercession on behalf of those who would believe, of His petitioning God for their blessing, of this "Lord's prayer." We find here a summary of Jesus' teaching, and as it is summarized, it is explained in concise terms. And if we have been following along, in fact, even pulling from the epistle of 1 John, if we have pulled these truths together, then all we are reading now is unfolding gloriously before us.

We ought not be surprised that Jesus continues with this theme of union. It bears pointing out, although it hardly needs to be, that this idea of union with Christ seems to be the culminating point of all of the teaching of Scripture. We know that when Jesus talks about His being the light of the world, or if He talks about Him being the bread of life, we know as to those particulars how they apply in helping us understand the person of Christ and His ministry and His mission. But when you begin to gather all of these strands of teaching, and you begin to pull together all of the different ideas and the different theologies that are presented in all of Scripture, you find there is nothing greater except the proclamation of God in His own person than this idea of our union with Christ when properly understood. Our union with Christ. Our communion with the Savior.

All we've learned so far seems to validate Rainsford's conclusion about union:

> "Union with God Almighty is the greatest and the fullest of all conceivable blessings and the source and spring from whence all other blessings flow. And our union with Christ and God's ever-lasting purpose is the source of all blessing which has been or is or shall ever be bestowed upon us, and of all the glory to be revealed to us or in us, whatever that glory may be." (405)

What would bring such a conviction from such a learned, lifetime minister as Marcus Rainsford where he would consider union with God Almighty the greatest and fullest of all conceivable blessings? Consider these words: the people of God are united spiritually with God the Father in union.

What is the difference between union and not being in union? We might say observation would be different from union. We can say we observe the Lord's Table. That would mean we watch it, we learn something from it, but there is no union or genuine communion there. We might say that in the Church, we observe one another in our spiritual walks, but if we are a divided people or if we are a scattered people, if we are not in union in Christ, then we're not truly a family of God, for there is nothing that links us together.

We observe one another in our individual spiritual journeys, but we are not one in Christ, and so, we are not truly a Body in Christ, for a body that is dismembered is no longer a body. So, this idea of union plays out in a proper understanding of almost every other part of theology. You can't have a true theology of the Church without an idea of what union in Christ is. You can't truly have a theology concerning the indwelling of the Holy Spirit unless you also have an idea of union with Christ, for it is the Spirit of Christ who dwells in us. Unity with God is transformative in its theological importance in our thinking and in our walk.

We cannot consider ourselves independent spiritual agents doing what we will, exercising individual wisdom over and above the Body for example, for we understand God is working with the community of people just as He did with the nation of Israel. Granted, working through the elders who were placed over the nation of Israel, but nevertheless, each part of the body having its function. Not one co-opting the other because it would have to abandon its own function to co-op the purpose of another and then not be able to fulfill that purpose, for one part of the Body is not made to perform the function of another, anymore than you might replace a kidney with a liver. You could fill the gap, but the liver would not function in the same way. We understand that biologically, but do we understand it in the Body of Christ? Do we understand our unique calling, and are we functioning in that calling? Are we satisfied in that calling? Are we serving Christ because of the union and the fellowship which is the Body?

Verses 22 and 23 continue to push this idea of union, carrying forward the teaching of Jesus which we would find throughout the Scriptures, but certainly John 14:23. "If anyone loves me, he will keep my word, and my Father will love him, and we will come to him and make our home with him." Is Jesus talking about moving in next door, or is He speaking of the coming of the Holy Spirit where we become the temples of the Holy Spirit because it is the Spirit of God who resides in us? And if we have the Holy Spirit residing in us, there is no division in God, is there?

Then we have the fullness of the triune God dwelling within us. We can't separate the Trinity anymore than God Himself would separate them, and He has not. He has kept them together as being one in essence though they are three in Persons. And so, to have the Spirit of Christ is to have the Spirit of God, which is the Holy Spirit, the Comforter, the Advocate. So, we are made to be the temple of the Holy Spirit.

In verse 22, Jesus is praying to the Father, and He prays and mentions in His prayer that God has bestowed glory on Him, and He has bestowed glory on us on account of that glory which God gave to Him. And on account of that glory, we are considered qualified for union and communion with the Father. In other words, our union with the living Christ—rather than our religious ideas about him—is grounds for our union with the Father. It's not having a religious philosophy but a genuine spiritual rebirth. And that rebirth is *only* by the power of the Holy Spirit which brings life into that which was dead. And so, by that rebirth we are brought into union with Christ.

We are not made individual agents again. We are brought into union with Him by that birth. When a baby is born, that child is brought into the community of mankind, but there is no spiritual union. There is familiarity, there is likeness or sameness in the way of life, in what sustains life. So, there is some kinship, but not true spiritual union. We must be born again, born of the Spirit to obtain spiritual union.

To grasp the concept of unity in the Scriptures, consider these four unions that are described in the Bible. We understand unity because we are given these four examples. The first being the Trinity itself, the incomprehensible union of the Trinity, all three Persons, Father, Son, and Holy Spirit, who are dwelling in an inseparable union as to Their essence because They are one. This idea of Trinity presents to us the idea of union.

Then, there is the union of God and man in the Person of Christ by virtue of the incarnation. This is called the *hypostatic union*, which is the joining of God and man, two natures brought together as one, not divided, not split, no less God, no less man, all man, all God, yet there is man in God in union. Not side by side; in union. One man, one mind, one will, this will of God found in Christ who came to do the Father's will. He was not immune from anything that had to do with man. And so, this also presents to us the idea or the picture of union as deity and man are made one. God descended in the Person of Christ, and we ascend by Christ. The Father is the beginning and the end, and Christ is the means.

Then, there is thirdly, the union of the Holy Spirit with believers. This union of the Holy Spirit with believers gives us that spiritual union which is primarily the topic of Jesus' prayer that we've been studying together. It results in life for the believers. The body is made the temple of the Holy Spirit, and each believer is then a part of Christ's Body, and He Himself is one with us so that whatever we do as the Church or to the Church, we do unto Him. That bears repeating, for whatever we do as the Church we are doing with Christ, and whatever we do to the Church we are doing to Christ.

The last is the communion of the saints. Whether we speak of those believers who have left already for heaven or those who have not yet been born or those who are our contemporaries, we are in union with them by virtue of our union with Christ. Thomas Manton said, "All believers are united into a Body by the communion of Christ's Spirit that by Christ they may perform service to God" (John 17:22–23). All believers are united by virtue of the Spirit of Christ. If we are in union with Christ, then we are in union with all who are in union with Christ, hence, the term the *communion of the saints*. Believers of every age are united into one Body, making one kingdom of God.

Now, Jesus spoke of a glory that He gave to us. He says, "It's on account of this glory that we are considered worthy of being received by the Father." The glory that Jesus is talking about is a glory that comes from the Father because it comes from the Father's own glory. By the virtue of Jesus being one with the Father, He now shares that glory with us who are in union with Him. It's a practical expression of the result of that union that He would share that glory with us.

Jesus states that the very same glory that is His Father's will be shared with His own people. By our own mystical union with Christ in the Spirit of Christ, we're made partakers of that glory which is from the Father. As you try to grapple with this in your own mind, think in terms of God the Father who has given His glory to the Son because there is unity in the Trinity. The glory already existed with the Son. In fact, Jesus prayed, "Father, restore to Me that glory which I had with You in all eternity past," that is, at the time of His resurrection, "that it would be known to all people."

That glory was hidden for a time in Christ, except for those who had eyes to see as Jesus was performing the miracles and as He was teaching from the Scriptures. There were some who perceived that glory, and yet it was masked, it was veiled for most of human flesh. They could not see with their eyes the indwelling of God within that Man, Jesus Christ. And He says, "Restore to Me that glory."

Perhaps it's the glory like the apostles saw as they were on the Mount of Transfiguration when Jesus was glorified and He was radiant before them, and they knew instantly they were in the presence of God. Whatever Jesus means as far as the manifestation of that glory, we know He possessed that glory because He is one with God, and God never has lost His glory. And now, on the other side of that, the Father shares His glory with the Son, and we find ourselves in union with the Son. That same glory of Christ must be communicated to His own people because it is the Spirit of Christ who indwells the people.

And if the Spirit of Christ indwells the people because there is union with the Spirit and with the Son and with the Father, they share the same glory. The Spirit doesn't leave His glory behind when He indwells the believer. And so, where is the glory within the believer? Now, it doesn't emanate from us as to the flesh, but it is within us because we are in union with Christ. If it is not in us, then we cannot be in union with Christ. We are called together selflessly as a Body, the Body of Christ. Does Christ's Body not have glory? Of course, His Body has glory, and so Jesus in His prayer says, "On account of that glory, receive them. On account of that glory, provide for them. On account of that glory, protect them. On account of that glory, call them Your own." We have glory because the Spirit is within us, but it is not a glory of our own. It is the glory of the Father that is within us.

If we could only pause to meditate upon that, it will have to stagger you. If you know anything of God the Father, it will have to stagger you to consider that the Father's glory as God is within His people, the Church. Because He has given the Church to Christ who is the Bridegroom, He has given Him a Bride, and that Bride is glorified by the Father for the Bridegroom. Is it because we deserve it? It's absolutely because we *don't* deserve it that it comes from the Father.

The fullness of the Father flows to Christ, and the fullness of Christ flows to the Church. When we come to understand union and communion as the whole frame of the gospel, we realize our justification is a blessing that flows from our union with Christ. Our sanctification also flows from our union with Christ. Jesus says, "I in them. . . ." That is not to exclude the Father, but it shows He is our Mediator. He is Jacob's Ladder. Too often I have heard people talk about Jacob's ladder as something that we climb. There is even a hymn we dare not sing about us climbing Jacob's ladder as if we will somehow attain ourselves to the very heavens by our own effort, by our own strength, by our own climbing of Jacob's ladder. Jesus is Jacob's Ladder. The angels ascend and descend upon Jacob's Ladder. What man in Scripture is ever shown climbing a ladder? It is Christ Himself who is Jacob's Ladder. We are united to Him and to one another that we may be perfectly one.

In book three of Calvin's *Institutes*, Calvin shows the centrality of union in his own thinking. And perhaps it should also occupy that in our thinking as well. Concerning faith, Calvin says, "It does not reconcile us to God unless it joins us to Christ" (McDonnell 178). In other words, there can be no real faith unless it is faith that is joining us to Christ. What other kind of faith is there?

We have faith in all sorts of things. We have faith that tomorrow will come. We have faith, at least some hope, that we are able to retain our jobs or our work or our families. We have faith in other people's love for us. Sometime our faith proves to unfounded, but we exercise faith in many things. In fact, when it comes to religion, people oftentimes have faith in faith, meaning that their faith really has no objective substance. They believe they are saved by the act of belief itself, but we are not saved by faith in our own faith. We are saved by faith in Christ and Christ alone.

Calvin goes on: "How can there be a saving faith except insofar as it engrafts us in the Body of Christ?" G. T. Manley says, "As we draw nearer to Christ, we shall be drawn nearer to His people, and in our search for unity with the members, we shall be drawn closer to the Head" (McDonnell 178). Maybe this is why Calvin said there is no salvation outside of the Church because as we draw nearer to Christ, we draw nearer to each other. As we draw nearer to each other, we draw nearer to Christ. How can you picture that?

If you can imagine a triangle and have God the Father at the top and have the people of God on either side, as we draw nearer to each other, as we angle up onto the shape, we are drawing nearer to God. And that is an imperfect illustration, but perhaps it gives you some idea that as we draw nearer to Christ, we are drawing nearer to each other, and as we draw nearer to each other, we draw nearer to Christ.

Killian McDonnell wrote, "A grafting into Christ cannot be separated from being grafted into the Church. The Eucharist," that is, the Lord's Supper," is the visible expression of this present and enduring union with Christ, a union which is in His Body, the Church" (185). When we celebrate Communion, as we take of one loaf and as we symbolically drink from one cup, we recognize that that is symbolic of our union in one Christ. There is one Christ. We who are gathered together here as His Body, sharing our spiritual gifts with one another here as His Body share also at the table symbolically that we are one in Christ.

Jesus said, ". . . that they may all be one. . . ." The prayer of our Lord is not limited to the mature, to the studied, or the accomplished theologian. His prayer is for the weakest. His prayer is for the most ignorant of all believers. "That they may all be one." So, it is not for those of you who perhaps have not attained to some great theological repository of knowledge. It is not simply for those who are mature and have been around for a long time. It is for the youngest, the weakest, the newest, the one who just now is beginning to understand. Perhaps you've been warming a pew for many, many years, and just now you're beginning to realize there are some things you might not know. Jesus says, "*All* will be one."

There is not a club that you have to work your way into by learning a lot. He prays for all those who have childlike understanding of the Scriptures, those who have a very elemental understanding of the Scriptures and those with the most sophisticated theology. They *all* are made to be one in Christ. Weak and strong together are brought into one.

They're undivided to become His Church. All are purchased with His blood. All are atoned for by His life. All are clothed with His righteousness. And all have God as their inheritance. Rainsford observes that "Even Christ Himself could ask no more, and God Himself can give no more" (416). Do you hear that? There is nothing greater that Christ can ask for than our unity with the Father, and there is nothing greater that the Father can give than to bring us into unity with Himself. What could be greater than that? What could we ask for that would be greater than to be unified with Him?

Jesus speaks not only of being with us, not only being for us, and not only being near us, but being in us. Just as the Father is the strength and power of Christ, so Jesus is the strength and power to preserve His people. Hence, we read in Jude 1 that we are "in God the Father and kept for Jesus. . . ." We are preserved for Jesus because we are in God the Father. Just as Noah was preserved in the ark, so we are safe in Christ.

The Lord mentions two objects that result from this union as we now begin to open up verse 23. The first concerns those who are believers united to Christ, and the second involves the world that will be convinced. We've already dealt somewhat at length with the world's being convinced because of the testimony of the Church which is in union together, so we'll look primarily at the object of union in Christ for believers, that we are loved by God as Christ Himself is loved by God.

Jesus says, ". . . that they may become perfectly one." The idea of perfection is one that we don't usually consider. When God created the angels, He made them perfect. When God created man, He made him perfect. But both angels and man were created and possessed an independent will, and hence, they were able to fall, and both did. Why did they fall? Because they were not perfect in One, that is, in God. They were made perfect in the sense of being without sin, but they were not at that time in union with the Father. With our being perfected in One, there will be no fall in our future. God Himself will be the center of our existence. He was not the center of Adam's existence. He was not the center of the fallen angels' existence. But He will be the center of our existence because we are in union with Him.

As Rainsford observed, "God Himself must fail before His children can fall. Christ's fullness must be exhausted before the members of His own Body can fail. The Holy Spirit must be overcome before we can be snatched from the Father's hand" (419). This perfection is union with

God and Christ and union with each other. That is what Jesus is speaking of—"that they may become perfectly one." Perfection is union with God because in Him there is no fault.

The culmination of that union is the last sentence of verse 23: "You sent Me and loved them even as You loved Me." He isn't saying He loves us because of Christ here, but *as* Christ. We can't deny He loves us because of Christ because it's on account of the atonement that we're called sons and daughters of God, but here He is not talking about the merit of Christ's bringing to us the love of God. He is here saying that God loves us *as* He loves Christ. Boice says, "It means that God's love for us is in some measure and is exercised in the same way as His love for Christ."

Note 1 John, chapter 3, verse 1. "See what kind of love the Father has given to us, that we should be called children of God." It's a relational love. It's a love that brings us into union with Himself. People naturally long to love and be loved. But with half of all marriages ending in divorce, and half again continuing in misery, how can we understand this love of God? How can we understand the love of God which is to us the same love as He has for His Son Jesus Christ? It means we have to examine the love of God for Christ if we are going to understand the love of God for us. If we want to know the measure of His love, we don't have anything to compare God's love to in our own lives except for the love of God for His Son.

God's love is infinite. There is no limit. There is no way to exhaust His love. Not only can we go to Him daily, not only can we ask of Him all that we need, but He commands that we do so, and He places no limit on our coming. He loves us in Christ as being part of Christ, and therefore, not only is it infinite, but it is eternal. Not only is His love without limit, but it is without end. The Father will never cease to love Jesus, therefore His love for us will not cease. God will never change, and His love isn't conditioned on changes in us. Consequently, not even sin can separate us from the love of God that is in Christ Jesus our Lord. We will fail; God will not. His love is not conditional upon our acts of obedience. It's conditioned upon His own character, and He has declared that He loves us. God's love is not withdrawn. He doesn't give it by mistake, and then take it back.

George Newton, who was preaching God's Word around 1655 said, "When He gives over loving Christ, then and not 'til then, my brethren, will He give over loving you. When He withdraws His heart from Christ, the Darling of His own bosom, He will withdraw His heart from you too" (337). God will never stop loving His Son, and so, He will never stop loving us. His love is infinite, His love is eternal, and His love is perfect.

We love within the context of families, but not perfectly. In Ephesians 5, men, husbands, are commanded to love their wives as Christ loved the Church. But marriages struggle and children rebel, and often in counseling I'll ask a couple who are sitting there in conflict whether they would still love one another if their disagreement were removed. I ask them, "In the very beginning, did you love one another? Is that why you got married?" Or, "Did you know you weren't in love and got married anyway?" They believed they were in love. Usually, they will affirm almost always that yes, if their issue were removed, they would still love one another.

God's love though is perfect. There is no issue to remove. It was removed at the Cross. God's love is perfect, and perfect loves serves to provide for what is absolutely best for the one who is loved no matter the cost—no matter the cost. What did it cost? "For God so loved the world, that He gave His only begotten Son." How can we measure that cost for His love? Because He loves us even as He loves Christ, He will uphold and protect us just as He did Christ.

In His life, the life of Jesus, many tried to destroy Him. They tried to pull Him away, they tried to stone Him, they tried to kill Him, but God did not allow it because it was not yet His time. As He said in Isaiah 42:1, "Behold my servant, whom I uphold, . . ." His enemies could do no harm to Him until His appointed hour. This was also the promise to Abraham in Genesis 15:1. "Fear not, Abram, I am your shield." Though Jesus encountered times of great trial and stress, so great He would sweat His own blood, God remained His strength, even sending angels to minister to and strengthen Him. It must be the same in our callings in life. The weakest among us shouldn't fear the hardest calling of service.

The consequences of this love are not only redemptive, but practical. How do we apply it? We must love one another as God has loved us in Christ, for to reject one another is to reject the Christ who is that person. And to reject the Christ who is in them is to reject Christ, and so, to bear the testimony of our own being outside of Christ. We must love one another as God has loved us in Christ. We must learn to love impartially and beyond just giving love to others as it serves our own interests or as they deserve.

This love serves to perfect the Body. It is a testimony to the world of God's love. The burden of Christ's prayer in the hours before His crucifixion was for unity. Remember the context of Jesus' prayer. What is it that Jesus is pressing for in His prayer with God in the moments before He would be carried off for His crucifixion? Unity! Unity! Unity with Him, unity within the Body, unity with the Father, that the world would know His glory because it would shine forth from the Body of Christ. Unity with Him and with one another. Unity so that we would know the love of God as He knows it.

Let me conclude this chapter with a passage from First John 4:17. "By this is love perfected with us, so that we may have confidence for the day of judgment, because as He is so also are we in this world." It doesn't say so *ought* we to be. It doesn't say so *will* we be, speaking post resurrection. Perfect love is that as He is, so *are* we. We are not maids in waiting. We are the Bride of Christ. And we are indwelled fully with His Holy Spirit, not a piece, not partially, not sentimentally, but with the true Spirit of Christ which has the glory of God. And so, we are made to be able to be loved by God.

On judgment day, we will have no fear because Christ Himself has no fear. As God loves the Son, so He loves us. "Perfect love casts out fear," does it not? And perfect love is found in our union with Christ who is loved perfectly by the Father, and as we love one another, not with a love of our own, but with a perfect love which is from the Father.

There is a beauty and magnificence in the Church of Jesus Christ that is not because we've made it so, but because it is the Body of Christ, and it shines forth most boldly as the light of the world when God's glory is made front and center to shine forth. We don't need to decorate it as we do our trees at Christmas. Those shine forth in our homes, and they beautify our homes. But the glory of God is not an ornament to be put up and to be taken down. The glory of God shines forth as the Church of Jesus Christ gets out of the way and lets God shine forth through them that the world may behold His love for His people, their unity in Christ, and the glory of God that shines forth from them. The Church belongs to the Father. We belong to the Father. We are His own, and He loves us as He loves the Son who dwells within us.

19

Being where Jesus Will Be

(John 17:24)

"Father, I desire that they also, whom you have given me, may be with me where I am, to see my glory that you have given me because you loved me before the foundation of the world."

WE LIVE IN A time of decline—declining morality, a declining dollar, a declining of our individual rights, a declining in personal wealth, church membership, scholarship, piety, manners, respect, national power, and hope. We live in a time when it seems that everything is spooling down around us, whether it's your investments, or your health. Most of us have gone through a time of life, and if you haven't reached it yet then you can look forward to it, when we begin to feel that something is just not right ourselves. We experience fatigue, a lack of motivation, sometimes weight gain. It happens, I'm told, when you turn 40, and the doctors can't do anything about it except console you.

You get a sinking feeling in your body, as comedian Bill Cosby said, "For me it's a time when our hair begins to slide off the top of our head and down our back." If this were all that we had to look forward to in life, we might struggle to find a reason to press on. What would be the use? What would be the purpose in pressing on when there is nothing ahead but decline? When there is nothing ahead but erosion? When there is nothing ahead but aging and infirmity and ultimately, death? If all we had to look forward to is the struggle of life, we might be all the more tempted to give up.

What we know is that while we are in decline, we are actually getting closer to our very best time because the closer we come to our grave, and in fact the moment that you are dropped and descending into the grave is when you come near to paradise. Only Christianity holds out this expectation, the expectation that our greatest tragedy will in fact be our greatest triumph. This hope defies evolutionary, it defies humanistic, philosophical thinking. There is nothing that is natural or ordinary about this way of talking. At the very moment you experience your worst, at that very moment you have your very best. This is nothing less than an act of God.

At the very start of His prayer, Jesus acknowledges that the Father had given Him authority over all flesh to give eternal life to all that the Father had given Him. Every one of His sheep, Jesus who is the great shepherd, has promised this great reward that they (that is that we) will be with Him. Augustine said, "Listen and rejoice in hope that since the present is not a life to be loved, but to be tolerated, you may have the power of patient endurance amid all this tribulation."

Would that we could hold this perspective ourselves—that while we applaud the leisure of life and the wonders of medicine, we do not forget that simply relieving pain or suffering does nothing to actually change our circumstance and situation. The relief helps us to not feel it as keenly, but in not feeling it we also rob ourselves of opportunity to think more clearly about it. Jesus prayed, "Father, I desire that they also whom you have given me may be with me." To put this very simply, Jesus desires to keep those the Father has given Him with Himself in paradise. Verse 12 of this same chapter (17) showed us as much when Jesus prayed this, "I kept them in your name, which you have given me." So we can say at this point that our previous studies of divine election and union in Christ make it a logical and foregone conclusion that those whom belong to Christ remain in Christ. They are given to Him by the Father, and Jesus has a right of ownership, if you will, over those souls which are the elect, which belong to Him.

Our Westminster Confession of Faith in chapter 3, the fifth paragraph says, "Those of mankind that are predestinated unto life, God, before the foundation of the world was laid, according to his eternal and immutable purpose, and the secret counsel and good pleasure of his will, hath chosen, in Christ, unto everlasting glory, out of his mere free grace and love." *Everlasting glory*—the confession captures this same teaching that the Scriptures hold before us that those who are in Christ are bound for everlasting glory. The day we encounter our worst will be the day that God gives us the very best, an everlasting glory.

That's the great Christian hope, isn't it? Not just that we are somehow equipped and empowered to get through in this life, which is accomplished by the grace and the blessing of God, but that at the end of our trials, at the end of our life, whether it be long or whether it be short, that there is something even better that is laid up for us; it is a glory, a sharing in the glory of Christ. That's our hope. Not simply that we will be saved from death, but that we will be given a wonder of a future.

Jesus prays, "Father, I desire. . . ." It's a very unique way that Jesus has of phrasing this. No other place do we find this type of address. There are places where God is called *Father*, but no other place does Jesus speak in such a way, and no one else would dare speak in such a way. You might remember throughout the gospel that it was simply calling God *Father* that got Jesus in a lot of trouble with the religious leadership. So take this a step further now, and Jesus is saying, "Father," and then being very assertive, "I desire. . . ." Or in some translations, it says, "I will. . . ." It's not so much a request here as Jesus is laying out His own will. There is no other place that this sort of address is given in a prayer language.

If we begin simply with *Father*, we might note that titles are often used to address God, and they're normally suited to the context or to the matter at hand at the time the prayer is being uttered. Jesus is petitioning God as His only begotten Son that we, the adopted sons and daughters, would be kept with Him. It's no small matter that Jesus presents this as a family matter, as He calls Him *Father*, and He is talking about the sons and daughters of God that He wants to have kept there with Him. He presents it as a family matter for what we receive is an inheritance, not a wage. We're not given what we're due; we're given an inheritance.

"Knowing that from the Lord you will receive the inheritance as your reward" (Colossians 3:24). Our waiting to receive the inheritance is described as waiting to receive adoption by Paul in Romans 8:23. Not only the creation, but we ourselves, who have the first fruits of the spirit grown inwardly as we wait eagerly for adoption as sons, the redemption of our bodies. You hear all this familial language, and so Jesus in His prayer, says, "Father, I desire that they be kept with Me." He is appealing like one would within a family. Some of us understand this in the context of family. In almost every family there is an uncle or there is an aunt, or there is a sibling who has walked a path that has not been complimentary to the vision of the family or the values of the family. If it were a stranger we might be tempted to turn and walk away, but when it is family, we tend to have not only more compassion, but we tend to have a sympathy, a desire to keep them in the family.

We don't want to turn them out. The offense that is required for a family member to be turned out is usually far greater than when one is simply an acquaintance or a co-worker or a stranger. When one is family, there is a striving, there is a work to keep the family member in the fold. Jesus is appealing in just that way, "Father, I desire that they be kept with Me." He had every right to make the request because God had given them to Him. They were His by possession, and He now is saying, "Father, as I go to glory Myself, I desire that they also would be kept with Me."

We know when Jesus says *be kept with me where I am,* He is not talking about the place where He is making the prayer. He already has frequently made reference to the future as if it were present because He is so close here to the Cross, there is nothing really left except for Him to experience the worst that He also would receive the best. The next words, "*I desire,*" that follow His address of God as Father are constructed as one might expect of a person's last words.

Marcus Rainsford said, These words, they ". . . express the last will and testament of God's Son whispered into His Father's heart concerning His redeemed" (428). It's not phrased, and it's not constructed as a request. It is in the moments before Jesus is to be arrested, tried, and crucified. This is His last will and testament. Father, my last will and testament is that these will also be with me where I am. All that Jesus has been praying for up until this point was to prepare His people that they might be with Him and to behold His glory.

The prayer for unity with God the Father and with Him and with one another, all of that is to prepare them that they would behold His glory. The prayer for their safety and for their mission was so that God's people could be gathered in that they might, after their own perishing in this life, after their flesh fails, raise glorified and be with Him and behold His glory. Some would wonder, *Is that it for us? Is that all that we're going to look forward to—just to see His glory? Is that what being saved is all about? Is that what the resurrection is all about that we'll wake up, we'll be resurrected, there will be a moment of excitement, we'll see His glory and then it's all over? We'll have seen it, been there, done that in heaven and then there is nothing left?*

Some won't understand that the object of preaching is the same as the object of Christ, and it is to show the people the glory of God in Christ, to show the people Christ. I had a discussion with a person about whether a sermon is classified as a work of teaching or whether it's classified as a work of preaching. The whole issue seemed to be, Well, what is there in it for me to take out here? What do you want me to do with it? You have to give me some action I need to take as a result of this.

That seemed to be the distinction that was being made. Preaching is in the most elemental way of expressing it, continuing the mission Christ gave the church, which is to show the people the glory of God as it is found in the Scripture. It's not a class in ethics. It's not a class in morality. It's not a class in Christian behavior. It's not a class in getting along with one another. Those are fruits of our lives, which are the result of the indwelling of the Spirit, and as we come to see Christ and as we come to see the Father more and more, we find ourselves living more and more like Christ, but it's not a place for dispensing rules and regulations. There is a preaching that is appropriate when there is an emphasis on the law in Scripture. There is a proper emphasis on conduct, and there is a proper emphasis on our behavior, and how we order our lives. But the purpose of opening the Word of God is that we would see God.

Jesus says as much when He says, "I have made known to them your name, and will continue to make it known," in verse 26, "that the love with which you have loved me may be in them, and I in them." If we don't attend to this most vital function, which was Christ's own function in His preaching, then haven't we abandoned the role and the task of the church and become like so many classes in schools simply telling folks what to do or how they're supposed to behave when they leave. But as people who belong to God, we desire to see His glory. That's what we're doing.

We're showing His glory. How did Christ do it? He says, "I made known to them Your name." That's how I've shown them you. He left us His Word, and He says, "Make it known. Make God known to them. Make them to know the Father. Make them to know the Son. Make them to know the Spirit, to know them through the revelation which has been given to us, and so we preach." So why should we see His glory? If that's what it's all about, why should we be bothered by that? Why should we see His glory?

First of all, it's the satisfaction of all of our hopes. We can't find a satisfaction for our hope in this world. This world will not bring it to us no matter how hard we strive and no matter how high we climb. Romans 8:24–25, "For in this hope we were saved. Now hope that is seen is not hope. For who hopes for what he sees? But if we hope for what we do not see, we wait for it with patience." Our hope is for what we don't see. The purpose of the preaching is so that you know what it is that Paul is talking about.

The tragedy of the current ministry of the Christian church is that it is such a poor steward of the people's time that after sitting through hours and hours of not preaching, but lecturing on Christian behavior, they have no idea what Paul is talking about. They see, but that's not what our hope is to be fixed on. Our hope is to be fixed on that which we do not see and it's for that that we wait. It's for that that we endure patiently.

Why do we not have endurance? Why are we so impatient as a Christian people? Why do we want to get in and get it done when it comes to church and religion? Because we don't see what it is that Paul is talking about. We don't have patience because we don't have the object set before us, clearly the glory of God in Christ. In many ways we are like the righteous and devout man Simeon, who waited to see the Messiah with his own eyes who said in Luke 2, "Lord, now you are letting your servant depart in peace, according to your word; for my eyes have seen your salvation that you have prepared in the presence of all peoples." Here this devout man, this Jew, who had his own labors and his own services and his own work, found satisfaction when he saw the glory of God in the salvation of his people by the coming of the Messiah.

Our faith is dependent on a resurrected Christ and that Christ must be at God's right hand in glory. The sight of Jesus in His glory is the satisfaction of every question and every accusation railed against the church and against God. You bring whatever protest you want, and on that day when the glory is revealed, every single one will burn away like chaff because what question could hold up to the sight of the glory of God? None. What accusation can stand when it is shown? Ask yourself this if you want to know the objective of why we gather and why we open the Word and why we preach or why we teach, whichever word you chose. Accusations can still be brought if we want to argue six-day creationism and evolution. Accusations can still be brought if we want to argue that we should live according to the Beatitudes.

Accusations can still be brought if we bring forward the Ten Commandments and we preach them faithfully; accusations can still be brought to say, "That's your law, that's not my law." But when the glory of God is revealed and the resurrected Christ, who will have a word to say? Who will have anything to say when Christ, the resurrected Christ at God's right hand, is shown? It will be the definitive word. So what should we preach to an unbelieving world? Anything else but that? We preach Christ and Him crucified. We preach Christ and the gospel of Christ. We preach Christ and His glory seated at the right hand of God even now, which is our hope. Once that glory is revealed, there could be no other answer except that the one true God of grace has brought salvation in Christ. That's the only answer that can be given. It doesn't even need a question.

Just as an athlete who comes forward to receive a crown if that crown is placed upon their head, isn't the body also glorified with the head? Of course it is! Even if it is an intellectual tournament, can the head be glorified without the body? We are the body of Christ, and by union with Him, His glory will also be shared by us. Colossians 3:4, "When Christ who is your life appears, then you also will appear with Him in glory."

"So is it with the resurrection of the dead. What is sown is perishable; what is raised is imperishable. It is sown in dishonor; it is raised in glory. It is sown in weakness; it is raised in power. It is sown a natural body; it is raised a spiritual body. If there is a natural body, there is also a spiritual body" (1 Corinthians 15:42–44). That which is sown in dishonor will be raised in glory. Sharing in His glory by virtue of our union with Him, we will be transformed into the same image—from glory to glory is how Scripture puts it. Isn't that what John tells us in his first epistle in 1 John 3:2, "Beloved, we are God's children now, and what we will be has not yet appeared; but we know that when He appears we shall be like Him, because we shall see Him as He is."

> We will be like Him because we shall see Him as He is in His glory. We'll be like Him in respect to His character for in that day all the sin, ignorance, and folly that characterizes our lives here will be gone. We will be like Him in love, holiness, knowledge, wisdom, truth, mercy, and all His other attributes. Then again we'll be like Him in respect to His body, for we shall receive a resurrection body patterned after His own. In short, we will be like Him in all respects. We were created in the image of God and we will be shaped into His own Son's image who has a resurrected body. (Boice)

This is Paul's comfort in Philippians 3. Paul, who was writing from a prison in Rome, and wanted to encourage the Philippian church while he himself was facing an uncertain future said, "But our citizenship is in heaven, and from it we await a Savior, the Lord Jesus Christ, who will transform our lowly body to be like His glorious body, by the power that enables Him even to subject all things to Himself." If we're convinced this is our future, then what do we have to enjoy now? That's our hope. That's our future. But what about now? Is there anything now, or are we just waiting for the future to come?

A verse in Second Corinthians 3:18 holds a key for us. "And we all, with unveiled face, beholding the glory of the Lord, are being transformed into the same image from one degree of glory to another." We, this very day, are being transformed when the Word is preached to a people who are indwelled by the Holy Spirit; God is at work transforming us. When the Word is preached and it falls upon deaf ears, there is no change except perhaps to heap up guilt by hearing the law. They do not hear grace; they only hear the law. But where there is indwelling of the Spirit, there where the Word is preached there is a transformation.

What we're able to enjoy today is the transforming effect of Christ's glory if we behold it. Do you behold it? Do you see this glory? Beholding God's glory is a gift in itself. As an act of judgment against Israel who turned not to God, but to Egypt for protection He said this in Isaiah 6, "Keep on hearing, but do not understand; keep on seeing, but do not perceive. Make the heart of this people dull, and their ears heavy, and blind their eyes; lest they see with their eyes, and hear with their ears, and understand with their hearts, and turn and be healed." Israel had turned away from God for their help and their salvation, and so they became like the lifeless idols of Egypt. Israel was condemned to become just like those lifeless, sightless, and deaf idols that were the gods to the Egyptians. They, just like we, became like what they worshipped.

We become like what we worship. Ponder that for a few moments. Ponder your own life. You become like what you worship. If you want a life change, change what you worship because you will become like what you worship. That judgment that God pronounced against Israel in Isaiah is reversed in Isaiah 32, "Then the eyes of those who see will not be closed, and the ears of those who hear will give attention. The heart of the hasty [people of God] will understand and know, and the tongue of the stammerers will hasten to speak distinctly."

The judgment will end when according to Isaiah 32:15, "Spirit is poured upon us from on high." Isn't that the intent as Paul in 2 Corinthians 3:18, when he said, "And we all, with unveiled face, beholding the glory of the Lord, are being transformed into the same image from one degree of glory to another. For this comes from the Lord who is the Spirit." We are being transformed by the Word and the Spirit. Our transformation occurs as the Spirit takes up an abode with us, and as we, with eyes that can see, behold the glory of the Lord.

In times of sorrow, temptation, deep despair, it's the brightness of His glory that remains our hope and our joy. Our transformation is caught up in our beholding His glory until the day of His return when we shall be like Him and we shall see Him as He is. This is now how we would hear Jesus' prayer, "Father, I desire that they be with Me and that they would see My glory," because we are being transformed. We will not be foreigners and aliens and outsiders, but we are adopted sons and daughters and we will be with our Lord.

So let me ask you this. How do you measure Romans 12:2 in your own life? *"Do not be conformed to this world."* When you read the Scripture that says, "Whether you eat or drink or whatever else you may do, do so to the glory of God," how do you perceive glorifying God in everything that you do? Do you see and enjoy the light of the gospel of the glory of Christ who is the image of God? Do you take pleasure in hearing the Word of God read? Do you find your joy there because God has opened and shown to you? Are you confirmed in your hope for the future because of the activity of the Spirit of God that is transforming you from glory unto glory today? Or have you remained relatively unchanged even as the Word of God has been all around you? Is it for that that Jesus is praying? Did Jesus pray for you that you would see His glory and be where He is when the sun sets on your own life? Is it you He's talking about?

20

Jesus Is Still Working on You

(John 17: 25, 26)

"O righteous Father, even though the world does not know you, I
know you, and these know that you have sent me. I made known
to them your name, and I will continue to make it known, that
the love with which you have loved me may be in them, and I in
them."

CHRIST HAS BEEN SPEAKING so plainly to the Father as to make it so
clear what His relationship is to His people, but what are His expec-
tations for His people? What it is that we are to anticipate as we continue
to grow in His life and in His love?

Our whole identity is caught up in Christ. There has been no confusion between the persons of ourselves and of our Savior and yet, we
are one in Christ. This truth of this union defines our salvation. It gives
direction to our sanctification. It gives purpose and life to the Church,
promising us that the Church herself will receive glory with Christ as His
own Body, that is, His Bride.

Ephesians 5:29 is nothing more than an expansion on the idea when
it says, "For no one ever hated his own flesh, but nourishes and cherishes
it, just as Christ does the Church." So organic are we to Christ that He
cares for His Church just as we care for our own body.

We learned of our High Priest's love for His Bride, the Church, as He
petitioned the Father in gracious terms of endearment. He calls repeatedly
upon God as *Father* and He appeals to God as *Father* because of His love
for us, that we would be protected and never separated from Him till we
are gathered with Him by His throne in the heavens. Jesus opened His

prayer with a simple address to His Father when He said, "Father, the hour has come; glorify Your Son that the Son may glorify You."

Again, in verses 5 and 21 and 24, He calls upon God as *Father* and then in verse 11, He calls Him *Holy Father* as He emphasizes our separation unto God out of the world. He calls upon God again in verse 25, saying, "O righteous Father, even though the world does not know You, I know You, and these know that You have sent Me." He here calls our attention again to the fact that we are called out of the world. We are to be separated from the world. The world doesn't even know God, but we know God because we are in Christ.

And now in verse 25, He uses a different title, one that hasn't been used before, the title of *Righteous Father* in His prayer. These last two verses could be somewhat set apart from the rest of the prayer. Jesus isn't praying for those who will believe through the apostles' testimony. He's making a statement about what He has done and the purpose with which He is opening His appeal to the Father.

We ourselves will often pray to our *Holy Father*, to our *Gracious, Loving God* or *Merciful Father*. Sometimes we pray with the terms of *Creator God*. We particularly like *Loving God and Father* in our prayers. But I have not heard an appeal from one of God's children, in prayer, to God's righteousness, as the way they begin their prayer, calling upon God in His righteousness to hear their prayer.

Why would we not call upon God's righteousness? Because when we say *righteousness*, we are talking here about God's perfect judgment and justice. When we call upon His righteousness, we are now saying, "Holy, Righteous Father, look to us with Your perfect eye of perfect justice." Rather, when we pray, we prefer to appeal to God's grace. *Gracious God. Loving God. Merciful, Heavenly Father.* We appeal to God in terms of His mercy and His love. I have not heard someone appeal to God as Judge in their prayer. *Righteous Father.*

But Jesus does. When we come before God, we want to be treated with mercy and grace and love. So what would prompt an appeal by Christ here to a just and righteous God in the closing of this prayer? After all, we have, in our minds, that great passage, Romans 3:23, which humbles us when we read that "All have sinned and fall short of the glory of God." Isn't it God's righteousness that's vindicated in the judgment of the wicked? Isn't it God's righteousness that was vindicated in the punishment of sin?

Jesus addresses the Father as the Head of the Church. Jesus is showing us on what basis the Father may be known and trusted by the Church when He appeals to Him as *Righteous Father*. Jesus is calling upon God in covenantal terms. Man was judged for his sin by a righteous God who promised a Redeemer would come, by which man would be saved. In Jeremiah 23, verse 6—and it repeats the same in Jeremiah 33:16—the promise of a Redeemer is described in these terms, "In His days Judah will be saved, and Israel will dwell securely. And this is the name by which He will be called: 'The LORD is our righteousness.'"

And we know the gospel itself is laid on a foundation of God's righteousness, which Paul teaches in Romans, chapter 1, verses 16 and 17, "For I am not ashamed of the gospel, for it is the power of God for salvation to everyone who believes, to the Jew first and also to the Greek. For in it the righteousness of God is revealed from faith for faith, as it is written, 'The righteous shall live by faith.'" *Righteousness* is used 35 times in Romans. With that sort of frequency, you might say it is the word that might best be used to describe Romans. Romans 3:21–26, put the gospel in perspective in the light of righteousness:

> "But now the righteousness of God has been manifested apart from the law, although the Law and the Prophets bear witness to it—the righteousness of God through faith in Jesus Christ for all who believe. For there is no distinction: for all have sinned and fallen short of the glory of God, and are justified by His grace as a gift, through the redemption that is in Christ Jesus, whom God put forward as a propitiation by His blood, to be received by faith. This was to show God's righteousness, because in His divine forbearance He had passed over former sins. It was to show His righteousness at the present time, so that He might be just and the justifier of the one who has faith in Jesus."

The purpose of gospel itself is to manifest and make known the righteousness of God. Note Paul's introduction in Titus, as he introduces his role to them in the first couple of verses, "Paul, a servant of God and an apostle of Jesus Christ, for the sake of the faith of God's elect and their knowledge of the truth, which accords with godliness, in hope of eternal life, which God, who never lies, promised before the ages began."

When we consider how we address God and how we have come to know God, is it important that we understand the issue of *Righteous God*? Taking from what Paul has said in his letter to Titus, if we were to simply preach godliness, we would be preaching a prideful legalism and a moralism. If we were just teaching what it is that we should do to obey, then we would end up with a pharisaism, which would be built upon the pride of man as he would manifest and say, "My, look how godly I am in my conduct and in my life."

But consequently, if we were to also simply preach knowledge without godliness, then we would also be appealing to the pride of man and promoting a Gnosticism or, the philosophy that people could be saved just by knowing enough stuff, a scholasticism. And so there is, in Paul's own self-description, a twofold purpose. There is a knowledge or an understanding that leads to godliness. We might say by implication, there could be no genuine godliness without understanding. So when we come before God, is it important we understand the Righteous Father so we can understand our place in Him?

Paul certainly understood it as we've already read in Romans, chapter 3. He says that the entire gospel itself is nothing more than a manifestation of the righteousness of God for His people. Jesus calls upon God's righteousness as the guarantee of all that He has asked for, coming to pass. And we might scratch our heads and we would wonder, *How is appealing to His righteousness a guarantee of everything He's prayed for coming to pass? How is it that an appeal to God as Judge, as the One who will condemn sinners and save the righteous—how is it that an appeal to that is a presentation of the gospel?*

"So when God desired to show more convincingly to the heirs of the promise the unchangeable character of His purpose, He guaranteed it with an oath, so that by two unchangeable things, in which it is impossible for God to lie, we who have fled for refuge might have strong encouragement to hold fast to the hope set before us" (Hebrews 6:17–18).

Do you realize how much we depend upon the character of God for salvation? It's not just legal terms, except that those legal terms were established by God and because God is righteous and faithful to His own Word, we have the assurance of faith, that God will keep His promises. He does what is right. His Law is perfect.

And so we might say then, "Well, that's well suited to Jesus, who kept the Law perfectly, in whom there was no sin or defilement of any kind. But what about us? Didn't we earlier confess that we're sinners? And if we're sinners, we certainly are not righteous in the flesh and in our conduct every day. So how is it that we would have any sort of draw to appeal to God as Righteous Father? Isn't that simply to call down His judgment upon us?"

Have we so quickly forgotten all of the teaching Jesus gave us on our unity with Him, how we are in union with Christ? Jesus calls upon the Father to look at Him and to us, the Church, according to His righteousness. And those He finds to be righteous will be saved according to His promise, just as it says in James 2:23, when he reminds us, "Abraham believed God, and it was counted to him as righteousness." That righteousness was not Abraham's to offer. It was imputed to him by God, the imputation of righteousness, a righteousness given to him by God. And that's the righteousness by which Abraham was judged and found to be faithful.

It is impossible for God to show favor or justify anyone who isn't really just. However, since no human being has a perfect righteousness in himself, it must be sought out for us by the intervention of someone who is perfectly righteous.

What does that mean? We're not going to be righteous. So our salvation, which will be based upon righteousness, must be found in another, and we know who that is. It is Christ Jesus, our Lord. Our righteousness is not our own, but as we are bonded to and in union with Christ, the righteousness of God is imputed to us as the active obedience of Christ who kept the whole Law and was without sin. When we say *active obedience*, we mean that all through His life, Jesus actively kept the Law. He kept all of God's commands. He kept every aspect of God's expectation. Christ fulfilled the covenant given to man.

The passive obedience of Christ, who lived His entire life in perfect surrender to the will of the Father, led to a vicarious atonement for our sins at Calvary. That simply means that in His life, not only did Jesus perfectly keep the Law, but He surrendered Himself completely to the Father's will. C.S. Lewis on that vicarious atonement, that dying in our place, said, "'He saved others. Himself He cannot save" (Matthew 27:42). That's the definition of the kingdom. All salvation everywhere and at all times, in great things or in little, is vicarious.

William Shedd, a great theologian, explains, "Christ's atoning death for sin is not the sinner's atoning death for sin, but God imputes it to him. That is, He calls or He reckons it his. 'Abraham believed God and it was counted to him as righteousness'" (795).

Jesus is praying to His Righteous Father, who will give Him every blessing for His perfect obedience. Jesus kept perfectly the Law and is declared righteous. Hence we are declared righteous as we are found in union with Christ. And so for us, in reflecting upon the gospel, we have to ask ourselves, *Have I died to self that I would live to Christ? Have I truly disregarded the flesh and the things of this world or do I still treasure them and hold them? If so, then the Righteous Father will judge me accordingly. But if I have completely become surrendered unto Christ, then I will be judged righteous because of the imputation of Christ's righteousness to me.*

Marcus Rainsford sums it up so pastorally and so beautifully, "It was pure mercy in God to provide a Savior when man had sinned. It was pure mercy in God to promise that Savior. It was pure mercy in God to send Him. But having provided, having promised, having sent Him to be the propitiation through faith in His blood and having accepted His offering and raised Him from the dead, it is no mere mercy in God to give the benefit to those sinners who believe on Him. It is justice to Christ, though it is mercy to them" (441).

Ponder that. It is justice to Christ and mercy to us that He would regard us in Christ, according to righteousness. Why is it justice to Christ? If God is not going to regard us in Christ by His righteousness, then why the Cross? If it's not by righteousness we are to be regarded, why the atonement? Righteousness was to be satisfied. Righteousness was to be fulfilled and Christ fulfilled those. If it were not necessary, then oh, the Cross was in vain!

And so Jesus, in calling out to the Father as *Righteous Father*, is calling upon God in His obligation to honor the promise which is to save all of those whom He has given to Christ. He is calling upon it, presuming upon it, that those who are His, whom the Father has given unto Him, will in fact be saved because God will view them according to His righteousness, as is His obligation. Also those who are not in Christ will not be saved because they also will be viewed in righteousness.

Continuing with Rainsford, "The Lord promised Christ that He would do this. It was pure grace in the Lord to make that promise, but now, Christ was come to fulfill the conditions of the covenant and make an end of sin, and He appeals to His Righteous Father to secure to Him and to His believing people all the benefits of His passion" (441). Jesus in calling upon his *Righteous Father* is calling God to now fulfill all the benefits of the covenant to His people. When He says *Righteous Father*,

He is saying, "The time has now come and these people which are mine are now to receive the benefits of salvation, according to the promise of Your covenant." As 1 John 1:9 would teach, "If we confess our sins, He is faithful and just to forgive us our sins." *Faithful and just*—that means it is right that He would forgive our sins if we confess Jesus Christ.

If we confess that we are sinners, if we appeal unto the Lord, based upon Christ and His Cross, it is God's faithfulness and justice to forgive us because it is no longer we who live, but Christ who lives in us. This is what we take away from this. This is the end of the gospel. It is the revelation of God's righteousness and the salvation of men through Christ.

There is no use at all for the old man who's dead in the flesh, the so-called righteousness of man. There are no shortcuts that satisfy perfect salvation, and there is no shortcut to God's righteousness in Christ, which is imputed to us. And the very same righteousness is our promise as well, for God cannot lie and has promised that whoever confesses with His mouth the belief of their heart that Jesus is Lord will be saved. His promise is sealed in the covenant blood of His own Son.

May we each learn God's righteousness the way it's pictured for us in Isaiah 32: 17, 18. "And the effect of righteousness will be peace, and the result of righteousness, quietness and trust forever. My people will abide in a peaceful habitation, in secure dwellings, and in quiet resting places." Those in Christ have no fear of God's righteousness. In fact, we rejoice in it because it is the guarantee of our salvation, that God will do that which is right, according to His own Law, which God, who cannot lie, has promised.

But those who are outside of Christ have every reason to fear righteousness. Yes, they pray for mercy. Yes, they pray for grace, but will they receive mercy and grace? Not outside of Christ. They will receive only righteousness. They will come to know the Righteous Father, but only in the end. We who are in Christ know the righteousness of God now. We seek to obey His Law now, not because we are judged according to law or works, but because we who are in Christ seek to live the life of Christ who lives in us, to be conformed to the image of God and to be image bearers of the Lord Jesus Christ in our own bodies.

And so Jesus appeals to the Righteous Father as He closes out His prayer, appealing now in this last prayer to the Father while He's with His disciples and saying,

"Now the time has come, Father, to fulfill the terms of the covenant because I, by My now taking a step toward the Cross, will fulfill those terms and I will end the reign of sin and the hold of death upon these people. Fulfill Your righteousness and grant to these people whom You've given Me, forgiveness and salvation, Righteous Father."

Our Lord is good and He is righteous. He is faithful and just. That's to whom we pray. That's to whom we live as we are found in union with Christ.

2 1

Running Against the Wind

(John 17:25–26)

"O righteous Father, even though the world does not know you, I know you, and these know that you have sent me. I made known to them your name, and I will continue to make it known, that the love with which you have loved me may be in them, and I in them."

WE COME TO THE end of the Lord's petitions in this prayer. Jesus is now pressing those reasons that His prayer will be heard. He has already prayed to the righteous Father, appealing to God's righteousness, and we noted how, ironically, we often will not pray in the same way. We pray to a merciful and a graceful and a holy God, but we don't intuitively appeal to a righteous Father because we associate righteousness with judgment. Jesus was not in error. Jesus also understood the righteousness of God, but having fulfilled the covenant obligations, He now called upon God's righteousness because God always does what is right. He was connecting His Person in prayer to God's covenant because He Himself had fulfilled it in His own life. It's right that God will honor Jesus' prayer because Jesus has satisfied both the justice of God and the obedience of man to God's Law. And so He prayed to the righteous Father.

The second appeal which we discover is based on the sonship of believers and the Sonship of Christ Himself to the Father, both His and ours together with Him. Jesus begins by distinguishing the groups of people who are under God's view. He distinguishes those who believe and are united to Him, and by virtue of their union with Him have had their sins removed, and those who are not of the Father.

Jesus says, "The world does not know you." And the Father is righteous in His judgment of an unbelieving world. Again, the world, which we so often hear as we read and study Scripture, is being cast as the lost, the reprobate, the ungodly, or those who are damned. We hear this theme often repeated.

> "Every spirit that does not confess Jesus is not from God. This is the spirit of the antichrist…They are from the world; therefore they speak from the world, and the world listens to them" (1 John 4:3,5).

> "We know that we are from God, and the whole world lies in the power of the evil one" (1 John 5:19).

In the face of such a scathing judgment, we wonder how it could be that the world would not know its Creator. Scripture says that only the fool has said in his heart that there is no God. Since the fall and after, man was cast out of God's presence, and there has been an estrangement. There has been an ignorance of man concerning God. There has been an ignorance and a blindness of God in the world.

> The ox knows its owner, and the donkey its master's crib, but Israel does not know, My people do not understand. (Isaiah 1:3)

Now certainly Israel was aware that there was a God. When it says that Israel does not know, we understand the word *knowledge* to indicate something more, something relational, not just a simple bare awareness. For we know that when the damned are also cast out, the Lord will say, "I never knew you." Certainly, the Creator knows of them, but He does not have that relational knowledge.

If the world does not know God, it's not for a lack of evidence. Nature bears testimony of God. "The heavens declare the glory of God, and the sky above proclaims His handiwork" (Psalm 19:1). This is what we often refer to as *general revelation*. It's a revelation because it points to God. It testifies of God. It's general in the sense that it's broad, and it's vast in its scope, and it's available to all who have eyes to see the revelation of God's handiwork in creation.

Our Westminster Confession of Faith in the very first chapter acknowledges this because it's so important and vital as we build an understanding of God's revelation of Himself. It says in the first paragraph, "Although the light of nature, and the works of creation and providence do so far manifest the goodness, wisdom, and power of God, as to leave men inexcusable; yet are they not sufficient to give that knowledge of God, and of His will, which is necessary unto salvation:"

So here our Confession acknowledges what the Scripture teaches, and that is that there is enough in the world to convict a man or a woman that there is a God, and yet we don't find the gospel itself so clearly presented in creation that we might know how it is we would be saved. And so God has testified through nature, but He also has testified by sending messengers who proclaim His name. "God spoke to our fathers by the prophets, but in these last days He has spoken to us by His Son" (Hebrews 1:1). He has not left us without a word. He has not left us without some way of knowing, some way of hearing Him speak, some way of showing us how we might be saved or come into a relationship with Him.

This is the very truth that John began his Gospel with as he introduced the Savior in John 1:10 through 11 when he said that "He," that is Jesus, "was in the world, and the world was made through Him, yet the world did not know Him. He came to His own, and His own people did not receive Him." Our minds can't help but marvel at the disbelief of those who would declare themselves to be atheists, believing there is no God.

G. K. Chesterton said, "If there were no God, then there would be no atheist." It's a bizarre thing that people would believe that there is no God. Truly we understand and hold the conviction that at the most base level, the fool is the only one who would say in his heart there is no God. Second Corinthians 4:4, as we consider why this is so, teaches us "the god of this world has blinded the minds of the unbelievers, to keep them from seeing the light of the gospel of the glory of Christ. . . ."

Romans explains that men are intent on suppressing the truth about God. Still, we wonder why. Why such a vigorous effort to suppress the truth about God? Is there any sadder condition described in the Bible than that of a world which has forgotten its Creator? How could the creation forget its Creator?

In the Scripture, when we read about knowledge, and we read about knowing God, this word *knowledge* carries with it the idea of an affection. Unbelievers are those who do not have a knowledge of God that includes the heart and affection, so it cannot be properly be called knowledge. We can't say they have a knowledge of God if they have no affection towards

God. If the knowledge does not also include a heart that is given to God, then it can't be called a knowledge of God.

The Bible says that a man doesn't know that which he doesn't love. Unbelievers possess is what Paul calls in Romans 2:20 a "form of knowledge." There seems to be an awareness or even an acknowledgment. There even seems sometimes to be religious action, but no real affection of the heart, no real absolute commitment unto the Lord in life. In Psalm 95, verse 10, regarding the Jews as they were in the wilderness, God made this observation: "They are a people who go astray in their heart, and they have not known my ways." Even as God led them through the wilderness, their hearts went astray, and that going astray is being described as a lack of knowledge. They have not known God, and they have not known God's ways because their heart is astray.

When Scripture says Jesus knew no sin, we don't mean that He didn't believe that there was sin in the world, but that He treasured and desired no sin in His heart. The mind is the seat of precept and of speculation and of principles. The heart is the seat of action. Actions speak louder than words. We can profess to believe anything, but when our lives are moved to action upon what we profess to believe, then we might have some idea or some sense of understanding that we know the Lord, not just of the Lord. The heart tells the story of what we believe. Hence, God's covenant promises that He will put a law into our inward parts and write it on our hearts. We shall not only know it, but have it in our hearts to live it and to desire it. "I have stored up your word in my heart, that I might not sin against you" (Psalm 119:11).

So what about us? What do we know of God? Do we know Him as our righteous Father? Do you have a genuine fellowship with the God of Scripture? Do you have religious practices and a general conviction that there is a God and that perhaps Christ existed in history? The resurrection is a historical event. What impact has the resurrection had upon you? What knowledge of God do you have within your heart that compels you to action, to godliness, to sanctification, to changed life? Jesus is washing His Bride with the water of the Word. Are you being washed and cleansed, sanctified daily by Christ?

Ignorance of God will mean exclusion from heaven. And that sets us to understand Jesus' second concern in His prayer here—those who do know the Lord. "His divine power has granted to us all things that pertain to life and godliness, through the knowledge of Him who called us to His own glory and excellence" (2 Peter 1:3). He has granted to us all things that pertain to life and godliness through the knowledge of Him, through genuine, authentic knowledge of Him, heart knowledge of Him.

It's as Augustine said, "For what else is the knowing of Him but eternal life?" There are many who can talk of Christ, but the knowing of Christ is as Augustine has reminded us, eternal life. To know God, genuinely know Him in the sense that God Himself would frame the use of that word, to know God in that way is eternal life.

Jesus explains how we come to that knowledge. We're not talking now Gnosticism. We're not talking learning that leads to salvation. We're talking the conversion of a heart. As the Spirit of Christ dwells within the heart, we come to know God affectionately. We come to know God intimately, not simply facts or about Him. Again, Jesus explains how we can come to that knowledge; He knows the Father, and by virtue of Him, we also know the Father. The order is plain and important. Jesus knows Him immediately, and we know Him through Jesus.

"No one knows the Father except the Son and anyone to whom the Son chooses to reveal Him" (Matthew 11:27). Our knowledge of God, our saving knowledge of God, is through the Son. No one can pry open the book that is sealed in Revelation 6 except the Lamb who is worthy, and if He had not done it, then its contents would remain unknown. Neither can any man be saved by what he is able to learn, but by what Jesus shows him. This is why the Law can never save because Law can never capture the heart. Law can never grasp love from the heart. It can only cause us to have a sense of duty. It can only drive us out of fear and sense of duty.

But Jesus gives us a knowledge of God, and He does this in two ways: by His Word and by His Spirit. It's significant that these become two pillars in your own understanding—the Word and Spirit. Returning again to Hebrews 1, we are reminded that "in these last days He has spoken to us by His Son." As the hymns instruct us, "Jesus is God in flesh appearing."

As Jesus instructed Philip in John 14:9, "Whoever has seen me has seen the Father," Jesus has shown us the Lord's holiness and His righteousness. And His life has given us an understanding of God's grace and mercy and love. His works and miracles have shown us God's power and authority over all of His creation. His resurrection has shown us His power over death and assured us there is a life that comes beyond the grave. So we can agree with 1 John 5:20, "We know that the Son of God has come and has given us understanding, so that we may know Him who is true."

But not only did Jesus teach us, He continues to teach us. How? Through the work of the Holy Spirit. And this knowledge of God isn't simply an awareness. It is a saving knowledge. And what we learn is that God has stooped down to show us saving grace. Donald Grey Barnhouse, a great pastor, taught that, "Love that goes upward from the heart of man to God is adoration. Love that goes outward from one heart to another is affection. Love that stoops is grace" (72). That stooping to save reveals to us that God is love.

Nature bears testimony that God is real. While there is natural beauty that inspires, nature cannot love. There are many I have heard say, "I can worship God in the woods. I can worship God on the lake. I can worship God in some sort of a sporting environment. I can worship God in the quiet place in my own home." You can observe God's creation, and you can be thrilled and filled with joy because you revel in God's creation, but God has revealed Himself in His Word. God has revealed Himself through His fellowship within the Church.

Nature cannot love you. Nature will never love you. And if you love nature beyond being a faithful steward and having an appreciation of God's own creation, know that nature will never love you back or even know that you love it. But God loves you, and God has ordained where His people and how His people gather, and what they do when they gather for His own glory. He hasn't left it to our imaginations that we would fall into error without being aware. God has a call on His people, and so when we say that we would desire to commune with God in some place foreign to God's own instruction, we need to know that while natural beauty inspires, that natural beauty will never love us back.

So take up Christ as you find Him in the Scriptures. Learn from Him of the Father who grants forgiveness and salvation to whom He will. And pray with Philip, "Lord, show us the Father, and it is enough for us." Let that be our prayer. "Lord, show us the Father, and it is enough." Jesus says as much. "I made known to them your name."

God has shown us His love in that while we were dead in our sin and estranged from Him, He sent His Son to die for us. When Jesus hung on the Cross, God saw us hanging there. As Barnhouse has said, "When our time came to live, the Spirit of God told us that we were sinners. Our minds recognized the truth of the accusations, and the Spirit of God pointed to the Cross of Christ."

Jesus says, "The world does not know you, but I know you, and they know you." We know God through His Son, and His Son is in union with us by virtue of the indwelling of the Spirit and His death on the Cross. Do you know the Father? You know of the Father? Do you know about the Bible? Are you a scholar? That is all well and good. Do you know God? The affections of your heart, do you love God? Are you content simply to observe God in creation, or do you hunger for His Word? As the deer pants for water, do you also hunger and thirst for the Scripture, for God's Word, to commune with Him by Word and by Spirit that we might know Him? Do you know God?

22

I Will Show Them Your Name

(John 17:26)

"I made known to them your name, and I will continue to make it known, that the love with which you have loved me may be in them, and I in them."

I N THE FINAL VERSE of John 17, Jesus continues speaking of the abiding benefits to the apostles which flow from Him. He continues his declaration of what He has done and will continue to do. First, in this passage, we notice what He has done. He has manifested the Father's name to them. We know that from a previous verse where Jesus has simply declared, "Father, I manifested your name to them." Now Jesus repeats, "I made known to them your name, and I will continue to make it known." Jesus has manifested the Father's name to them.

Secondly, to whom did He manifest it? To the apostles and through the apostles to believers in every age. And thirdly, Jesus tells us what He will do. Not only what He has done, not only to whom He has done it, but what He will do. He will continue to reveal the Father by the outpouring of the Spirit. What does He mean by God's name? "I have revealed to them, or made known to them, or manifested to them your name."

It was the privilege of Israel to know God by His names. We know that on Mars Hill Paul sees all of the different idols that were placed there, the one that is to an unnamed god, or an unknown god. Man has an intrinsic desire to know God. Not to simply know that there is a God, but to know God. And names are those personal attributes that are put into words that tell us of God.

The Old Testament Hebrew Scriptures give us several names for God. I'll only survey a few. The first is simply *El*. You hear *El Shaddai* or *Elohim*. The first *el*, if you were to put it that way, is actually a name for God. It simply means *God*. It doesn't give us any description. It simply means God—One who is mighty, One who is strong, One who is sovereign.

Then *Elohim* is God in a plural sense. And here we take our understanding of the Trinity, and we begin to look into the Old Testament, and we see it actually supported in the names of God. *El Shaddai*, God Almighty, or God All-sufficient. *Adonai*, which is translated as Lord in our English Bibles. All these are frequently used names of God. Returning to the Old Testament, we have *Jehovah*, which is also translated LORD in our Bibles.

Jehovah Jirah, the Lord will provide. Or *Jehovah Rophe*, the Lord who heals. *Jehovah Nissi*, the Lord our banner. All of these are names of God which are given to us in the Scriptures. I know that you've heard *shalom*. *Jehovah Shalom*, the Lord our peace. *Jehovah Elohim*, the Lord God. *Jehovah Rohi*, the Lord our Shepherd. *El Elyon*, God most high, speaking here of God's exalted nature, or most high nature. *Abir*, the mighty One. *Kadosh*, the holy One. *El Roi*, the God who sees all. And in the Psalms, we're often told of His eyes which are roaming to and fro, back and forth across the world as He is *El Roi*, the God who sees. No heart is hidden from *El Roi*.

Kenah, the God who is jealous. *Megan*, who is our shield. *Sadik*, He is the righteous One, the God who is righteous before us. *El Olam*, the everlasting God. *El Berith*, a particularly significant one in our understanding of our construction of a theological system. He is the God of covenant—*Berith*. *El Gabor*, the mighty God. *Melech*, He is our King. *Father, the First and the Last, Emmanuel*, God with us.

And then in the New Testament only a few. *Kurios*, which is Lord. Or *Theos*, which is God. He is the *Great I Am*, which is carried over from the Old Testament. He is called the *Word* and *Almighty*. All of these varied descriptions of God tell us something about the person of God. A name serves to identify an object or an individual. At creation, Adam named every animal according to its kind to distinguish one kind from another, according to their class, or according to their herd which they gathered in.

A personal name was reserved for man, however. Man was created more excellent than others, and he was given a stewardship over all of the others. So man is not known according to his kind, but by his name. Perhaps that is one reason prejudice or social profiling is so offensive to people. It's offensive because a person is not considered according to their uniqueness or individuality. They're regarded merely as a class of people, or, to go back to the days of creation, because of the herd which they are a part of. It takes away their humanity, that uniqueness of being created in the image of God, this act of prejudice which tends to lump people according to their class rather than the unique personhood which is discounted.

We might wonder why God even needs a name however. God is one of a kind. There is no confusion between God and another. He is Spirit. Where there are many names to distinguish individuals, there is only one God. So why a name? Why is it so important in Jesus' dialogue that He says, "I manifested your name to them"? Why would they need Jesus to manifest the name of God? Because the name by which God is called separates Him both from the creatures and from other ideas of gods which are invented by men.

I, like you, am exposed to people's ideas of God all throughout our days. The names of God inform our ideas of God. The One who searches out the hearts of men, the One who provides, the One who is the shield, the One who protects, the One who is in covenant with us—these are definitions of God's person that are given to us through the names of God that are provided.

"For you shall worship no other god, for the LORD, whose name is Jealous, is a jealous God" (Exodus 34:14). That helps to explain Hebrews 12:29, which says, ". . .for our God is a consuming fire." We are told to worship in reverence and awe because our God is a consuming fire. He wants no false notions, for to worship a false notion is to worship a false God. We will not conjure up an idea of God from our own mind because God has gone to great lengths to detail who He is and how He is to be worshiped.

There can be no doubt that God has intended His people to know and to comprehend and to relate to Him on the basis of His name. "I bow down toward your holy temple and give thanks to your name for your steadfast love and your faithfulness, for you have exalted above all things your name and your word" (Psalm 138:22). And Jesus says, "I've manifested that name to you."

Creation tells us much about God, but the Scriptures teach us who God is. For the Christian, knowing God's name is one of the great privileges of salvation. It distinguishes us from ancient followers of God such as we read of in Judges 13, verse 18. "Why do you ask my name, seeing it is wonderful?" Here the angel of the LORD has been asked, "What is your name?" The angel of the LORD is a pre-incarnate appearance of Christ, often called a *theophany*. Here the angel of the LORD is asked His name, but it cannot yet be revealed. He says, "Why are you asking me my name? It's too great. It's too marvelous. It's too wonderful. I can't tell you that name which you ask of."

We know God has given Israel names as well by which they may know Him, but it remained to the unveiling of the gospel in Christ for all to be made known. Israel had names of God, they had ways of relating to God, they had understanding of God, but they still had questions, questions that were yet unanswered until Christ. And when the Word became flesh and was manifest before them, so the name of God was manifested to them, and now we know God. Until then, God taught His people gradually through history of redemption about His own person and His name.

In Exodus 6:3, God speaks to Moses, saying, "I appeared to Abraham, to Isaac, and to Jacob, as God Almighty. . . ." A name, ". . .but by my name the LORD I did not make myself known to them." So it is in the plan of God to reveal Himself progressively through redemptive history to His people, and at the coming of Christ in the incarnation, He is fully made known.

"In His days Judah will be saved, and Israel will dwell securely. And this is the name by which He will be called: 'The LORD is our righteousness'" (Jeremiah 23:6). But we only have to back up a couple of verses to be reminded that Jesus in praying even says, "O righteous Father." And how was He to pray, "O righteous Father"? He was calling on God to recognize the righteousness satisfied in Christ, the promises that there will be One who is called "the LORD is our righteousness." Christ is our righteousness. "I've manifested your name before the people." So in His Person, this name of the Lord is manifested before the people, *the LORD our righteousness* in fulfillment of a great prophecy given to Jeremiah.

He is Creator. He is Lord. He is the God of Abraham, the eternal, the infinite, but in the gospel we discover even more because it is in the gospel we discover and it is made clear that He is also the God who is triune, Father, and Son, and Holy Spirit. Here we see the Old Testament made clear by the New. The truth was before them even in the account of creation when we read of God creating by the power of His voice and of the Spirit who hovers over the waters. And in Colossians, we learn of Christ who was there at creation because it's in Him and by Him that all things are made. So even in the creation account, the Trinity is present.

For the Old Testament paradigm of understanding, without it being made clear, it remained a mystery though it was present. But now, because of the unfolding of the New Testament in Christ, that truth which has always been before God's people has been made clear by the shining of the light of Christ upon it. It was not until the incarnation, the descent of the Holy Spirit at Jesus' baptism and the thundering voice of God that said, "This is my Son in whom I am well pleased," that we were able to say, "Ah! All three are present there, a Father, and a Son, and the Holy Spirit." Then it became clear that God is one in essence and three in Persons.

Another great benefit that we have as New Testament believers is in the incarnation itself. "He was manifested in the flesh, vindicated by the Spirit, seen by angels, proclaimed among the nations, believed on in the world, taken up in glory" (1 Timothy 3:16). God Himself, was manifested in the flesh, made visible by all, seen by angels and men, proclaimed, and then taken up into glory.

God's mercy, His justice, and truth are explained time after time throughout the Scriptures, but Jesus is the wisdom and power of God, and in Him all the fullness of the Godhead dwells. So it is with Jesus that God is best made known. Thus Jesus can say, "I have manifested your name." Only Jesus could have shown us God's name. No name that man could give God could reveal God except those names that He calls Himself.

Proverbs 30 challenges the notion that prideful man can know anything except what God reveals to him. "Who has ascended to heaven. . ." we are asked. "Who has gathered the wind in his fists? Who has wrapped up the waters in a garment? What is his name, and what is his son's name? Surely you know!" Only the Lord has done this. No, man cannot know except that Christ has manifested His name. We cannot guess about God. Only as it's been manifested and revealed to us can we know the truth about God.

Jesus manifested that name before them, and He will continue to manifest it. Did you miss that in the passage? "I made known to them your name, and I will continue to make it known." And if we read ahead in the

Scriptures, we see that what comes very quickly is Gethsemane, betrayal, arrest, trial, crucifixion, resurrection. *When* is Jesus going to continue to make known the ministry of revealing God's name? He will manifest the Father's grace as He is hanged on the Cross. When He is resurrected, He will show the God who is the Lord of life and of glory. And it was Jesus who had shown them and He would show them—and us—still more.

When we turn to the gospel, whom do we imagine is showing us its truth? There is no saving knowledge that comes from any man no matter how great or how poor the preaching any more than the truth of God comes from a man. It doesn't spring from the wells of a man's mouth or his own heart, this truth that is put forward for God's people to take in and to digest. It springs from the Scriptures. But the Scriptures remained veiled to the unbeliever. They remain mysterious to them, a stumbling block, a yoke around their neck.

Marcus Rainsford says, "Whatever we shall know of God in time or in eternity, Jesus will be the Teacher. Whatever we shall see of God, Jesus will be the Manifestor. Whatever we shall enjoy of God, Jesus will be the Mediator" (448). And as we learn from Hebrews 1:2, ". . .in these last days He has spoken to us by His Son." We repeat Jesus' promise, "I made known to them your name, and I will continue to make it known."

Every day that we open the Scriptures we read, Jesus is continuing to make known His name. "For God, who said, 'Let light shine out of darkness,' has shone in our hearts to give the light of the knowledge of the glory of God in the face of Jesus Christ" (2 Corinthians 4:6). The incarnation is the character and the Person of God manifest in the flesh of man. Not that the flesh came first and God infused it into man, but God came to man in the Person of His only begotten Son, Jesus Christ, the second Person of the Trinity, who was fully God, one hundred percent God though He was also one hundred percent man without confusion. And being one hundred percent God, He manifested God's Person, God's name, before them.

Some day our eyes will behold what we see now only by faith. We read and we believe, and we believe sincerely in our heart with an uncorrupted faith as it is given by the Spirit of God. Until that time, it's the Scriptures that provide God's self-portrait. We want to know God. Where will we turn? Not to the skies, not to the trees, not to one another. These all support an understanding. It's to the Scriptures and the Scriptures alone that we turn. Any other place that we seek to define God will build for us idols of our own design and our own making. The Scripture is God's self-portrait. It's the record of what Jesus has declared concerning God. It's the means by which God grants to us a knowledge of Himself. We are living in that phrase that reads, ". . .and will declare it." As long as there are people, Jesus will continue to declare it.

Remember initially Jesus declared it only among the Jews. Jesus told the Canaanite woman seeking relief for her daughter who was possessed by a demon in Matthew 15, "I was sent only to the lost sheep of the house of Israel." He later tells her to go, that her faith would cause her prayers to be answered. In Matthew, chapter 10, when Jesus sent the apostles out on their own, He gave them these instructions, "Go nowhere among the Gentiles and enter no town of the Samaritans, but go rather to the lost sheep of the house of Israel."

After the resurrection however, as the Spirit was poured out, He said in Mark 16:15, "Go into all the world and proclaim the gospel to the whole creation." The restriction was that it would only be shown to the Jews in Jesus' life when He dwelled in flesh here with man. But after the resurrection, the Spirit would be poured out, and we are to go out into all nations and tell them of the Lord.

We have the wonderful example of Paul who wrote in Romans 15:20, "Thus I make it my ambition to preach the gospel, not where Christ has already been named, lest I build on someone else's foundation." Paul understood. He understood, "I'm not here to preach to the choir. I'm here to take the gospel to places where the people have not heard of the wonders of Christ."

To this end, Jesus has appointed ministers in His Church of all sorts. In 1 Corinthians 12, we read that "God has appointed in the church first apostles, second prophets, third teachers, then miracles, then gifts of healing, helping, administrating, and various kinds of tongues." We know that God has appointed those and given spiritual gifts for the purpose of proclaiming the gospel. And they go out, not in their own strength, but in the strength of Christ who promised in Matthew 28, "And behold, I am with you always, to the end of the age."

"I have proclaimed. I will continue to proclaim." As we go out, it is Jesus who goes with us, and Jesus continues to proclaim through His Body, the Church. He continues to declare God's name by Word and Spirit—His Word and His Spirit proclaimed in His Body to all nations. This was His explanation in John 14, which we've already studied. Judas asked Him directly, "'Lord, how is it that you will manifest yourself to us, and not to the world?' Jesus answered him, 'If anyone loves me, he will keep my word, and my Father will love him, and we will come to him and make our home with him.'"

This keeping of the Word is where Jesus is found to dwell. The Father will love Him. It sounds much like the prayer of Jesus when He says, "That the love with which you have loved me may be in them, and I in them." Here we have a beautiful tie in with what we have already learned regarding the unity with God which we find in the Son.

The word *that* cannot be overlooked. "I will continue to make it known, that the love with which You have loved me may be in them." It can't be overlooked because here we have a promise that the love of God to Christ will be the same love given to us as Christ who abides in us. But it is conditional on the name of God being continually known, that Jesus will proclaim it in order that the love of God will be given to us.

This verse is a strong case for the salvation in the gospel that is available only in that great theology which we refer to as a theology of the Word and the Spirit. The Word is the continuing testimony of Christ who manifested the name of God in His Person and work. The Word is read, and it is heard, but as man can't create God, neither can he raise his soul from death, and so God sends His own Spirit, the Spirit of Christ who gives life and the knowledge of God. This Word of Christ goes out, and the Spirit of Christ causes the Word to be active and alive, sharper than a two-edged sword, piercing to the very bone and the marrow of man. The Word of Christ goes, the Spirit of Christ goes, and coming together in the heart of man, life begins.

He is the wonderful Counselor, the mighty God, the everlasting Father, the Prince of Peace. This is the message that is still proclaimed today by Christ in His Church through the Word. He still proclaims. He still manifests the name of God which is salvation to His people. So I conclude with a simple question—*have you heard the name of God? Have you heard Christ proclaim the name of God?*

About the Author

M.E. CANNON IS AN ORDAINED minister in the Presbyterian Church in America and serves as an Army Chaplain. He has authored several other books including *A Christian Soldier's Catechism*. A graduate of Columbia International University, he lives with his family in South Carolina.

Bibliography

Barnhouse, Donald Gray. *The Cross Through the Open Tomb*. Grand Rapids: Eerdmans, 1961.

Benhoeffer, Dietrich. *Life Together*. Translated by John W. Doberstein. San Francisco: Harper, 1954.

Boice, James Montgomery. *Gospel of John: The Peace in Storm (John 13–17)*. Grand Rapids: Baker, 2005.

———. *An Expositional Commentary on The Gospel of John*, Vol. 4. Grand Rapids: Baker, 1999.

———. *Foundations of the Christian Faith*. Madison: Intervarsity Press, 1986.

Bruce, F.F. *The Epistle to the Hebrews*. Grand Rapids: Eerdmans, 1990.

Brunner, Emil. *The Word and The World*. New York: Scribner, 1931.

Calvin, John. *New Testament Commentary, John 11–21*, Vol. 18. Grand Rapids: Baker, 1993.

Carson, D.A. *The Gospel According to John*. Grand Rapids: Eerdmans, 1991.

Eliott, Charles W., ed. *Confessions of St. Augustine*. New York: Collier, 1909.

Godet, Frederic Louis. *Commentary on the Gospel of John*. Grand Rapids: Zondervan, 1987.

Hazlett, William, ed. *The Table Talk of Martin Luther*. London: H.G. Bohn, 1857.

Hendrickson, William. *Exposition of the Gospel According to John*. Grand Rapids: Baker, 1954.

Ironside, H. A. *Address on the Gospel of John*. Grand Rapids: Kregal, 2006.

Keiper, Ralph. *Ralph L. Keiper and James M. Boice: Is Prayer a Problem?* Philadelphia: The Bible Study Hour, 1974.

Lange, John Peter. *Commentary on the Holy Scriptures: Critical, Doctrinal, Homiletical*. Trans. Philip Schaff. New York: Scribner's, 1879.

Lewis, C.S. *The Quotable Lewis*. Carol Stream, IL: Tyndale, 1990.

Lloyd-Jones, Martyn. *The Assurance of Our Salvation*. Wheaton: Crossway, 2000.

———. *Spiritual Depression*. Grand Rapids: Eerdmans, 1965

Manser, Martin. *The Westminster Collection of Christian Quotations*. Louisville: Westminster John Knox, 2001.

Manton, Thomas. *The Complete Works of Thomas Manton*. Vestavia Hills: Solid Ground Books, 2009.

McDonnell, Kilian. *John Calvin, the Church and the Eucharist*. Princeton: Princeton University Press, 1967.

Newton, George. *The Banner of Truth & Trust: An Exposition of John 17*. Avon: Bath Association, 1995.

Morgan, G. Campbell. *Webster's Quotations, Facts & Phrases*. Icon Group International: Online: http://books.google.com/books.

Pink, A. W. *Spiritual Union and Communion.* Lafayette: Sovereign Grace, 2002.

Rainsford, Marcus. *Our Lord Prays for His Own: Thoughts on John 17.* 5th edition. Grand Rapids: Kregel, 1985.

————. *Straight Paths for Your Feet.* London: Hodder and Stoughton, 1885.

Roberts, Maurice. *Union and Communion with Christ.* Grand Rapids: Reformation Heritage Books, 2008.

Ryken, Philip G. *The Communion of the Saints.* Phillipsburg: P & R Publishing, 2001.

Ryle, J.C. Holiness. London: James Clark, 1956.

Schaff, Philip. "The Nicene and Post Nicene Fathers." *St Augustine*: First Series, VII. Grand Rapids: Eerdmans, 1956.

————. *St Augustine of Hippo: Homilies on the Gospel. John* 1–40. Grand Rapids: Eerdmans, 1956.

Shedd, William. *Dogmatic Theology.* Phillipsburg: P & R Publishing, 2003.

Spurgeon, (from a sermon manuscript). "Christ's Pastoral Prayer for His People." September 1, 1889; http://www.biblebb.com/files/spurgeon/2331.htm.

Water, Mark, ed. *The New Encyclopedia of Christian Quotations.* Grand Rapids: Baker, 1984.

Wells, David. *The Bleeding of the Evangelical Church.* Edinburg: Banner of Truth, 1995.

Williamson, G.I., ed. "Westminster Confession of Faith." P & R Publishing: 2nd edition (December 2003).